France

DOUGLAS JOHNSON

with 28 illustrations and a map

WALKER AND COMPANY
NEW YORK

Library of Congress Catalog Card Number: 75–78381

First published in the United States of America in 1969 by
Walker and Company, a division of the Walker Publishing Company, Inc.

Printed in Great Britain by Hazell Watson and Viney Ltd, Aylesbury, Bucks

Nations and Peoples

France

Contents

Preface

IT IS NEVER EASY to write about France. It is particularly difficult for someone who is not French. It is especially hard at a time of great perplexity. And yet one persists. France is a country of great attraction. Perhaps this is because, historically speaking, France has had the mission of posing many of the problems of civilization in a direct and challenging manner.

At the moment there is a malaise in France. More than ever before, the French are aware of uncertainty. The nature of the régime that will follow General de Gaulle; the uncertain future of the plans to divide the country into some twenty-one different regions, each with its own assembly, and the plans to reform the Senate; the future evolution of French schools and universities, now that they are moving away from their Napoleonic rigidities; the way in which a diverse economy will develop; the role that France will choose, or might be forced, to play in Europe. All these, and more, are subjects of unease. As Sir Denis Brogan remarked a long time ago, no one knows what a young France will be like. Perhaps the symbol is the schoolteacher who today begins the education of a young pupil without knowing what sort of examination will be set at the end of the school year.

Yet France has always been a country of uncertainty. The French state has always been both strong and weak. The future of all régimes has usually been in doubt. It has invariably been easier to define French writers in terms of what they were against rather than what they wanted. The French have looked at the present with regret, at the disappearing past with nostalgia. In the freshly whitened façades of today's Paris, dominated by endless streams of traffic, people look back to the days of deserted highways and peaceful river banks, when hopes ran high for some political cause, when Gide and Joyce lived in a Paris of almost provincial calm, when war was a memory and a rumour. People look back too, to the days of the Liberation, and they regret the passing of its bitter triumphs, its dynamic violence, its aspirations. There can be little doubt that in the future there will be many who will look back nostalgically to the days of Gaullism, its excitements, its exasperations, its greatness; even its uncertainties. Each age is a decline; but each age is also a renewal and a development.

The pages that follow seek to form an interpretation rather than a compendium of information. In them, General de Gaulle figures largely. For a time at least, it was as if French history had identified itself with this one man (*'s'est engouffrée dans ce dernier vivant'*, as François Mauriac has put it). We should be generous towards him, Robert Escarpit tells us, since his faults are those of the French. And yet one knows, it is almost an historical law, that in the future, he will appear less important than he does today. Already one must see him in the perspective of the past. As he told Malraux, *'D'abord, le passé'*.

I would like to thank the relatives, friends, colleagues, students, exstudents, typists and publishers who have helped me to write this book.

Birmingham; SaintServanssurmer; London.
April 1969

1 The beginning

Il en coûte cher pour devenir la France. L'histoire abat les prétentions impatientes et soutient les longues espérances. Guizot

IT HAS OFTEN BEEN SAID by geographers that France is an abridged version of all Europe. There are few countries in the world which can, in a few hundred kilometres, demonstrate such diversity. When such remarks are made, one is often thinking of the conditions of physical geography, with the hills of Brittany resembling those of Cornwall, the Ardennes of eastern France continuing the mountains of the Rhineland, the plains of French Flanders merging into Belgium and the Low Countries to become part of the green plain of northern Europe. The Paris basin appears as the equivalent to the London basin, the Vosges and Alsace are symmetrical to the Black Forest and the Baden plain, the Massif Central has many resemblances to the mountains of central Germany, and the great mountain chains of southern France and Corsica continue throughout the Mediterranean.

Pursuing this sort of comparison, the delta of the Rhône is like that of the Po; much of Sussex is like Normandy; there is something of Zealand in the Poitevin marshes and canals; the inhabitant of Quercy would not feel a stranger in Castile; the nature reserve of the Camargue is strangely like the Scandinavian island of Öland; the Jura are both French and Swiss. France is thus an accumulation of the rest of Europe. But within France itself, there is little similarity between the contrasting plains of Flanders, of the Landes, of Alsace, of Burgundy or of the Camargue; there are only differences between the hills of Aquitaine, the volcanic chains of the Puys, the mountains of the Vosges and the Limousin, and the Alps and the Pyrenees.

9

France is intensively penetrated by maritime influences, having coasts which face four different seas (the Mediterranean, the Atlantic, the Channel and the North Sea) and it is said that there is no part of France more than about 400 kilometres away from the sea; but at the same time France is profoundly continental, and with Strasbourg being nearer to Berlin than to Brest, France's destiny is forcibly European.

This geographical diversity is emphasized by a complicated river system, and by the fact that France is the meeting-place of different types of climate, oceanic, mediterranean, alpine and continental. At first sight it is difficult to find much in common between the inhabitant of the rich lands of Normandy (the story is told that one night a Norman farmer dropped his stick, and when he went out the following day to look for it the grass had already grown over it) and the inhabitant of the heart-breaking, barren soil south of the Loire. There is not much that is common to the climates of Brest, of Strasbourg or of Marseilles. There is little similarity between the ways of life of a fisherman in the North Sea, a wheat-farmer in the fertile plains of the Beauce, a wine-grower in the south-west, or a shepherd in the mountains of the Dauphiné. Hippolyte Taine is supposed to have said that if he were shown the map of a country, then he would be able to tell its history, and it is not surprising that the formation of the French nation, and the constitution of a French state, within these 213,000 sq. kilometres of varied terrain, were the results of a long and complicated history.

The first civilization in France was probably that of the south-west. At a time when much of the country was covered with glaciers, the hunters and fishermen of Périgord, like those of north-western Spain, took refuge in their caves and grottoes, on the walls of which they expressed their religious preoccupations and described the animals which they knew. One can find a testimony to this civilization in the decorations and paintings of the Eyzies, of the Mas d'Azil, of Cro-Magnon and Lascaux, some of which are 20,000 years old. It is in Brittany that one can most clearly see, in the thousands of megaliths and dolmens, the civilization which later developed, that of cultivators, cattle-farmers, traders and artisans. About the year 1000 BC the Celtic Gauls established a number of states in France. They developed their agriculture and their trade, and although they had not established any unity over the territory, they had created an active and prosperous ensemble by the time when the Romans invaded France. It was in 52 BC that Caesar overcame Vercingetorix, at Alesea.

For the first time France was given a form of political unity, and felt the impress of a relatively unified civilization which was to leave profound traces. It could be that one has under-estimated the importance of the Greek impact on France. The Greeks are usually thought of as confined to the Mediterranean coastline and to Provence, leaving relatively small traces of their presence in ports such as Marseilles and Nice but, if legend be true, introducing the cultivation of the vine. Recent excavations in Marseilles demonstrate that the extent of settlement and fortification were much larger than has been thought and suggest that Greek Gaul as a whole was more important than has been assumed.[1] But the impact of the Romans was dramatic none the less. Even the far west of France, Brittany, felt the effect of the Romans when Caesar defeated the Breton fleet in the Gulf of Morbihan. In spite of its division into provinces, Roman Gaul achieved a rough form of unity and received the adherence of many Gallic chiefs. Numerous towns became the centres of commercial and cultural life and Lyons became the centre of an ambitious social system. There are still many remains of Roman buildings connected with religion, with entertainment, with transport and with irrigation. A massively impressive construction like the Pont du Gard is testimony to the nature of the Roman presence. Just as certain place-names show the existence of Gallic tribes, like Paris (which refers to the Parisii) or Bourges (to the Bituriges), so there are many place-names of Roman origin, such as Orleans (Aurelianum) and Grenoble (Gratianopolis), names which reveal the presence of water (Aix, Aigues-Mortes, Fontenay), or which evoke a natural feature of the landscape (Verneuil, from the Latin *verna*, an alder tree, or Rouvre, from *robur*, an oak tree).

One should not exaggerate the nature of Gallo-Roman unity.

There were regions which felt the force of Rome more than others; there was a great variety of social and cultural life within the framework of Roman administration, all the more so since the appearance of Christianity in the second and third centuries. But there was a contrast between Roman Gaul and the Gaul which was invaded by a variety and mixture of peoples, Franks, Alamans, Burgundians, Visigoths, Ostrogoths and others. Out of these moving populations and shifting administrative frameworks, one king, the Frankish Clovis, succeeded in winning, by force of arms, a position of supremacy. His conversion to Christianity (supposedly in 496) gained him the support of the Gallo-Roman populations and the clergy. Something like a French state tentatively emerged, unified from the North Sea to the Mediterranean, from the Alps to the Atlantic. But this unity was precarious, and Clovis's authority was not accepted in Brittany, in parts of Normandy, Burgundy or Narbonne, and with his death in 511 the kingdom fell apart.

At least four main regional divisions can be seen. There was Neustria, from the Loire to the Meuse, containing important Gallo-Roman towns, such as Paris, Rouen and Tours; Austrasia, a mainly Frankish region, stretching across the Rhine, and including Rheims and Metz; Burgundy, the kingdom of the Burgundians; and Aquitaine, which remained very Roman, with the towns of Poitiers, Toulouse and Bordeaux. All these regions were further diversified as the Arabs advanced into Narbonne, Aquitaine (until their defeat at Poitiers in 732) and Provence, as the Hungarians roamed through Lorraine and Provence, and as the Vikings appeared on the Seine, the Loire and the Garonne.

The unification imposed by Charlemagne (768–814) was a striking achievement. His was a kingdom which extended far eastwards, beyond the frontiers of what is now called France. Charlemagne is a figure in German history as much as in French. He considered himself to be a champion of the Church and its rightful head. He frequently intervened in matters of doctrine and he himself appointed bishops. He appointed counts and sent special officials (*missi dominici*) throughout his empire who had considerable powers of enquiry and inspection. He encouraged vassalage, with the idea of making his authority felt indirectly throughout the hierarchy of feudal relationships.

It is not certain how effective some of these measures were. The *missi dominici* might well have been more efficient in theory than in practice. The attempt to cement society together by the man-to-man bond which one calls feudalism was a move away from the old Roman concept of state authority, and was eventually to establish territorial regionalism and bring about the elimination of a powerful central ruler. There is no dispute about the purely temporary nature of Charlemagne's work. The dislocation of the Carolingian empire became obvious after his death, and during the reign of his son Louis the Pious, whilst vestiges of strong government remained in the east, there was little sign of this in the west, where Viking raids became more numerous. The Vikings pillaged Paris four times and by a treaty of 911 an independent Viking province, the Duchy of Normandy, was established.

By the end of the tenth century it is difficult to define France, other than that part of the dismembered Carolingian empire which lay to the west of the Meuse. Divided into hundreds of fiefs and principalities, it is the most important of these feudal rulers that catch the eye, the counts of Flanders, Champagne, Poitou and Toulouse, the dukes of Normandy, Brittany, Burgundy and Guyenne.

Amongst them Hugh Capet was only a minor prince, living at Orleans, Etampes, Poissy or Senlis, and going from one of these towns to another, sometimes with difficulty, since his estates were penetrated by other feudal dependencies. In Paris he owned only a Palace, on the Ile de la Cité, and even this could be threatened by his neighbours. His election as king, in 987, was partly accidental, occasioned by the early death of Louis V, and by the reluctance of the French aristocracy to have the natural heir, Charles of Lorraine. But his election was also accomplished because he had the support of the Church, and because his family was well-related (Hugh was the brother of the King of Burgundy, and the brother-in-law both of the Duke of Normandy and the Duke of Aquitaine). And if it is sometimes said that, from this time onwards, attempts by the mon-archs to extend their authority and to unify the kingdom were directed against the feudal lords, this is something of an anachronism. The policies of the Capetian kings were in themselves feudal, seeking by all the well-established means (through conquest, confiscation, marriage, purchase, gift, legal subterfuge, etc.) to acquire further estates and to improve communications between them.

The first of the line, Hugh, started the custom of preserving the succession within his family, by anointing his son, and all the monarchs insisted on preserving the unity of the royal domaine by applying the custom of primogeniture (and they were fortunate in having male heirs). By virtue of their duty to maintain justice they enhanced their prestige and increased their power. As the appropriate machinery developed the tradition grew up that in a feudal dispute the weaker of the parties could appeal to the king, and the chroniclers always spoke about the Capetians as givers of justice (*droicturiers*).

In these ways the monarch affirmed his position. He was outstanding because although he could, as landholder, be someone's vassal, it was early established that he did not pay homage; he was important because of his title and because of his religious consecration. Yet one cannot imagine any of the Capetians seeking to rule over the whole territory which one now calls France; one cannot conceive that any of these kings wished to accomplish the ruin of the feudal system. At the most the king could aspire to being on the top of some sort of feudal pyramid.

But at the same time, within the variegated patterns of feudalism, one can see the emergence of certain national forms. The feudal set-up within France had already become more complicated when the Duke of Normandy became King of England after the successful invasion of 1066, and became more so when the Plantagenets succeeded to the throne of England in 1154. Henry Plantagenet became Henry II, inheriting England and Normandy from his grandfather Henry I, inheriting Anjou and Touraine from his father Geoffrey Plantagenet, and Aquitaine came to him through his wife Eleanor. This acquisition naturally created a good many problems, and it also underlined the question of the relation between the north and the south of France. The populations which had formed France differed considerably from the north to the south of the Loire, and by language (*langue d'oïl* to the north, *langue d'oc* to the south), custom and tradition, there was a contrast between these two regions, which the Norman invasion in the north, and the Arab invasion in the south, only emphasized.

So great was this difference that it was as if two civilizations were in confrontation, and it seemed possible that the Count of Toulouse, ruling over possessions which stretched from the Garonne to the Rhône, would triumph over the more limited King of France. During the twelfth century the Albigensian heresy found its fullest expression in Languedoc, whilst at this time Catalan influence expanded into southern France. But the Count of Toulouse's ally, the King of Aragon, was killed fighting against Simon de Montfort, and later on the King of Aragon withdrew definitively across the Pyrenees, so that the troubadour songs lament that they have been deserted. By 1271 the hazard of inheritance brought the immense estates of Alphonse de Poitiers and Jeanne de Toulouse into the royal domaine, although this did not end 'the southern question'.

To the east, affairs were often more dramatic. In 1124 the Emperor Henry V marched his armies against Rheims, and all the barons of France forgot their rivalries with the king in order to resist him. In 1214 a similar unity was demonstrated against the English attacking from the west, and against invaders from the north and east. By the end of the thirteenth century it could be said that the French monarchy was based upon a successfully consolidated domaine, and also upon something approaching a sense of country, an idea of France, which was threatening to break out of the con-strictions of feudalism.

Perhaps it is typical of French history that hardly had this consoli-dation been achieved, when it was destroyed again, with the struggle between the royal houses of England and France which is generally known as the Hundred Years War (one which is 'officially' dated 1337–1453). These were terrible years for France, and although historians nowadays react against the over-sombre picture which used to be drawn about this 'waning of the Middle Ages', it remains a period of such generalized suffering and devastation that it is difficult to distinguish the effects of plague from those of wars and

15

economic decline. There was no sealed frontier between Aquitaine (or Gascony) and the rest of France, and with uncertain boundaries and shifts in fortune, local magnates were frequently doubtful as to where their loyalties or their interests lay. A type of feudalism emerged which threatened the unity of the kingdom more severely than before; the dukes of Orleans, Bourbon, Anjou, Brittany, Alençon, Foix, Armagnac, Albret, Luxembourg, and above all Burgundy, constituted rivals and enemies, who in the complications of international diplomacy, had to be defeated in battle, outwitted through negotiation, or won over by marriage agreements.

If providence had favoured all the Capetian monarchs with sons and heirs, this genetic good fortune ceased when the sons of Philippe le Bel had only daughters, and the arbitrary choice of Philippe de Valois as king was an occasion for a general decline of loyalty and an incitement for the formation of factions, whilst at the same time bringing to the throne monarchs who were far from capable. The bourgeoisie of Paris, firstly under Etienne Marcel between 1355 and 1358, and then again in 1413, also represented an element which sought to moderate the power of the throne. It seems likely that the lowest point in the fortunes of the King of France was reached in the years after 1410, when the King was mad and the monarchy, surrounded by antagonistic clans, seemed completely discredited, and when invasion, schism, violence, poverty and famine seemed to have achieved a certain permanence.

The reorganization of France under Charles VII was accompanied by the unusual epic of Joan of Arc. The story of this peasant girl who sought to save the kingdom (and who was burnt by the English and the Burgundians in 1431) represents a moment of transition in French history, since it is partly religious and partly nationalist. To fight for Joan of Arc was partly to fight for a religious cause, and to die for one's faith; but it was also to fight for France and to die for one's country. The last battle of the Hundred Years War was fought at Castillon in 1453 when the French army was victorious and proceeded to capture Bordeaux. The English had lost all their possessions in France except Calais. After the death of Charles VII in 1461 the feudal leagues failed in their assaults against his successor,

Louis XI, and Picardy and Burgundy became part of the royal domaine in 1477. In 1491 Anne de Bretagne married the king of France, and although Brittany remained a separate duchy, when her daughter Claude married Francis d'Angoulême (who later became Francis I) in 1532, France and Brittany were declared united.

From this time onwards, in France as in other countries, the tendency was economically towards a greater prosperity and administratively towards a more centralized and effective monarchy. Diplomatically France became involved in wars with the other great powers of Europe and envisaged conquests in Italy and in Lorraine. Religiously there had been internal conflict, particularly in the years from 1559 to 1598, and the conflict between Catholic and Protestant threatened to destroy the unity of the kingdom once again. Politically there were the civil wars, known as the Frondes, from 1648 to 1653. But in 1661 the existence of a powerful monarchy was dramatically established. It was then that Cardinal Mazarin died and that Louis XIV, who was aged 22 and who had officially been king since 1643, announced that there would no longer be any first minister and that he himself would rule. It seemed to be the beginning of a new era for France and for the monarchy.

If, looking back, it is asked why it was that the monarchy prevailed, then a series of details could be considered. The size of France made it difficult for an Estates-General to meet; the nobles were mainly concerned with their fiscal privileges; the monarchs succeeded in building up the royal domaine. Or one could eschew detail, and put forward a large generalization, to the effect that the economic trends of the times, towards a greater movement and consumption of goods, was bound to destroy the essentially small unities of feudalism and demand the creation of some bigger organization.

Between the points of detail and the generalization there are two considerations which should not be forgotten. The first is that the Crown's long delay in attacking the great feudal principalities encouraged a deep-grained regionalism; by the time the Crown absorbed them they were fully consolidated entities. Hence regionalism was strong and remained strong. Conversely, however, the Crown benefited from this delay, since the king had no need to build up an administrative machinery; this had already been done for him by a Duke of Normandy or by a Count of Anjou. He merely stepped into his shoes.[2] In this way the successes of regionalism and of centralization went hand in hand.

The second consideration concerns Paris and the Ile de France. Too much has been made of the smallness of the region which the Capetians first controlled. It is too often forgotten that, economically, this was an outstandingly prosperous region. The importance of the Seine and the ease with which communications between the north and the south were effected through Paris made this a magnet which drew immigrants from a far distance. By the time of the Hundred Years War, Paris and the Ile de France were the most densely populated region of the country.[3] The 'Capetian miracle' was in many ways that of the Paris region. Both these considerations, that of the region and that of Paris, are continually to appear and reappear in the study of modern and contemporary France.

2 The Ancien Régime

French patriotism needs a permanent expression, which can be nothing but a king or, more correctly, a succession of kings. Charles Maurras

THE REIGN OF LOUIS XIV (d. 1715) has for a long time been studied within a certain tradition, the tradition that this was the apogee of the monarchy and of French greatness. Just as the palace of Versailles was the model for all royal palaces, so it seemed that in terms of power, or culture, or ideas, France was the master of Europe, and therefore of the world. It is curious that, even with the advantages of hindsight, this view should have persisted. Everyone knows that within less than a century of Louis XIV's death the French monarchy collapsed and was never permanently, or fully, re/instated. We have therefore to bear in mind that there are certain reasons why the reign of Louis XIV should have been extolled.

One reason undoubtedly was because when, in later years, Germany had become politically united and seemed to be the permanent enemy of France, then Louis XIV appeared to have been a patriotic king, the first to figure consistently against what was later to become Germany. And after 1870, it was remembered that he had also been a victorious king. He extended French frontiers eastwards, adding Strasbourg to the French state and confirming the general possession of Alsace, FrancheComté and French Flanders (including Douai, Lille and Dunkirk). Although less successful in his later wars, he maintained the essential of his continental gains and France assumed its modern, hexagonal, shape; his purpose seemed clear and reasonable, and Marshal Turenne's remark that Frenchmen could neither rest nor sleep as long as a single German remained in Alsace was to be quoted in all the school textbooks of modern times. Culturally, too,

19

the reign of Louis XIV was regarded as a particularly successful period, and it has been claimed that the remarkable group of writers, and architects and artists, from Molière and Racine to La Bruyère, from the Mansarts and Lebrun to Le Nôtre and Rigaud, were as instrumental in bringing about the formation of France as were marshals such as Turenne and Vilars (although it is worth noting that the greater part of the plays of Corneille had been written before the death of Mazarin, and that both Molière and Racine belong to the early part of the reign).[1]

But however plausible such suggestions, one is tempted to believe that historians have been attracted towards the reign of Louis XIV – and have called it *Le Grand Siècle*, although there are plenty of other centuries which could warrant being called great – because they, like the contemporaries of Le Roi Soleil, have been hoodwinked by the *mise-en-scène* of Versailles and of kingly rule. Everyone knows that the life of Louis XIV was a continual public performance, in which every detail of ceremonial procedure was laden with signifi-cance. Although the emblem of the Sun King had been used by kings before Louis XIV, the ritual of his life was greater than that of any predecessor. From the ceremonial of his getting up, through the procedure of eating and drinking, by the ostentatious display of procedural etiquette, and in all the festivities and the devotions, every-thing revolved around the king.[2] The careful planning of both the town and the palace of Versailles rendered the king's bedroom the centre of life. Louis deliberately sought to make himself a sign and a symbol rather than an ordinary mortal king. This was not a personal conceit, it was a deliberate calculation and a political decision, and one which owed much to his predecessors.

Its essential reason for existence was the insecurity and uncertainty of the throne. Louis XIV never forgot the humiliations which he had suffered as a child, when the throne had been a sort of play-thing in the hands of rival coteries. He always feared that the same thing could happen again. So he chose Versailles as the back-cloth to his performance; he gave official power to men from the ranks of the middle classes; he insisted that the aristocracy should be caught up in the details of court ceremony; he pursued an active and warlike policy which would emphasize the national interests of France and he encouraged his once over-mighty subjects to identify themselves with a great cause. He pursued a foreign policy in which the question of the Spanish succession was always present (from the wars of his Spanish queen's rights which brought him conquests in Flanders, to the wars of the Spanish Succession where he attempted to win an enormous heritage), so that the fortunes of France were linked to the interests of his family; he became the repressor of heresy, so that his rule was aligned to the cause of the Catholic Church; his govern‑ ment was associated with the principle of mercantilism, whereby France would amass wealth and would endure as a national econo‑ mic unity. In all these ways the supremacy of the crown was meant to be associated with all the qualities and all the aspirations of the country. As one can read today on the face of the Versailles palace: *A toutes les gloires de la France.*

In all this there was a firm grasp of reality and an effectiveness both of policy and of rule. But there was also a façade. Just as the grandeur of Versailles concealed poverty and squalor, just as the religious devotion of the court was only an act put on to please Louis and Madame de Maintenon, so the unity and centralization of monar‑ chical France existed in appearance rather than in reality. Louis XIV was not a great captain of war, and he did not like real battles. He preferred sieges where the results had been worked out in advance, and he liked victory to be set in a décor, so that he could arrive in a coach with the Queen, Madame La Vallière and Madame de Montespan ('les trois reines'), and make a solemn entry into the captured town, with the bells ringing and the magistrates presenting him with the keys. It is very far from the reality of warfare and we must take care not to be deceived by the *mise‑en‑scène* in this or in other sectors of French history during this reign.

Provinces that were joined to France did not become French simply because of an administrative arrangement. The force of local customs and particularisms did not disappear because a representa‑ tive of central authority suddenly appeared in the locality. It is true that this was the golden age of the *intendant* who was the chief agent of the King in the provinces. But the powers of the *intendant* varied both in theory and in practice. The very essence of the *intendant* system was its flexibility, and according to circumstances the *intendant* could develop from being just a supervisor of other officers, to assuming the function of almost all the other officers. Some provinces were slow in acquiring *intendants*; Béarn did not have one until 1682, Brittany not until 1689. Sometimes an *intendant* arrived in a vast province which was unknown to him, he had no records and no bureaucracy at his disposal, and with bad communications he had difficulty in getting to know the area which he was to administer. Sometimes he only stayed for a short time, and in these circumstances it is difficult to think of him as an effective force. There were *intendants* who did stay for longer periods in a province, like Lamoignon de Baville who was thirty-five years in Languedoc or de Bagnols who was twenty-four years in Lille. These could become powerful, domi-nating figures. But everywhere the *intendant* was obliged to take account of the local notabilities. As his tasks grew he was obliged to rely increasingly on various officers, most of whom had bought their offices and who represented local interests. The privileges and immunities of private right and the obstinacy and conservatism of provincial tradition (sometimes incorporated in the Estates or in a *parlement*), meant that the work of the *intendant* was often that of laborious and persevering negotiation rather than the assertion of royal supremacy. Towards the end of the reign, in particular, the most that the representatives of central government wanted was money. Once this demand was satisfied they cared little about the principle of a unified state. The actual enforcement fell far below the pretensions of Versailles and the king had assumed responsibilities far greater than his real power.

The reign of Louis cannot be considered as a unity in itself. Several divisions after 1660 have been suggested as useful and appropriate. At first there is the period up to 1664, which opens at a moment of economic crisis, but which concludes with the establishment of royal magnificence. Then from 1664 to 1672 there is the organization of the administrative monarchy and the great reforms of Colbert. From 1672 to 1678 the picture becomes more sombre. War against Holland and war against the first European coalition mean the abandonment of many reforms in favour of expedients whereby money can be raised. After 1678 the king abandons his licentiousness and he is converted to a more austere faith. He leaves his mistresses, he marries Mme de Maintenon, he persecutes the Jansenists and the Protestants, he organizes a crusade against Algiers. After 1686 there is a period of twenty-four years' continuous war, the most important and extensive wars that Europe had yet known, in which Louis was gradually moving towards capitulation and negotiation, giving up his hope of ruling the Low Countries, giving up his quarrel with the Pope, giving up the ambition of acquiring the whole of the Spanish inheritance.

From 1700 onwards there is a period of expedients and improvisations, concessions alternating with aggression, hesitation alternating with determination. The king was unable to work as effectively as in the past and he had no great ministers who could work for him. The court, which was sad and introspective, was cynical about protocol and was divided into various cabals concerning the succession. The government was desperately short of money; commerce and industry were stagnating; one of the worst famines ever to hit France was accompanied by plague and whilst perhaps one-tenth of France was reduced to beggary, the population probably fell by about a million in the last twenty years of the reign. There was widespread criticism of the government; in some parts of the country there was open defiance, and bands of men roamed at large, looking for food and pillage. The worst of the military defeats was salvaged in the last years of the war, but when Louis died on 1 September 1715, having reigned for 72 years, he died unwanted by courtiers and unloved by the population.

It was true that he had created a standing army and a bureaucratic state, that France was less profoundly rebellious than at his accession and had greatly increased in size. But he had found no remedy for the chronic disorders of the country, provoked too often by famine and by the forceful collection of taxes. He had carried out few innovations and he had allowed his despotism to exist alongside most old institutions and many old privileges, thus combining the abuses of arbitrary state power with those inherent in the social structure.

By the standards of the time, much of his rule was particularly violent and oppressive, and in spite of its mystique, it is doubtful whether this royalty was successful. There was a world of meaning in the remark made in 1715, that those who had witnessed the death of a king believed that anything might happen.[3]

When one examines the records of the French administration, say of the *intendants*, under Louis XIV, one has the impression of being much nearer to medieval than to modern times. But when one looks at the social history of France, towards the end of his reign particularly, then one is much nearer to the time of the French Revolution. The financial difficulties of government, the hostility between the bourgeoisie, growing in wealth and power, and the aristocracy, a class that is hardly renewing itself, the existence of a large rural population that is permanently on the verge of catas- trophe through shortage of food, all these were the symptoms of the pre-Revolutionary period. So near was the France of 1715 to that of 1789 that the Regent (there had to be a regent since Louis XV was only five years old) considered summoning the States-General; a debate took place on what were the real powers of the central government. It is important to note that there was no longer the movement of Versailles to deceive the eye into thinking that an effective and magnificent centralized government still existed; the boy-king was brought up in the Tuileries, the royal palace in Paris.

The claims of the provincial nobility were based upon their historical and legal rights and upon an interpretation of how a state should be organized. It was thought that powers in a state should be distributed so as to create a harmony, and it was suggested that a contract existed between the central government and the provincial institutions, and that both sides derived advantage from this association. If the central government increased its power then it was not only encroaching on historic rights, it was destroying the benefits of the contract. What was a debate became an administrative crisis when the financial needs of the central government made it imperative to raise more money from taxation. This was because of a number of developments, the most important of which were the wars of the eighteenth century, in which France's dual role as

24

both a continental and a maritime power involved her both in the continental and the colonial wars (especially in India, where the French establishment dated from 1702, and in Canada where the French establishment dated from 1603) and in a consequential heavy expenditure; there was also the general rise of prices throughout the eighteenth century which increased costs without correspondingly increasing receipts. It looked as if bankruptcy were inevitable. The government was not strong enough to reform the taxation system by insisting that the nobility should increase their contribu‑ tions; and the government was not weak enough simply to disappear.

The Revolution of 1789 has been attributed to many causes, and it was the outcome of many crises: there was the administrative crisis as there was the financial crisis; there was a crisis which arose from a slump in economic activity, roughly coinciding in time with the reign of Louis XVI, who succeeded to the throne in 1774; there was a social crisis which is to be explained essentially by hostility to the privileges of the aristocracy; there was the crisis of famine, and the fear of famine, as the growing population stretched the resources of agriculture and as the small landholders, when the harvest was bad, found it impossible to meet their own food requirements, let alone sell their produce; there was an urban crisis, when the high prices of food affected purchasing power and when industry, banking and credit began to weaken. But all these crises were, in the long run, insoluble because they represent a crisis in the organization of the French state.

Although, theoretically, the power of the French king began no‑ where and ended nowhere, and although, in practice, there was no such thing as a republican before 1789, there was an important section of the nobility which saw no reason why they should accept the rule of the king, except in the most general terms, and the nobility in Dauphiné and in Brittany began the revolution when they vio‑ lently flouted the royal authority in 1788. A bourgeois saw no reason why he should accept the ascendancy of an aristocrat simply because he had taken the trouble to be born. A peasant had no reason to like the privileges of the landowner, whether aristocrat or bourgeois. There were many, from all the groups and classes, who felt no loyalty to the Church, just as there were many parish priests whose enthusiasm for the aristocratic, and frequently absentee, bishops was secretly lukewarm. There were many who felt no interest in the colonial wars. In times of food scarcity there was a natural antagonism towards those who controlled the distribution of food. In times of economic crisis, there was criticism of those who were thought to be responsible. At all times there was a reluctance to pay taxes and in times of hardship there was a direct refusal. Before the storming of the Bastille in July 1789 the excise barriers and the tax collectors were the frequent victims of violence.

Thus it was possible for each section of the population to insist upon its own interests. There was no mystique whereby France was held together, no authority which was easily accepted. The writers and intellectuals were conscious of this disaggregation and they themselves contributed to it as they appeared increasingly to be a class apart from others, working within their own community of interests and objectives. By 1789 France was in danger of disintegra-tion. The Revolution was one way of saving the state and the nation.

3   The Revolution

Cette France, d'où se répandaient sur le monde tous les nobles sentiments, toutes les pensées généreuses. Constans, 1891

IT HAS OFTEN BEEN pointed out that the crisis in France at the end of the eighteenth century was not unique – other countries had experience of national debts, economic crisis, famine and revolution, and it has been suggested that these were characteristics common to those countries that bordered the Atlantic. It is not a complete rejec-tion of these theories to concentrate upon France and to describe the French Revolution essentially in French terms. In French terms the crisis that culminated in the events of 1789 meant that absolute monarchy was ended and that France was searching for a new form of government. The Revolution proposed several new forms. It proposed one when the Third Estate, representing that portion of the population which was neither clerical nor aristocratic, meeting in the general convocation of the States-General, proclaimed itself the National Assembly. The Revolution proposed a form of govern-ment when the constitution of 1791 divided France into 83 depart-ments. The Revolution put forward a system of government when the revolutionaries assumed that what was good for one part of France was good for another. They were later to assume that what was good for France was also good for Europe, and France, which had recently incorporated Lorraine (1766) and purchased Corsica (1768), was to absorb Avignon and to proceed to a more general expansion.

The year 1789 marks the period when centralization became permanent and, since it could no longer be rejected, successful. This is all the more striking since the Revolution, far from beginning

27

with the rising of the people in Paris as is often suggested, actually began as a movement of the provincial aristocracy, rejecting the incursions of the King and insisting on their privileges. One of the most active of the political organizations of the revolutionary period was based upon provincial strength, and demanded that Paris should be reduced to one eighty-third part of its existing influence. One of the great centres of opposition to the Revolution was centred in the Vendée, the bastion of Catholic Brittany. But the Revolution became a force which overcame all this opposition and it was able to do so for three main reasons.

Firstly, because after 1792, the Revolution became caught up in war, and to defend France was to defend the Revolution. The enemies of France were not only outside the frontiers – Prussia, Austria, England – but they were also inside France itself; the aristo-crats who were in league with the foreigners and who refused to give up their privileges, the priests who refused to co-operate with the government, the provincials who yearned for provincial rights and autonomy. It was the revolutionary armies which instilled the princip-les of patriotism into the distant provinces and it was the revolution-ary tribunals and *représentants en mission* who terrorized people so that they dared not doubt their loyalty both to the Revolution and to *la patrie en danger*.

Secondly, the same financial and economic problems which had beset the governments of the Ancien Régime continued to haunt the governments of the post-1789 era, and the solution which was proposed and accepted, that of seizing Church lands and issuing government bonds based upon the value of land, was one that was heavy with consequences. Not only did it create an ideological division within France, those who were loyal Catholics opposing the Revolution which had become the despoiler of Church property and the usurper of Church authority; but the bonds, or *assignats*, began to circulate as paper money, and the excessive issue of these notes, and their devaluation, made normal economic life difficult and hampered the ordinary exchange of goods. The mobile of revolution was economic uncertainty, especially the shortage of food or the fear that food might be short. For as long as there was an

28

apparent danger of such a shortage and a continued economic apprehension, then there was the danger of popular uprising, violence and bankruptcy, before which all the governing classes trembled. They looked to Paris for support and help, or they sought to remedy the situation by making changes in the government in Paris.

Thirdly, in spite of its popular aspects and the flurries of popular excitement which accompanied it, the Revolution was a bourgeois revolution. It put the concluding touches to a process which had been going on for a long time and virtually inaugurated a period of bour-geois power. The upper bourgeoisie, under such a constitution as that of 1791, was able to control most of the governing forces. Even when the Revolution seemed to be entering a socialist phase, with the period 1793 to 1794 which is usually associated with Robespierre, the upper bourgeoisie did not lose its ascendancy. At worst it was a temporary crisis, and this was overcome once the revolutionary armies were victorious and had stopped the foreign invasion; Robespierre was executed, the economic controls were lifted, the rights of property re-affirmed. The Directory, from 1795 to 1799, ushered in a period when the upper bourgeoisie was again supreme and Michelet, then a small boy, marvelled at the wealth and splen-dour of the carriages which were waiting outside the Opera.

The Revolution gave the bourgeoisie the opportunity of acquiring vast areas of land, of opening up the economic wealth of the country unhampered by aristocratic or local privileges, of populating the growing administrative services. The force of the Revolution was the force of the bourgeoisie. The peasantry, once they had received their land-rights in 1789, became a largely conservative force. The proletariat, whether urban or rural, remained at the bottom of the social pyramid. Their situation had not changed since 1789 except that at times it had grown worse; they had hardly been revolutionary, they had only been revindicative, wanting the certainty of cheap food rather than a re-distribution of wealth. Only on isolated occasions, like the Babeuf conspiracy of 1799, does one find the emergence of thorough-going revolutionary ideas. But the bourgeoisie had gained its opportunities through crisis and violence. It feared social revolution and it feared counter-revolution. Therefore it felt the need for a state which would safeguard its interests and permit further prosperity and progress. And for all these reasons the revolutionary state suc- ceeded. However much people outside France are apt to dwell upon the violence and the bloodshed of the Revolution, emphasizing (and exaggerating) the popular risings of 1789, the September massacres of 1792, the execution of the King the next year, the Terror of 1793 to 1794 and the repressions of 1795, the bourgeois view of the Revolution was that it was successful and that it represented progress. It stood for the rejection of absolute monarchy and aristocratic privilege and it promoted the ascension of the bourgeoisie and the rational organization of the state.

It has often been pointed out that the Revolution established an order of society, but did not establish a political system. And it should not be thought for a minute that because the Revolution was a bourgeois triumph, then subsequently everything happened accord- ing to some bourgeois plan or that all events can be fitted into some coherent process. The Revolution was filled with contradictions and was directed by men who often were unable to act rationally.

Nor would anyone claim that the coming to power of Napoleon in 1799, or his method of holding power and governing until 1815, was either foreseeable or arranged by the bourgeoisie. The whole movement of events under the Directory (1795–99) gave consider- able importance to the army. Once again France was at war; politically the country seemed to be at the mercy of extremists, either to the right or to the left; economically there was still no satisfactory organization of credit or of exchange; in personal terms, it was the young and able generals who were to be preferred to the corrupt and mediocre politicians left behind by the devastations of the Revo- lution. It was natural enough that one of these generals should seize power; but it was an accident that the particular general who came to the front should have been someone endowed with such per- sonality and imagination that he made a lasting impression upon France.

Even so, Napoleon (as he became after he had proclaimed himself Emperor in 1804) governed France in the interests of the bourgeoisie.

With the creation of the Bank of France he organized a workable system of credit and put an end to the period of unstable currency; with the introduction of the Civil Code he tried to unify legal procedure in the country, but he also sought to give legal backing to the existing distribution of property, and to assert the rights of males over females; with the development of foreign policy he tried to make the continent of Europe a vast colony for the benefit of the French manufacturer. The rights of the employer were asserted and the rights of working men were rejected. Paris, like other big towns, was carefully supplied with food, to prevent the recurrence of popular disturbances. There was an attempt to end the political quarrels of the past and to bring together all good Frenchmen under the rule of one enlightened despot, who would protect the achievements of the Revolution.

But the phenomenon of the Empire, if it was to the advantage of the bourgeoisie, was also a sign of weakness. Guizot once said that if the Revolution was a violent way of breaking out of the Ancien Régime, the Empire was a violent way of breaking out of the Revolution. And it is true that if the Revolution had permitted the assertion of bourgeois power, it had not provided a secure political base for it. Napoleon attempted to provide that basis. He emphasized administrative centralization and created the appearance of a direct link between the mayor of the smallest commune and the Emperor in his palace; he devised constitutions which were deliberately obscure so that his own authority was concealed amongst other institutions and appeared less solitary and less naked; he attempted to create a new monarchy, with a new court and a new aristocracy. But he was not successful in any of these things. His administration was not effective; the art of government for him was continued improvisation; he was never secure on his throne and not a year went by when he did not have the conspiracies of dissident generals, discontented business men, former Jacobins and nostalgic revolutionaries. The only system that Napoleon devised of dealing with them was to leap into his carriage, ride to some battlefield and gain some resounding victory outside France.

The Napoleonic system was, from the beginning, dependent

upon the Napoleonic legend and upon the myth that Napoleon's victories abroad made him impregnable at home. His situation was paradoxical. He was only sure of a large body of firm support when the achievements of the Revolution seemed to be in danger, and he often had to create the appearance of danger. He wanted all French-men, whether royalists or Jacobins, to be proud that they wore the uniform of Bonaparte. But he knew that they would weary of war and would wish to return to the comforts of home. He himself was not a man who gloried in battle, and he would have welcomed a prolonged period of stability, in which he could have made laws and lectured his compatriots about history and literature. He was always aware of the fragility of his power. 'The Emperor of Austria leaves his capital and fights and loses a battle. Yet when he returns to Vienna he is still Emperor.' This was the thought that haunted him. He knew that one day the 'divine spark' would desert him and that he would return to Paris, not in triumph but in defeat. And for all Napoleon's unequalled will to persist, it was clear that the Empire could be little more than a passing moment.

Just as in administration, or diplomacy, or in the conduct of a battle, Napoleon had neither the time nor the resources to do more than improvise, so the Empire itself was only a temporary expedient. What was unexpected was that Napoleon, who was not an attractive man, and who at times was very unpopular amongst his con-temporaries, should have impressed himself so firmly in the imagina-tion of the generations that followed. Perhaps this is a tribute to the need to remember him rather than a sign of anything truly remarkable about his achievement. It is a commentary on France rather than on Napoleon.[1]

1 A remarkable collection of prehistoric wall-paintings were discovered in the grotto of Lascaux in Dordogne, in 1940. This bull's head was painted by a Stone Age artist some 20,000 years ago.

2 The region of Carnac, near to Auray in Brittany, is rich in stone monuments, representing the civilization of 2500–1500 BC. Particularly striking are the rows of menhirs, or standing-stones.

3 Detail from the Bayeux tapestry, now to be seen at Bayeux in Normandy. It was probably made by Anglo-Saxon workers in the 11th century to decorate the cathedral at Bayeux. It illustrates the Norman conquest of England. Here Duke William ('Hic Willelm Dux') leads his men to the ships which are to carry them across the Channel.

4 The Pont du Gard, near Nîmes, is one of the most impressive monuments of Roman Gaul. Built a few years before the birth of Christ, it formed part of an aqueduct system which brought water to Nîmes from the region of Uzès.

5 Saint John the Baptist: detail from the west porch of Chartres Cathedral (late 12th to early 13th century). On visiting this cathedral, Napoleon is supposed to have said, 'an atheist would be ill at ease here.'

6 Left: the church of Saint-Philibert at Tournus in Burgundy (10th–11th century), famous for its austere simplicity.

7 The lower chapel of the Sainte-Chapelle in Paris (below). This was used by the servants of the royal palace. Built about 1247 by St Louis, it is a fine example of Gothic art.

8 One of the characteristics of the French renaissance was the building of châteaux in the Loire valley. Blois (opposite, above) contains a variety of different architectures; the early 16th-century staircase shows Italian influence.

9 Vaux-le-Vicomte, near Melun (opposite, below). Built by Louis le Vau, 1656–1660, it is said to have given Louis XIV the ambition to construct Versailles.

10 *La Liberté* (detail) by Delacroix (1758–1863), in the Louvre. This picture represents the barricades of the revolution of July 1830. It was in these days, 'les trois glorieuses', that the people of Paris accomplished one of the most romantic of revolutions, but one that was soon 'confiscated' by Louis-Philippe and the upper bourgeoisie.

11 *The Third-Class Carriage* by Daumier (1808–79), a subject which he painted and drew several times. Versions in oil are in New York and Ottawa.

12 *The Boating Party Lunch at Bougival* by Jean Renoir (1841–1919), now in the Phillips Collection, Washington. Painted in 1881, and concluding a period in Renoir's development, it represents a constant theme in French life and art.

13 War memorial at the Ecole des Beaux Arts in Paris. Almost every commune in France has such a memorial. Sometimes the names of those who fell in the three wars against Germany are recorded together.

4 Post-Revolution

La lutte des factions et des partis ne permet jamais à la France de disposer que du tiers de ses forces. Ernest Renan

THE HISTORY OF FRANCE in the nineteenth century underlines the failure of the Revolution to establish an accepted and workable principle of government. The instability of the régimes was proverb/ ial. Napoleon's abdication in 1814 was followed by the restoration of the Bourbon monarchy, and then, when there was an apparent danger to the revolutionary settlement, by Napoleon's return from exile for the so/called Hundred Days. The allied victory at Waterloo (18 June 1815) brought the Bourbons (Louis XVIII and Charles X) back again but the revolution of 1830 removed them definitively from the French throne; the revolution of 1848 then removed the Orleans branch of the royal family, which had replaced them. The short/ lived second Republic (1848–51) was followed by the second experience of Bonapartism with Napoleon's nephew as Emperor until the Franco/Prussian war and the proclamation of the Third Republic on 4 September 1870. This was to last until June 1940.

But even within these dates, which mark the different régimes, there was a further instability. When the country had a form of parliamentary government, from 1815 to 1848 with a monarchy and from 1870 to 1940 without one, it proved difficult for govern/ ments to stay in power for any length of time. Between 1830 and 1848 for example, the reign of the Orleanist Louis/Philippe, there were some seventeen different governments; between 1870 and 1940, over one hundred. To register the instability of the régimes and the instability of governments still does not exhaust the list of instabilities. 1815, 1830, 1848, 1851, 1870, these are the dates when the régime changed, but there were moments of crisis and uncertainty within those dates. In 1830 France might have become a republic if the leading republican, Lafayette, had been a determined and competent believer in political change. The authoritarianism of Napoleon III knew many oscillations. The Third Republic had many uncertain, ties and seemed occasionally to hover on the brink of fundamental change, as at the time of the social revolt known as the Commune in 1871, the movement in favour of General Boulanger, the division revealed and accentuated by the long,drawn,out quarrel over the alleged traitor, Captain Dreyfus. Modern France was a country of political uncertainty and occasionally of national scandal.

This story has been told many times.[1] It is more useful here to analyse the period and to try and determine what characterized it. First of all one finds that the political development of France is not dominated by a few powerful, nationally,organized political parties, as happens in other western European countries. In spite of the almost continuous existence of assemblies and of many different electoral laws, there is hardly an example of a single political party gaining a complete electoral victory and there are no examples at all of a political party gaining a victory for any appreciable length of time. Elections in France throughout this period tended to bring to the fore groups and tendencies which derived their strength from local rather than from national organizations, and the assemblies were usually made up of a wide selection of these groupings. It is rare for a group to be completely eliminated, and it is quite common for some tendency, which has apparently suffered a decisive electoral defeat, to re,appear in a short space of time, possibly under a new guise. Governments therefore became an affair of coalitions. The mainspring of political life often consisted of the negotiation between the different groups. The type of politician who emerged was one who was skilled at manœuvre, who avoided committing himself decisive, ly to any policy or organization, who saw national affairs through the spectrum of the great game of politics. And government tended to become a short,term affair. It is true that many politicians had a long life, and that within the different régimes it was often the same small pack of names that was continually being shuffled. But political

42

life had its own momentum, and sometimes seemed to be divorced from the realities of national life.

Another characteristic is that the system of centralization, that is to say the system of ministerial power and patronage and the internal organization of departments and prefects, was always maintained. There were moments when quite powerful movements in favour of decentralization could be discerned: under the Second Empire for example, opposition to the Emperor was often expressed in the framework of a desire for administrative reform. Whilst the political right objected to the whole of France being subjected to the tyranny of a Paris where revolutions took place, and would have preferred to see more power and influence given to local notabilities, men belonging to the left had frequent misgivings about the complicated apparatus of government emerging from the capital. But nothing was done to further change and the Jacobin tradition of centralization always persisted. It was thought that centralization was the only acceptable instrument of uniformity, and of justice, equality, reform and progress. Michelet, comparing the Italians to the French, thought that they were inferior because they did not have a system of centralization, and Edgar Quinet thought that it would be madness to try and diminish the greatness of Paris, achieved by centuries of history.

However, as Tocqueville and other reflective Frenchmen pointed out, the result of all this was that a representative system existed side by side with an administrative system, and the result was bound to be detrimental to the representative system, since governments naturally intervened administratively in order to further their political fortunes. This was not corruption, the actual buying of votes, but it represented a considerable force of persuasion and influence. And the effect of this administrative power was also to increase the gap between government and governed. One was not always on the side of the government and one's natural reluctance to accept, say, the fiscal demands coming from Paris were reinforced when the demands were associated with a political organization to which one was opposed. It became only too justifiable to be opposed to the state and its structures, and to assert values which existed before the state and which were independent of it.[2]

Such an attitude brings one naturally to a further characteristic of French political life at this time, and that is the persistence and growth of the religious quarrel which emphasized the ideological diversity of the nation. It is widely believed that this quarrel owed its origin to the Revolutionary legislation of 1791.

It seems likely that behind this confrontation lay a deeper cleavage: those who believed in progress, and who were confident of their ability to achieve this progress, saw the Roman Catholic church as an enemy to progress; whilst those who were Catholics doubted that the continual upheavals of France could be said to represent progress. The result was that many Frenchmen insisted upon the establishment of a state which could unify the nation and which would educate children as Frenchmen, not as Catholics; Catholics, on the other hand, insisted on their right to have their children brought up in their own faith, and claimed this as an elementary liberty. This endless quarrel about religion and about education, the sons of St Louis in conflict with the descendants of Voltaire, to use the vocabulary of one of the protagonists, sometimes became the main subject and the mainspring of politics. In village life, rivalry between the school-teacher (the *instituteur*) and the priest was the norm. In national life, the split between Catholics and non-Catholics (*laïques*) became particularly severe with the establishment of the Third Republic, when Catholics opposed the republic and when anti-Catholics passed a law separating Church and State (1905). There were few areas of French cultural life which were not affected by this quarrel.

A further characteristic of French political life during this period was the importance of foreign affairs. When Guizot was French ambassador in London in 1840, he was surprised to find the lack of interest which both the British public and British politicians showed in foreign policy matters. This was not to be his experience in France, where the greatest excitements were to be over France's position in various parts of the world. This can partly be explained by the political situation. If it was difficult for coalition governments to stay together, it was difficult for oppositions to work together. For both, questions of foreign policy could often be useful rallying

44

cries, convenient means of concealing the fundamental disagreements that threatened to stultify their action. Sometimes, an aggressive or bold foreign policy would make the French people forget, or it was hoped that they would forget, that they were Breton, or Catholic, or attached to some political grouping or interest, and they would remember only that they were French. In this way foreign policy could be a device which would compensate for internal divisions. But France's relations with the outside world were in themselves important, even inescapable. It could not be forgotten that the height of the Revolution had coincided with war, and many believed that the hope of all future revolutionaries was placed in war. Others pointed to the example of Napoleon, and claimed that whilst France had military victory, the population was indifferent to liberty. It could not be forgotten that France had been invaded in 1793, in 1814 and again in 1815, or that French frontiers had been fixed by a congress meeting at Vienna. There could be no indifference when revolution (or counter-revolution) took place in Spain, Savoy, Switzerland or Belgium, and the problem of French security became more pressing when, after another invasion of France and another military defeat, Germany and Italy became unified states.

The problem of France's role in Europe and in the world became more complicated as Europeans became more interested in Africa, Asia and Oceania. Sometimes there was a direct conflict between the protagonists of overseas empire, and those who thought that France had to direct all her attentions to Europe. Clemenceau urged Frenchmen to fix their eyes on the thin blue line of the Vosges, and he thought of the provinces that had been annexed by Germany in 1871, Alsace and Lorraine. The nationalist Déroulède spurned colonies. 'I have lost two children, and you offer me twenty servants,' he said. But others believed that France could compensate herself for defeat in Europe by victory in Tunisia and Indo-China. The man who dominated French foreign policy for many years, Delcassé, who was as desirous as anyone that Alsace-Lorraine should be recovered, thought that France should build up an alliance system in Europe (particularly with Russia and with Great Britain) and at the same time that France should affirm her position in territories

45

such as Morocco. At all events the debate on foreign policy was yet a further complication to the political system.

If one turns from this political scene to the economic and social life of nineteenth-century France, one moves to an area where the terms 'stability' and 'instability' are no longer applicable, where the contrast is rather one between what is stagnant and what is dynamic. Like all western European countries at this time, France equipped herself with a modern transport system of railways, and with new industries. As textile and metallurgical enterprises grew, corresponding developments in credit and banking, in imports and exports, took place. Towns grew in size, and certain areas of the country became specialized in the mining or manufacturing processes. Sections of the population transferred from agriculture to industry, first of all in seasonal terms and then permanently. In other words the general characteristics of nineteenth-century economic change, with the uncertainties, the abuses and the triumphs of capitalism, were present in France as in other western countries. But the particularity of the French experience was that all these changes were much gentler, apparently less important, than elsewhere.

It has become one of the well-worn themes of historical debate to discuss whether France had an industrial revolution or not. The French never experienced the sweeping changes which came, with apparent suddenness, to countries such as England and Germany. The expanding rapid growth of towns, for example, did not take place in France. The concentration of economic power, which caused the French historian Michelet, as he travelled from Birmingham to Wolverhampton, and from Manchester to Bolton, to reflect that he was at the heart of what was important in England, was less apparent in France. Considerable areas seemed untouched by change and whereas in other European countries industrialization was to be a process which eventually created a certain uniformity, in France industrialization was to add further diversifications to French society.

One has to explain why it is that France experienced only limited change, and when seeking explanation, one immediately comes upon another unusual characteristic of nineteenth- and twentieth-century

France, which might well have had some bearing upon the slowness of economic change. This is the movement of population growth. In the eighteenth century France had a large and young population. It was this population which enabled the country to withstand the revolutionary and Napoleonic wars. In 1800, with a population of about 28 millions, France was the most populous country of Europe, apart from Russia. But by the end of the century, although the population had increased to 40 millions, the populations of other countries had increased much more, and France was placed only fifth in Europe. With the exception of Ireland, France was probably the European country with the smallest population growth.

This cannot be explained by any suggestion that it was the revolutionary and Napoleonic wars which were responsible. In these wars the death-rate was not high, the degree of mobilization was not important, and it was not always Frenchmen who were fighting for Napoleon. Nor would it be true to say that emigration reduced the numbers of French within France; of the European countries France contributed amongst the least to overseas settlement, and the moments of organized schemes of settlement in Algeria were usually linked to particular episodes, such as the economic crisis of 1848, or the annexation of Alsace and Lorraine in 1871. In almost all the nineteenth century, there were more Spanish, Italians, Maltese and Germans in Algeria than there were French. Therefore, since one must discount death in warfare and loss by emigration, one is left with a consideration of birth-rate and death-rate.

There are three main theories. The one stresses the importance of the revolutionary and Napoleonic legislation, which ensured that all the children in a family would normally inherit their parents' property, not merely the eldest son. This made it disadvantageous for property-owners, and especially landowners, to have large families. The other sees family limitations as part of a more generalized cultural complex whereby a high rate of infantile mortality has to be considered alongside a bourgeois preoccupation with comfort and social ambitions. Finally, one can consider the reproductive rate of French women and suggest that variations in the rate are to be associated with particular crises in the French economy, especially in the rural areas. France was almost classically the country of food shortage, real or imagined, and a mystique concerning bread grew up and persisted, so that large families were thought to be dangerous. All these theories suggest that birth-control was practised, both by the populations of the countryside (as suggested by the novelist Zola) and by the bourgeoisie (as suggested by the Goncourt brothers in their novels).[3]

It is not easy to choose between these three theories. Fortunately it is possible to see some truth in each of them. The difficulty arises because French demographic history is treated as a whole, since it has some cultural unity. In fact, the different factors played a varied role, having importance at certain moments or in certain areas. It is still difficult to appreciate the role of religion, of alcoholism, of rural hygiene and medical services, or of various psychological factors, in all this. But it is certain that this decline of population disturbed many Frenchmen, many of whom thought that it was more catas-trophic than their political confusions and inadequacies. 'France is an island of sugar that is melting away,' commented a distinguished economist at the end of the century, and there were many who saw the population decline as part of a general decadence.

But the precise problem remains that of economic development. Those who wish to link France's failure to industrialize completely to France's demographic weaknesses, argue that if population in-creases then demand increases and the need to expand the amount of wealth available becomes more pressing. Hence, and the case of Germany is often cited as an example, economic expansion is a response to demographic pressure. Since that demographic pressure did not exist in France then there was no consequential economic growth. But once again it must be said that the economic history of France is not as simple as this. Those movements of rapid economic growth that did take place in France are not to be explained by exceptional moments of population increase. And twentieth-century experience suggests that a large and growing population is not always an incentive to industrial production, since it can overwhelm the economic structures and reduce them to ineffectiveness.

One has to look at the other explanations which have been offered for economic backwardness. For example, it has been suggested that France simply did not have the 'minerals in the blood' necessary for industrialization, and here it is essentially a good supply of coking coal that is meant. It has also been said that French industrialists did not have the necessary capital. Money was tied up in land, which was the most secure of investments and which had been underwritten by the 1789 Revolution. Otherwise French holders of capital preferred the bonds of some foreign government, or even simply to hoard money in the *bas de laine*, gold coins hidden beneath the mattress, in a general distrust of governments, banks and investments. The role of the family firm has also been considered as an element in the failure to produce large-scale enterprises. The family firm could be backward in its technology and in its financial organization. But above all it created a very limited ambition. It was not working for an unlimited future, it was working for a very foreseeable future, a calculable number of people, marriages and children. Werner Sombart's reflection that the Industrial Revolution took place simply because a handful of men wanted to get rich would not be applicable to these unambitious entrepreneurs. France did not progress economically because Frenchmen did not want to do so.

There are yet other suggestions for French backwardness. There is the consideration that labour, in constant demand on the land, was not available for large-scale industrial development; that there was something in the French national character that preferred small-scale, high-quality (sometimes luxury) production; that successive French governments, by a continued policy of protection, allowed small and inefficient firms to exist side by side with more modern and better equipped enterprises; or simply, that France, deeply divided within itself, simply could not adjust itself to a pattern of modern industrial organization. It is difficult to choose from amongst so many different suggestions. But once again it is possible to believe that there is something to be said for each suggestion. The error comes from over-simplifying a long and varied period, and from supposing that the same considerations applied at all times. In the 1840s, for example, there was little apparent incentive to modernize, the price of fuel was high, it was not easy or cheap to borrow money, and within a small, assured market there was no guarantee that modernization would be more successful than traditional methods. Later in the century, when development was more rapid, it is as if both bourgeoisie and government were easily satisfied with what had been accomplished and saw little reason why the expansion process should continue. Perhaps what links both periods is a certain self-consciousness, and, with novelists such as Balzac and Zola, a certain denunciation of the materialism and the degradation which accompanied the activity of money-making.[4]

Thus although the political world was unstable and changing, and although the economic system was only gradually being transformed, in both the structures were rigid. There is one factor which is part of both the political and the economic aspects of nineteenth-century France, and that is the growth and importance of Paris. Throughout the century the population of Paris continued to rise and came to represent a substantial percentage of the total population. As the administrative capital, the importance of Paris increased as the importance of governmental activity increased and extended itself to new spheres. Since the important decisions were taken in Paris, then it was important to be in Paris. The railway system was centred upon Paris, banking was concentrated in Paris, cultural life came to depend increasingly on the University in Paris, and on the Paris press, periodicals, theatres, salons, cafés and all the contacts and possibilities which existed in the capital.

Politics were centred in Paris. If the Revolution of 1789 began in the provinces, those of 1830 and 1848, the *coup d'état* of 1851, the proclamation of the Republic in 1870, the Commune of 1871, the episode of General Boulanger, the Dreyfus affair, all were essentially Parisian in their outlook and in their development. The provinces provided the spectators rather than the actors, and the apparent fragility of much French political life derived from the fact that whoever could control Paris could claim to control the whole of France. And the success of Paris, its growth and increase, brought about still further growth. Since Paris was a centre of consumption then it became a centre of production, and increasingly people were attracted to the high wages and to the possibilities of commercial profit. And as Paris grew and prospered so the provinces became less interesting and less important. The word provincial' took on a pejorative meaning. Life in the provinces became dull, petty and somnolent. From time to time attempts were made to revive the culture or the economic life of some province or region. But the inexorable progress of Paris continued. Madame Bovary, buying writing paper and having no one to write to, is a typical provincial figure. Her creator, Flaubert, on a visit to Rennes, noted that a seal was appearing in a circus there. Once the seal has gone, he wrote, there will be nothing of interest in Rennes. Paris became a world of its own, conscious of its superiority, often self-satisfied, sometimes nervous and uncertain. Much of the energy of the country seemed to drain out of the provinces as Paris absorbed too much and became a value of its own.

Thus, politically speaking, the France that entered the twentieth century was apparently unstable, subject to a constant political change and to a frequent threat of violence. But in social terms, it was a country where there was little change, where the structures of bourgeois and peasant power were firmly established. To such an extent was this so that to those who wished for changes and reforms, the rigidity of the social system and the power of the bourgeoisie appeared overwhelming. Since there was little expectation of reform by persuasion, it became common to believe in reform by violence and to place one's hopes in destruction.

Doubtless it was because of this that certain Frenchmen adopted a pessimistic attitude when they regarded the affairs of their own country. Voltaire said that there was a law whereby people always believed that the world was in process of degeneration, but however this may be, there is reason to think that the French were becoming more convinced of their decadence than they had been in the past. Men from different parts of the political spectrum had their visions of an ideal France, and sought to identify those who were responsible for the failure to achieve it. And different men chose different enemies, pointed to different groups in society as the perpetrators of all that had gone wrong, asserted different values. French political thinking was divided and revealed the differences, even the hatreds, that existed amongst the French.

5   The years of despair

'Pourvu qu'ils tiennent . . .' 'Qui?' 'Les civils.'   Caption to a drawing by Forain

THE FOREIGN POLICY of a state is rarely a matter of choice.
It is usually dictated by discernible principles. One can see that it
was the principles of physical geography which made France particularly attentive towards the eastern frontier, since seas, mountains
and hills provided natural and defensible frontiers elsewhere. Economic geography, whereby France maintained a more harmonious
economy than other countries, and human geography, recording
the relative decline of the French population, suggested that French
interests outside Europe, in terms of markets, sources of raw material,
or settlers, would not be considerable. Political geography showed that
amongst a collection of small or weak neighbours, only one, Germany,
was a potential enemy. The *coup de théâtre* of the French position was
that the one possible enemy was situated exactly where the frontier was
open. Thus, for every minister for foreign affairs, it was the German
question which threw the largest shadow. Without there being any
automatic preparation to recover Alsace-Lorraine, any cult of
revenge, it was the problem of Germany which had to dominate
French diplomatic preoccupations.

    It is therefore a commentary on French governments to notice
that it is in the years before 1914 that the French overseas empire
was acquired. Algeria, which had been partly French since 1830,
became a large and extensive establishment regarded as an integral
part of metropolitan France. Morocco and Tunisia became Protectorates. The huge areas of Western and Equatorial Africa, together
with Madagascar, were in the same colour on the maps. Cochin-

52

China, Cambodia, Tonkin, Annam and Laos were united in French Indo-China. This was an impressive achievement and more than once relations between France and England or France and Italy were imperilled as a result of these colonial activities. But imperialism was never popular in France. The empire was not acquired in a fit of absence of mind, but it was more often than not acquired in the absence of the Chamber of Deputies. If there was a rush of blood to the head at the prospect of imperial power, it was limited to a restricted number of Frenchmen. If, in England, it was the anti-imperialist Lloyd George who had had to take refuge from the indignation of the Birmingham crowds, in France it was the imperialist Jules Ferry, the man who had 'acquired' Tunisia and Indo-China, who was threatened by hostile crowds as he left the Chamber of Deputies. French imperialism was usually the affair of a minority and was often the outcome of governmental weakness. Governments were unable to withstand pressures, whether from interested groups or from 'the man on the spot'; they were always apprehensive of the charge that they were subservient to England or to Italy; they were too often hopeful that their problems would become easier as the colonial troops demonstrated their bravery or the administrators their skill and determination.

Another commentary on French policy arises from the relative unimportance of French diplomacy in the 1914 crisis. As the consequences of the Sarajevo assassination and of Austria-Hungary's determination to save their dynastic state were unravelled, one can see how the French position was not determined so much by the desire to work with her one ally, Russia, or to co-operate with her associate, England, but rather by the German insistence on the logic of military planning. The German High Command demanded that, as a guarantee of neutrality, France should surrender certain fortresses in the east. This was to act as if France had already been defeated and no French government could possibly have accepted this. Those who were opposed to war were reduced to warning the government about conflict by accident and were unable to put forward any positive policy of their own. And so it happened that without the French government taking much initiative, it was a united country which went to war with a determined President, Poincaré, and a mildly socialist Prime Minister, Viviani.

The atmosphere of July and August 1914 has often been recalled. The Minister for War always remembered leaving his ministry after signing orders for mobilization, and finding himself surrounded by the gay Sunday crowds, returning from a day in the country. Others remembered the excited, straw-hatted men in the streets shouting 'to Berlin, death to the Kaiser' and singing the *Marseillaise*. The newspapers spoke with confidence of the Russians being in Berlin within a month and fashionable writers, such as the Academi-cian Paul Bourget, explained how war had many beneficial effects. There might have been a political crisis had the socialist leader Jean Jaurès been arrested. This arrest was being called for by the right since the attitude of the socialists towards the war was allegedly unpatriotic, but Jaurès was assassinated by an unknown young man on 31 July. And in an almost light-hearted way France embarked on the most devastating war of her history. 1,300,000 men were killed or listed as missing; over 1,000,000 were so badly wounded as to be permanently invalid; the total of killed, missing, wounded and prisoners was well over 6,000,000; 600,000 French women became war-widows and 750,000 children became orphans.

The greater part of the fighting on the Western front took place on French soil, and apart from the annexed provinces of Alsace and Lorraine, the Germans occupied ten departments. Within a few weeks of the declaration of war, a French offensive in Alsace had been thrown back and the Germans had moved through Belgium into northern France and were advancing on Paris. It is true that the German attacks were badly co-ordinated and that the German command made many mistakes. But the French com-mander-in-chief, Joffre, and the area commander, Galliéni, showed impressive coolness. And behind them the nation, faced with danger, appeared to be united. The victory of the Marne put an end to Ger-man plans for a quick victory and made the war a long one.

When the war became a war of attrition, the French army found itself fighting a war for which it was ill-prepared. It had been trained to take the offensive but the war was one in which defensive weapons were superior. The French public, too, had not expected a war of this sort. They had confidently expected a rapid victory; they would have understood defeat, and they would have proceeded to find those who were responsible. But prolonged war, with its terrible losses, ironies and disappointments, was more difficult to understand and to accept. It was to be expected that the weaknesses which had been evident before the war would become more obvious and more fatal.

To some extent this did happen. The political confusions persisted, and without counting the frequent re-shuffling of cabinets, France had five different Prime Ministers during the war: Viviani, Aristide Briand, Ribot, Painlevé and Clemenceau. Political and religious quarrels extended themselves into military matters, and a general such as Sarrail received support because he was republican and anti-clerical, whilst the disastrous appointment of Nivelle is to be explained because he was a Protestant (and therefore more acceptable). Constitutional uncertainties persisted, and there were many who believed that General Galliéni would profit from his popularity in 1914 to seize power. Some sort of *coup d'état* was certainly meditated by Poincaré when he envisaged the possibility of being both President of the Republic and Prime Minister. Clemenceau's newspaper *L'Homme Enchaîné* had no difficulty in finding sarcasms for the unfortunate minister who closed the factories on Ascension Day.

There were frequent social troubles, particularly in 1917, the year of mutinies in the army and of strikes in the towns. The peasants, who were mobilized and exposed to the horrors of trench warfare in return for a miserly pay, resented the demobilization of industrial workers, who were able to earn large salaries in the civilized safety of the towns. There were those who professed that it was better to kill a French capitalist than a uniformed German worker. There were those too who pointed out that although Frenchmen were mobilized, French fortunes were not; the sanctity of bourgeois property remained and the income-tax law, although voted, was not applied without considerable delay. There was an only too obvious difference between the horrors of trench warfare and the ostentatiously frivolous

life of 'le Tout-Paris'. Scandals and mysteries persisted and the curiously convenient suicide of the so-called Almereyda, a newspaper
owner, is only the most typical. He was perhaps receiving money
from foreign sources; he certainly had friends in high places; his
career confirmed the constant impression of many that there were
Frenchmen who were not wholly French and that corruption persisted whilst the country was in danger.

But in spite of these appearances, the war did present new
characteristics in French history. Socialists, who before 1914 had
envisaged the possibility of a general strike in the event of war,
and who had always insisted upon the gulf that separated them
from the succession of bourgeois governments, now emphasized
their patriotism. They identified themselves with the Republic and
the most violent of their anti-militarists now became the most energetic defenders of the national cause. In much the same way the
war brought about a modification of the religious quarrel. Catholics
also identified themselves with the Republic. Priests went to the
front (4,000 of them were killed) and the government, ceasing its
persecutions of the congregations, appealed to the church for help
in raising money and in maintaining morale.

The fact that about 8,000,000 Frenchmen were mobilized meant
that the war saw a great bringing together of populations, workers
and bourgeois, Catholics and non-Catholics, peasants and town-
dwellers, men from different provinces, men with different political
and cultural ideas. And although there was all the bitterness and
cynicism that goes with war, and although the 1917 mutinies revealed
a whole world of despair and revolt, the very fact that these mutinies
could be contained (and kept secret) shows the degree of national
and republican unity that had been attained.[1]

There were many occasions which recalled the great days of the
Revolution. In September 1914, with the government evacuated to
Bordeaux and with the Germans less than thirty miles away, the
elderly Galliéni mobilized the people of Paris in defence of their
town. In November 1917 a suspicious Chamber of Deputies and a
reluctant collection of newspapers found themselves forced to enthusiasm for the anti-clerical, anti-worker, individualistic Clemen-

ceau. It had been said that Clemenceau would find it difficult to get men to serve as ministers under him; but he had replied that, in that case, he would appear before the Chamber accompanied by four private soldiers. From this time onwards the old and deaf Clemenceau, with his heavy tweed coat and battered hat, his gaiters and thick walking stick, tramping through the mud of the trenches, seemed to symbolize French vitality and determination.

And beyond the fighting and the killing, there were other changes. On the farms it was discovered that the work could be done with less manpower; in the factories new methods and techniques were introduced and the production of the Renault light tank, for example, was a considerable achievement; in society as a whole, women were called upon to play a more important role, the government intervened effectively in various economic and social affairs. There were many reasons to think that a victorious France would be a new France.

But this was not the case. The history of France between the wars was to be one of unrelieved frustration. There were *les années difficiles*, the years of despair, when all the hopes of the first war were disappointed and all the earlier tendencies which led to weakness and to disunity were reinforced. There was no political clarification or ministerial stability, and the succession of over thirty short-lived governments made French democracy something of a laughing-stock. There was little religious peace, and Catholics and anti-clericals resumed their quarrels over state and Catholic schools. There was no demographic recovery, and with the haemorrhage of the war (it must be remembered that if one calculates, in addition to the killed, the number of children who would normally have been born but who were not, then French losses were in the nature of 3,000,000) France faced real and literal depopulation. And whilst the census figure for 1921 shows a loss of population in France as a whole, they show an increase in the population of Paris, which continued to grow and to absorb the populations of the provinces. There was no economic revolution; after an impressive industrial expansion in the 1920s, French industry and agriculture stagnated worse than ever.

It can be argued that just as Clemenceau was not the only war leader to be jettisoned by his supporters once they had no further use for him, so France was not the only country to experience the disappointments of victory and the bitter disillusionments of peace. But in the case of France, the outcome was particularly unfortunate. The contrast between the country that had existed at the end of the nineteenth century, a country of scandal, crisis and decadence, and the France that had succeeded in surving the ordeal of the war, had been too great. To return to the same weary round of scandals and crises, the same fears and insecurities about the future, the same sense of division and decadence, was worse than a disappointment. It was a disaster.

And after 1918 there was much that was positively worse. Politically speaking there was a hardening of attitudes. The revolution in Russia created a complication for those who believed in socialism, and at the 1920 Socialist congress at Tours there was a clear split between Communists (aligning themselves with Lenin) and a minority of socialists who expressed hostility towards Soviet Russia and Russian interference in the internal affairs of other countries. Amongst political parties on the right, those moderates who tried to maintain their relatively privileged positions in the face of heavy taxation and public ownership found themselves under pressure from groups which aimed at more radical political change. France, it was said, had been within a hair's breadth of losing the war, because of the incompetence of the politicians. The same incompetence was revealing itself in the failure to cope with the postwar economic and diplomatic problems. The enemies were still the same: socialism, tradeunionism, anticlericalism, parliamentarianism, etc. Placed between these extremes, politicians were forced into uneasy coalitions which sometimes gave politics an air of unreality and invariably made governments ineffective. The public could only respond with cynicism or with violence.

French foreign policy was notably unsuccessful. After 1918 the main preoccupation was inescapably that of security. How could the threat of another war with Germany be avoided? It was suggested that Germany should be divided, but other powers, which were not so vulnerable to Germany, would not agree. It was thought that France should have her frontiers guaranteed by alliances with Britain and the U.S.A., but these countries refused to commit themselves. It was decided that France should put pressure on Germany and squeeze reparations out of her; but with the occupation of the Ruhr in 1923 France gained nothing other than international ill- will. For a long time France accepted the compromise satisfaction of the Locarno agreements of 1925, which guaranteed the frontiers of western Europe, but these arrangements did not prevent the victory of the Nazis and the revival of German militarism. In her search for allies France was forced to discover the complacent indifference with which most British statesmen regarded French insecurity (Austen Chamberlain being the most notable exception)[2] as well as British military unpreparedness. Russia was for some an undesirable friend and, for most, an uncertain ally; Czechoslovakia and other eastern European states were complicated allies with problems of their own. If France was to have any security at all then she would have to be ready to defend herself and so, as part of an enormous military effort, the Maginot Line of defence against Germany was constructed in the 1930's. But this implied an essentially defensive strategy. And statesmen of differing tempera- ments, Aristide Briand, Pierre Laval, Edouard Daladier, never ceased to promise peace. By 1939 French foreign policy was in a cul-de-sac. It was as if there were no policy at all.

Prior to 1914 France had at least enjoyed the stability of the franc based on gold. The story used to be told of one of the innumerable Premiers who was forming his government being obliged, for political reasons, to find a post for a man who had neither experience nor ability. After some reflection he decided to make him Minister of Finance, being confident that there he could do no harm. But after 1918 the franc was no longer stable, France was faced with a crushing public debt and between 1919 and 1931 there were more than twenty different finance ministers. The cessation of allied support for the franc, the working of the international monetary mechanisms, the failure of attempts to make Germany pay extensive reparations, the difficulty of increasing exports, the world economic crisis of

1929, all these were reasons which explain how it was that French politics came, at times, to be dominated by a new type of problem. And it was a problem for which the politicians were unprepared, and the public ill-informed. In France it seemed to be particularly intractable, since devaluation struck at the investments of the politically powerful *rentier* class, since taxation was complicated in a country where so many of the enterprises were small-scale, and since it proved difficult to borrow money and to pursue social reforms at the same time. It is unlikely that any government could have commanded the wide social support necessary for an energetic and effective policy.[3]

Many examples could be given of the lack of social coherence in France. The 'affaire Stavisky', for example, led to the dramatic events of 6 February 1934. A financier, Stavisky, was caught out in a series of frauds, but his disappearance, his mysterious suicide, and the realization that he had had important friends turned a petty case into a first-class political scandal. The resignation of the government and a subsequent re-shuffling of officials did not appease opinion; right-wing groups took to the streets and a massive wave of disorder led to the fall of the legally constituted government on 7 February. Left-wing counter-demonstrations suggested that the violence of a few Parisian streets and suburbs might lead to a fundamental division in the country. But the violence passed away. There was no general agreement on how public affairs could be conducted; there was little in the ideals of the revolutionaries for which they were prepared to fight; there was a tendency to attitudinize and to demonstrate rather than to proceed to the more serious business of seizing power. Both government and opposition, revolution and reaction, had demonstrated their weakness rather than their strength.

The accession of the so-called Popular Front to power, after the elections of May 1936, seemed to suggest a more serious and more principled revolution. The socialist leader Léon Blum, with the support of the communists, became Prime Minister of a left-wing cabinet which was hailed enthusiastically as a turning-point in the history of humanity. The celebrations of 14 July 1936 were compared, in significance, to the events of 14 July 1789. A workers' charter was drawn up in consultation with the employers; holidays with pay were instituted; the forty-hour week was decided. But the communists refused to participate in a government which, in their eyes, was still bourgeois; opposition leaders denounced Blum and his ministers as being gang-leaders rather than statesmen; the right-wing thinker Maurras proclaimed the reign of the Jew in France; gold was drained away from the Bank of France and business refused to have confidence in the government; measures to invigorate the economy failed and attempts to conciliate employers and workers were only partially successful.

By the end of the year, after only six months, it was obvious that the Popular Front was in full decline and that it was being smothered in an atmosphere heavy with disappointment and recrimination. Such was the bitterness and violence of politics that in November 1936 the Minister of the Interior, Roger Salengro, committed suicide in the face of allegations that he had been a deserter during the war. Blum resigned in June 1937; in October 1938 the radical-socialists broke with the communists and in November the government led by the radical Edouard Daladier marked the beginning of a new period in politics by making extensive use of the police and armed forces in order to break a communist-inspired strike.[4]

If there is some uncertainty about the actual achievements of Léon Blum, there is none about the man who was perhaps the most typical politician of these years, Edouard Herriot. He was a man who had had a distinguished university career and who enjoyed a considerable reputation as a literary historian. He had a quick, sharp intelligence and his comments, over a wide variety of subjects, always deserved attention. For the uncertainties of national politics he had a firm base in Lyons, his political fief, where he was mayor. But he was ill at ease dealing with economic problems which he had scarcely studied; he enjoyed and exploited the political scene too much to wish to change it; like many brilliant men, his daring tended to be verbal rather than practical and when faced with a crisis he used his talents to side-step the difficulties, not to overcome them. He rarely tried to dominate events; sometimes he did not even try to understand them.

It has been suggested that as Proust advanced in his great work, he moved from remembrance of the past to a realization that the France which surrounded him in the present was hollow and diseased. His concluding volumes have a sense of defeat and collapse, and take on a particular significance. Significant too was the fact that the great literary and intellectual figure of the times, the most noted and the most noticeable, was André Gide. Yet, although a perceptive and sensitive man, he can hardly be called a great inventive writer. It is as if his homosexuality paralleled a failure to be creative. Intensely cultured and eternally youthful, he was devoted to literature and to the problems of comprehending and expressing the sentiments of the individual. But he was rarely able to get beyond a preoccupation with himself, his own emotions and problems. Lacking in imagination, lacking in generosity, there is a selfishness and an ego-centricity in his work. Its success is often caused by the creation of a complicity between the author, his characters and his readers. The adventure of the Gideian character is often false, the drama factitious, the commitment a mere attitude. This is more a self-consciousness than a literature. As Gide said, in Les Nouvelles Nourritures, 'La chenille qui chercherait à "bien se connaître" ne devient drait jamais papillon.' (If a caterpillar were to attempt to put into practice the maxim of 'knowing oneself' its development into a butterfly would be arrested.) And it was appropriate that such a writer as Gide should have had such an eminent position in the France of his time.[5]

6   The Second War

S'il faut croire à un miracle pour sauver la France, alors je crois au miracle car 'e crois à la France. Paul Reynaud

THE FRANCE OF 1939 was a country with an elderly population. It was therefore all the easier for the declaration of war against Germany to evoke memories of the first world war and to foresee the cemeteries of the future. It had been the same in 1938, when the French, like other European nations, had welcomed the Munich agreement which had sacrificed Czechoslovakia but which had preserved peace. They had been particularly glad to be able to return to their card-games and to listen to the singer Tino Rossi (as Henri de Montherlant bitterly put it). But there had been other considera- tions. It hardly seemed logical to much conservative and moderate opinion to fight a war in order to preserve Czechoslovakia, which was a creation of the Treaty of Versailles, a treaty which was never popular in France since it had not provided the country with security. It did not seem possible that a divided public opinion could rally around Daladier, who was for some the creator of the Popular Front and for others its chief betrayer, in any policy save that of peace. There were those who thought that internally the only result of a war with Germany would be a new commune in Paris, but this time under the Soviet flag. Externally they saw France as isolated, since there was little confidence in either British or Soviet military preparedness.

In 1939 the situation was similar. There were those who refused 'to die for Danzig' and a campaign was launched by Marcel Déat. There were many, notably Pierre Laval, who believed that the diplomatic activities of the French government in 1939 had been singularly inept, and that there was a real possibility of ending the war in the west by means of a Franco-Italian agreement which would then be extended to Germany. The Prime Minister was still Daladier and the Chamber was still that which had been elected in May 1936. The signing of the German-Soviet pact reinforced the campaign against the communists; in September 1939 the communist party was dissolved and in January 1940 the communist deputies were expelled from the Chamber. It was politics as usual. In March 1940, alleging that Daladier had not been vigorous enough in aiding Finland in its resistance to Soviet invasion, Daladier's supporters abstained from supporting him, and a new government was formed under Paul Reynaud (with Daladier holding the position of Minister of Defence).

Yet there was no determined or concerted opposition to the war. And this was because there was a certain conception of the type of war that was being fought. In spite of many uncertainties, it seemed that the French army was magnificently reliable, perhaps the best in the world. The Commander-in-Chief, General Gamelin, had established the principle of defensive warfare behind the heavily fortified Maginot Line. The weakness of the French army in 1914 had been that it took the offensive in impossible conditions. This was now rectified, and it seemed that the army was effectively protected against enemy attack, and that it would only leave its superb positions when backed by superior artillery fire. The German army had also to cover long frontiers, and it seemed that these forces would have to follow something of the same strategy. When the Germans had liquidated the Polish front and yet made no attempt to take any offensive in the west, then this over-all view of strategy seemed to be confirmed. Although a number of possible French diversions were considered, there was no real attempt to break out of this predominant immobilism. The British military effort was placed under French command and played no role in the discussion.

It was this situation which was ended, firstly by the Norwegian campaign, and then by the German offensive into Holland and Belgium on 10 May 1940. The invasion of Belgium had been expected. It was thought that the Germans would repeat their strategy of 1914 and would try to roll back the left wing of the allied forces, whilst occupying the Channel ports. There were those who thought that this presented an opportunity for a French counter-offensive, and after some hesitation, French and British troops were ordered into Belgium. Others thought that to abandon an excellent defensive position was disastrous. At all events, two days later, the Germans attacked the French 9th Army across the Ardennes, and introduced a new element into the strategy.

It is still a subject for some discussion why the French forces under General Corap were unable to withstand this assault.[1] At all events, because of the element of surprise, because of inadequacies in the training of the French troops, and because of technological inferiorities, possibly along with the absence of any real determination to fight and to win, the French armies were forced to fall back. This presented a real crisis. The German advance threatened to outflank the units of the French and British armies already engaged in the fighting. And the French and Belgian populations, remembering the fate of the occupied departments during the first World War, began a movement of flight (the *exode*) which seriously hampered military operations and which presented complicated material and moral problems.

Reynaud found himself in a situation which was particularly difficult. This small, neat man had always impressed by the perception of his analyses and the precision of his speeches. He was looked on as a personality, as a conjurer, who could produce solutions to some complicated problems. He was not the leader of any important political party, and he was very sensitive to the limitations of his power. After all, he had only been voted into power by a majority of one, and he had never felt strong enough to dismiss General Gamelin, whom he mistrusted. But in the crisis of the German military advance, he affirmed his position by a lengthy series of cabinet changes. He replaced Gamelin by Weygand (who had been a colleague of Foch); he recalled Pétain (the hero of Verdun, then aged 83) and made him a deputy Prime Minister; he put Mandel, Clemenceau's former right hand, at the Ministry of the Interior; and whilst bringing in a number of civil servants to replace the politicians, he appointed a junior general, Charles de Gaulle, with whom he had been acquainted for some time, as under-secretary for war. This was to resuscitate the great names of the 1914 war, and to bring in an exponent of more modern strategy. But these changes did not stop the German advance. The most that could be done was to organize the evacuation of entrapped soldiers from Dunkirk to England, and to arrange for the transfer of the French government from Paris to Tours, and then to Bordeaux.

Hitler had always expected that the French would be defeated and would ask for an armistice. It was not long before this was being mentioned. Pétain seems to have spoken about an armistice before the German offensive had got under way, and others envisaged this possibility as early as 25 May. The replacement of Gamelin by Weygand had created a certain cynicism, since it came after a death-or-glory speech by Gamelin. The transfer of the government from Paris to Bordeaux had caused the government to lose its sense of control and direction. There came all sorts of pressure on to the government to conclude fighting. Some personalities urged that their towns should not be bombed. (Herriot, for example, was particularly anxious that Lyons should not suffer.) A sort of 'commune' of politicians in Bordeaux claimed that it was the government's duty to end the fighting.

Eventually, on 12 June, General Weygand stated in full cabinet that the French army could not continue the fight and that 'an honourable armistice' was the only possible conclusion to events. Marshal Pétain accepted this view, and although Reynaud continued to reject this suggestion, it was obviously becoming more powerful. Politically speaking Reynaud had only a small majority in the Chamber. Had he wished to insist on the fight he would have had to dismiss both Weygand and Pétain, and it is not certain that he could have ridden the subsequent storm. Events did not encourage him. Italy declared war; Roosevelt responded unhelpfully to Reynaud's broadcast appeal that America should help; the navy seemed surprisingly ready to accept the armistice terms, and Churchill was somewhat evasive as to what England would do if the French signed an armistice. It seems likely that Reynaud was in a minority in his cabinet on the issue of continuing the war.

He probably made a mistake when he revealed, on 16 June, the British government's proposal for a solemn union between the two countries. He saw this as a way of avoiding an armistice, but most of his colleagues rejected the idea outright. They saw it as an attempt to make France a British dominion, and those who were doubtful if the British alliance had been useful to France and who pointed at the disproportionate number of British and French evacu-ated from Dunkirk (200,000 British, 130,000 French) and the fail-ure of the British to use their full air strength in support of France, found further support for their viewpoint. When Reynaud resigned (on 16 June) Pétain had for some days been negotiating with various personalities, and it took no time at all for him to present his minister-ial list. After a week of negotiations, an armistice was signed on 25 June, a week after General de Gaulle had broadcast from London.

One need not give too sinister an interpretation to these events. It has been suggested that Weygand had no desire to defend the Republic; and it is true that he was nervous about communist uprisings and helped to spread rumours about communist activities. It has also been suggested that Pétain had for some time been in contact with right-wing political circles who were more hostile to the French socialists than to the Germans, and that for them the war was principally a means of liquidating the aftermath of the Popular Front. Léon Blum described the steady corruption of French deputies as they arrived in Bordeaux. 'I saw men go rotten before my very eyes' was the phrase he later used, and there undoubtedly was an organized attempt by a number of politicians to discredit those who wanted to continue fighting. It has even been suggested that Madame de Portes, a close friend of Reynaud's, played a conspiratorial role in persuading the Prime Minister not to insist upon resistance.

None of these allegations can be ruled out. But it is wiser to insist upon the prevailing uncertainties, which everyone shared (the Pétain government, for example, considered the possibility of going to North Africa for what now seems to be a surprisingly long time). And it is more significant to see how, in contrast to the first war,

67

danger and defeat in the second world war only accentuated the divisions that already existed within the country. There was no spirit of national unity, however temporary. Perhaps it was because defeat was more rapid and more total. It emphasized the sense of being weak, alone and deserted. 'Not enough arms, not enough children, not enough friends', as Pétain was to put it. The notion that modern warfare was particularly terrible encouraged a confused apprehension that complete annihilation was possible. But it is striking to see how 1940 reflects the pattern of the 1930s. Many of the working class saw the government as an enemy; the bourgeoisie did not see what it had to gain; the peasantry saw itself called upon to make endless sacrifices. The politicians failed to carry conviction, and in the continued and general search to identify the cause of the French crisis, there was no agreement that Germany was the enemy.

Who stood for France in 1940? Was it the prestigious figure of Pétain in Bordeaux, who said that the war must stop, or the little-known figure of de Gaulle in London who said that the war must go on? Was it the deputies who tried to escape from France and get to North Africa, or was it the communist leader Maurice Thorez who went to Soviet Russia? Was it Pierre Laval who said that he was only a peasant who wanted to keep his farm and who wanted to keep France? Was it some early resistance leader who already dreamed of ways of sabotaging the invaders? Or was it some unknown Frenchman, who lay still and who hoped that no one would notice him? The drama of French history is that it is not possible to give a clear answer to all these simple questions. If 1940 was a moment of clarification in England, this was not the case for France. At all events, after 1940 the course of French history was in three different directions: that of Pétain's government, in Vichy; that of de Gaulle, in London and, later, Algiers; that of the French resistance move-ment, in hiding. But all three were agreed that the time had come for a complete renovation of the state and the nation.[2]

There were two sides to the government which was installed at Vichy, the capital of unoccupied France. The one was made up of a number of skilful politicians who were working in the framework

of the 1930s and whose ability to negotiate, conciliate and compromise had been affirmed by the crisis of 1940. They maintained that
their idea was always to defend French interests, in every way possible.
Their leader was Pierre Laval, the lawyer from the Auvergne
(where people traditionally have the reputation of being cunning),
a man who had begun life as a socialist but who had manœuvred
his way through the confusion of the French political groups,
making himself indispensable by means of his talents and his
personality. For Laval, and probably for Admiral Darlan too, the
armistice and the German victory over France was simply another
occasion when he could bargain, intrigue, and eventually settle for the
best terms possible. The conditions of the armistice, by which France
was divided into an occupied and an unoccupied zone, as well as
into various zones of military regulations, provided ample opportunity
for this type of argument. France, amongst German-occupied
territories, was unique in having a semi-independent government.

The other side to Vichy was more idealistic and more theoretical.
One of the main preoccupations of the right-wing leader, Charles
Maurras, had always been to determine at what moment the counter-
revolution should be launched. It appeared that the armistice,
and the admission of French defeat, was a propitious moment for
the slate to be wiped clean, when everything could be started and
built afresh. Vichy would thus constitute a national revolution and
would bring in a new order. France would be given an organization which would be based on sound principles rather than upon
a series of political upheavals. The ideas of Maurras himself, the
ideas of corporatists such as La Tour du Pin, the ideas of such
a right-wing leader as Colonel Casimir de la Rocque (the enemy of
the Popular Front; 'raccourcir Casimir' had been one of the cries
of the left) were in the air. The journalist and historian Lucien
Romier (who became Minister of State in 1941), Raphael Alibert, an
associate of Laval, the businessman Jules Verger, the lawyer Tixier-
Vignancour, and the moralist Drieu le Rochelle, were all influential.

If one asks where Marshal Pétain stood in all this, it is important
to note that he participated fully in both aspects of the government
of Vichy. In terms of bargaining, he never ceased to believe that

he was enabling France to escape the fate of Poland. He believed that such acts of policy as meeting Hitler, at Montoire in November 1940, would protect both the French empire and the French people. At the same time he thought that France ought to undergo the experience of a new form of government and here he was influenced by his entourage, as well as by his earlier, but recent, experience as Ambassador to General Franco's Spain. In both respects he showed himself to be a clever politician. He had frequently been solicited by right-wing groups prior to 1939 but he had avoided committing himself. As the hero of Verdun he continued to enjoy the reputation of the general who had been anxious not to lose men, and he was therefore esteemed by many of the anti-militarists of the left. And with all this, he had made a mystery of himself. Like Napoleon III, much of his reputation rested on his ability to keep silent. When in power he could be extremely talkative, but when asked questions to which he did not wish to answer, his deafness became more pronounced and his forgetfulness more marked. He could easily become an old man, reminiscing about the past, remembering old speeches and quoting poetry. He could summon up a sharp tongue and a rough, soldierly wit. He revealed all the selfishness and egoism we often associate with old men, but he was careful not to fall under any one single influence. He always had several irons in the fire, making advances to the Americans, the resistance movement, the Germans, the French in North Africa and so on. Whatever the degree of apparent subservience, the Marshal liked to think that he was taking all the decisions himself, and his endless interviews in the Hotel du Parc made his headquarters a centre of rumour, uncertainty, hopes and disappointments. Hence everyone (French or German) had their own idea of the Marshal, their own idea of the leader whom they wished to see.

All this means that Vichy cannot be regarded as a simple, monolithic *bloc*. It was varied, and it contained a number of widely differing elements, ranging from fervent, even fanatical reformers, through a wide selection of moderates, administrators, generals and admirals to the opportunists and adventurers. It is difficult to equate Vichy with any simple doctrine. Sometimes, for example, it has been said that it stands for Catholicism. But if one examines the position of Catholics between 1940 and 1944, one is struck by the diversity of Catholic reaction and by the developments which took place within that period. Pétain himself was not a practising Catho-lic and his marriage had been a civil one with a divorcee. Nor were Laval or Darlan particularly interested in religious matters. The Church, therefore, was seen essentially as a political institution, a guarantor of order and stability. For some Catholic leaders the great enemy was Bolshevism, and for them, Pétain and Nazi Germany were protectors against that evil. Others (such as the Cardinal-Archbishop of Paris, Suhard) were more preoccupied with particu-lar questions, such as the future of Catholic schools. They were largely satisfied when the government gave subsidies to the schools and freed the religious congregations from restrictive laws. Some (such as the Cardinal of Toulouse) were cynical about the Vichy government, and there were many who feared that any apparent association between the Church and a government that was not altogether free and independent could only harm the cause of Catho-licism. There were Catholics in favour of compulsory religious education; others thought this unwise and tactless. Some Catholics joined in resistance movements in their early days, believing that it was their Christian duty to combat the evil of Hitlerism (the first number of the clandestine journal *Témoignage chrétien* dates from November 1941 and launched the warning that France was in danger of losing its soul). When the Vichy government adopted a number of measures against the Jews, from the end of 1940 and the summer of 1941, and when, in 1943, compulsory labour service was instituted for certain categories of young Frenchmen, then the Catholic opposition became strong in all branches of the resistance and involved both priests and the laity. Yet all the while there were many Catholics who remained fervent supporters of Pétain, who believed in anti-Semitism, and who preached obedience until the end.

The most usual remark made about the government of Vichy is that it was a government with many characteristics of the right in politics. It was authoritarian; by the vote of the two chambers meeting together on 10 July 1940, full powers were conferred on Marshal Pétain and the elective principle of government was abandoned. A form of monarchy was established in which the eventual successor was named by proclamation. At the same time the government of Vichy was nationalist. It adopted laws against those who were of foreign origin or who were Jewish. It was anti-revolutionary, since it abolished the slogan 'Liberty, Equality, Fraternity' and replaced it by 'Family, Work, Country', since it took issue with organizations such as the freemasons, repealed a certain amount of anti-Catholic legislation and changed the busts of the Republic for the portraits of the Marshal. The Republic was replaced by the French state. It was a traditionalist government, with an ostentatious attachment to the soil and to 'the eternal order of things', as observed by those who work in the fields. Finally it could be said that the Vichy régime was fascist, since it sought to reorganize the state through a number of corporations, and to replace the trade unions by workers' charters and by an association of capital and labour.

However, there existed a fundamental contradiction. The younger officials and technicians showed that they were dynamic. But at the same time Vichy was bound to be immobile, waiting on events, dependent upon the actions of others. The ever-growing demands of the Germans, and the Anglo-American landings in North Africa (8 November 1942) combined to make the Vichy government valueless. If Pétain was not prepared to join the allies then there was little he could do but hang on. His statement that every field that lay fallow was a defeat for France, and that every field that was cultivated was a victory for France, became the key to the régime. It was as if he had urged the French to pay no attention to what was happening in Europe and in the French empire. Vichy had begun in melancholy, but it had its patriotism and its hopes. It ended with inactivity and with the abandonment of all sense of the State. It was for this that it was not to be forgiven.[3]

General de Gaulle arrived in London on 17 June 1940, and on the following day (it happened to be the anniversary of Waterloo) he broadcast a message, asserting that whatever happened 'the flame of French resistance must not and shall not be extinguished'. France, according to de Gaulle, had not lost the war. France had only lost a battle. The war was a world war and France still had a role to play.

In this de Gaulle took exactly the opposite view to Pétain. But there were a good many resemblances between the two men. Indeed de Gaulle had for a time been Pétain's *protégé*. In 1940 both men were making personal appeals to the French. The '*nous, Philippe Pétain*' of Vichy was balanced by the '*moi, Général de Gaulle*' of London. They were both men of principle with high ideals, who had been progressively alienated from the régime of the Third Republic as it had demonstrated its decadence. They were authori/tarian, ostentatiously taking decisions themselves and at times, isolating themselves from their colleagues, deliberately allowing uncertainty and mystery to grow. They were clever politicians, skilful in private negotiation and remarkably astute in the use which they made of the radio. Pétain was something of a secretive figure, about whose right/wing political sympathies there was more rumour than knowledge, whilst de Gaulle's political sympathies were com/pletely unknown, except for some vaguely Maurrassien associations and a number of personal contacts (with Reynaud, for example).

Both men were anxious to stand apart from the ordinary political groupings, and it was part of the considerable pride which they shared, to believe that their patriotism placed them above the ordin/ary politicians. If Pétain saw himself as incarnating France and noted, with a certain complacency, his popularity with ordinary people, and if he encouraged the cult of his person ('*Maréchal, nous voilà!*' was a typical song of this cult), then de Gaulle was equally confident that he spoke for France. De Gaulle believed that the élite of the French state had deserted, since the deputies, senators, academicians, generals, trade/union leaders and so on remained in a France which was no longer free. Only the ordinary French people came to Lon/don, and it was the people who realized that he was now France. Both men had a rough and caustic wit, so that their idealistic apprai/sal of their exalted position was frequently tempered by a certain cynicism. There was a sense of adventure in the case of the aged

Marshal, well past retiring age, whose career was once thought to have ended with the first World War, becoming the head of State. There was a decided adventure in de Gaulle, relatively young and unknown, taking the path that led to London, and it is said that when André Malraux later asked him what it was like in 1940, de Gaulle is said to have seized his hands and with uncharacteristic emotion, to have said, 'it was terrible' ('*Malraux, c'était épouvantable*').

One could pursue this double portrait and insist on further re-semblances between these two men. This is not altogether surprising since, in spite of the difference of age, they were both military men who had been marked by the 1914 war. And there was a significant similarity in their situations. For both of them the crucial problem was one of relations with foreign powers. In the case of Pétain this was Germany; in the case of de Gaulle, it was Britain and, later, the U.S.A. Neither was in a strong position. There was no obvious reason why Hitler should give a defeated France a privileged posi-tion, and there was no obvious reason why Churchill should wel-come the claims of this unknown and junior general, when he would have preferred someone more famous to have come forward as the leader of Free France.

But this particular resemblance between the situations of Pétain and de Gaulle stops there. There was an important and intrinsic contrast between the one and the other. Pétainism was *attentiste*, obliged to play a waiting game, and whilst waiting to see what would happen, preparing for all eventualities. But Gaullism was obliged to be dynamic. De Gaulle had to demonstrate that whilst Pétain, and the Vichy government, were under German control and could not speak for France, he was able to act with complete freedom and independence. He had to show that he was not a puppet at the disposal of London or of Washington. And from this came all the bad relations with the allies, and the quarrels with Churchill and Roosevelt. De Gaulle had to be uncompromising when it came to French independence, otherwise there was no reason why he should be preferred to Pétain, no reason why he should oppose Pétain.

Another of the outstanding characteristics of Gaullism is that it

74

was essentially political. Here is another of the reasons why de Gaulle's relations with Churchill were so often bad. De Gaulle, who had the more logical mind of the two, started from the assump, tion that the war would be won. If the war were lost then he had no future and Gaullism would cease to exist. Therefore he concen, trated all his attention upon the circumstances in which the war would be won. Churchill made no such assumptions and he could not afford to make them. He was by no means certain that the war would be won, and he was anxious that politics should be suspended until the war was over. This, too, was the attitude of General Giraud, the French general whom the Americans preferred to consider as the leader of the French after they had occupied North Africa. But Gaullism could not have existed if this argument had been accepted. De Gaulle would have existed only as an individual and he would have been a junior general putting insignificant forces at the disposal of the allied commanders. He did not consider that this would have been of much use to France. If politics were, for Churchill, a number of attitudes which could be temporarily forgotten about, politics for de Gaulle were the means whereby the national identity of France was to be saved.

Gaullism therefore was a political force. Naturally, amongst the Gaullists there were different opinions, but it was de Gaulle who gave the tone to Gaullism, and he sought to make this political force a revolutionary one. He always proclaimed the continuity of the Republic, and he always insisted that government must be demo, cratic. He never ceased to promise that, when the time came, he would render account of his actions to the French people. But he also insisted that the events of 1940 constituted a break in the history of France, comparable to that of 1789. The break was, in the first instance, personal. The men who had led France until that time had had their day. To ask why such men would no longer be in French governments would be like asking why Turgot and Necker were not members of the Committee of Public Safety.

The idea was always present amongst Gaullists that once France was liberated there would be a meting,out of justice, and that only those who were worthy would be able to hold authority in the new

75

France. But this change in French history was not only personal. It had also to be social. So much had happened it was not possible to go back to the situation that had existed before the war. And the change could only be one whereby old privileges were overthrown. 'If there are still Bastilles then let them get ready to open their doors,' de Gaulle proclaimed in Algiers, in 1943. The Gaullists spoke about a new revolution and a new republic. This caused General Giraud to see the Gaullists as a continuation of the Popular Front and this also alarmed the Americans, since it seemed to have over-tones of socialism and violence. But it was somewhat vague and when in 1942 the socialist leader Felix Gouin reported to Léon Blum on the Gaullists, whilst thinking that de Gaulle himself was quite exceptional, he found the Gaullist conception of the revolution to be much like that of Vichy.

Naturally there was a strong element of tactics in all this. De Gaulle had many advisers who were quite conservative, and he himself had a background which suggested a moderate, liberal conservatism. But he was obliged to oppose Vichy, and if Vichy was a government of the right, then he would have to lead a govern-ment of the left; if the government of Vichy was particularly attached to the conservatism of rural France, then it was natural that de Gaulle should turn to industry and to the towns. He was increasingly deter-mined to rally the internal resistance movement which (as shall be shown) was increasingly left-wing. He was aware, especially after the move from London to Algiers, that he was opposed by the generals and the administration, and that the source of his power was the ordinary people of France.

Yet at the same time, there was something profoundly true about the revolutionary principles of Gaullism, something which went beyond the calculations of tactics and methods. It had been an act of great daring for a general to disobey his superiors and go to a foreign capital, proclaiming that he was the true government of France. Once this step had been taken, others were less difficult. De Gaulle, from 1940 onwards, had cast himself in the role of a rebel. And he was viewing France from the outside, with the eyes of an *émigré* (who had been sentenced to death by Vichy). Within his optic,

the one unacceptable possibility was that the existing French estab/
lishment, whether political, military or social, should remain in
power. In 1942 he said that national liberation could only be
accomplished if it were accompanied by national insurrection.
There is every reason to think that he believed this.

Thus Gaullism was a continuing element in the political dia/
logue of France. But it was a pointed and dynamic element, clearer
than the more muffled and hesitant voice of Vichy. If Daladier,
both before and after 1939, and to some extent Reynaud, and then
Pétain, had made up the counter/current to the Popular Front,
then de Gaulle stood for a kind of counter/current on behalf of the
Popular Front.[4] But this was not a role which was to satisfy the
General. During the years from 1940 one can see the Gaullist
preoccupation with unity. He wanted administrators, technicians,
politicians; he wanted socialists, communists, radicals, all types of
opinions; for a long time he hoped that some Catholic bishop could
be persuaded to join him. He was anxious that all men should
be Gaullists. And although, for a time, this policy had to be seen
within a limited framework, nevertheless it was, in embryo, a new
contribution to the political scene.[5]

The Resistance movement was an original episode in French history,
and one which is difficult to assess. The first members of the Resis/
tance were individuals, or small groups, and by their very nature they
were clandestine. But in the final days, as the defeat of the Germans
became clear for everyone to see, the Resistance appeared to consist of
the whole population of France. It is only natural that one should be
somewhat cynical about some of these aspects of the Resistance and a
trifle uncertain about the distinction between resistant and non/
resistant. It is only natural too that some episodes should be easier
to study than others or should appear more immediately significant
than others.

If both Vichy, and to a lesser extent Gaullism, represented diverse
and varied ensembles, the Resistance outdid them both in its diversity.
There were individuals; there were groups, some of which were
organized according to the place where their members worked, some

of which were purely geographical, and some had a doctrinal basis of organization. Individuals entered the Resistance out of a sense of adventure, out of a sense of patriotism, or because they were being pursued by the authorities, whether German or French. Groups emerged in the Resistance for equally varied reasons. Many communists were already in hiding before the accession of Pétain, and although there is a long-standing controversy about the role of the communists during the period of the German-Soviet pact, after 1941 the communist contribution to fighting the enemy of Soviet Russia and of the working class was considerable. For the first time, communists, whether workers or intellectuals, acted as a revolution-ary force, living the poetry of revolution. It was natural that youth, whether communist or non-communist, should be attracted towards the Resistance, but the invasion of the unoccupied zone in 1942 and the measures for compulsory labour in Germany forced many young men to become resistants. And within the Resistance there were a great many different roles to play. There were armed bands, the *maquis*, who fought the Germans and who sabotaged the German war effort, causing more effective damage than all the bombing of the R.A.F. There were organizations which specialized in main-taining contact outside France and in helping prisoners to escape. Some countered German and Vichy propaganda, distributed news and tracts, maintained the faith in allied victory. Simply to listen to de Gaulle on the B.B.C. was to practise the Resistance.

The Resistance as a whole tied down large numbers of German troops, guarding stores, communications and prisoners; it formed a huge and menacing reserve army. Above all, the Resistance made it impossible for anyone to regard Hitler's victory as lasting or Hitler's Europe as permanent. Soon all the elements of the Resistance had their martyrs, the communists with Gabriel Peri and Danielle Casanova, the Catholics with Estienne d'Orve and Francisque Gay. And like Jean-Paul Sartre's hero, Mathieu, there must have been countless who dreamed that some day a little square would be named after them.

The remarkable achievement was that these disparate forces should have been united. De Gaulle's representative, Jean Moulin, was parachuted into France, captured by the Germans and tortured to death by them. But he succeeded in creating the National Council of the Resistance in 1942, which accepted the leadership of de Gaulle. It is true that this Council did not put an end to the many disagree, ments and discussions which flourished during the next two years; after Moulin's death there were bound to be difficulties, if only between General de Gaulle's representative Parodi, and the elected President of the Resistance Council, the Catholic schoolmaster Georges Bidault. But the institutional unity was there. And a sort of doctrinal unity was also there, in spite of all the variety of ideas which appeared in the millions of newspapers, periodicals and tracts. The spirit of the Resistance was for a renovated France, for a democratic Republic, for social reform, for economic rationalism, for the government of France by an élite of merit rather than an élite of birth. Once again one sees the spirit of the Popular Front.[6]

It was 6 June 1944 that the allies invaded Normandy. In spite of the Americans and the British, who had hoped to eliminate de Gaulle, those areas of liberated France which were able to express themselves showed that they were Gaullist. Wherever de Gaulle went he was acclaimed as the head of state. In spite, too, of allied reluctance to liberate Paris in the early stages of the campaign, the rising of the Resistance in that city struck the imagination of everyone, and French forces under General Leclerc were sent into Paris to assist the insur, rection. On 25 August 1944 occupied Paris, 'the remorse of the free world' as de Gaulle put it, was liberated. The next day de Gaulle strode in triumph down the Champs-Elysées.

7 The post-war world

On n'imagine jamais les maux comme ils sont. Alain

THE WAR MEMOIRS which General de Gaulle has published are strangely impersonal and non-dramatic. One of the few dramatic moments is when he describes his return, in 1944, to the Ministry of War in the rue Saint-Dominique. He had not been there since 1940. But after all that had happened, he found little apparent change. Everything was as before, everything was in its place. Only one thing was missing, and that was the State. And so, he went to work.[1]

All that could be done was to improvise, to face up to the immediate and urgent problems of the moment. France was a devastated country. The problem of food and fuel supplies, the problem of communications, the need to organize credit and industry, the necessity to start a massive reconstruction, all these were vast enterprises in themselves, but they had to be undertaken in conditions of war and crisis. The liberation of Paris did not mean the end of the war in France, nor did it mean the end of de Gaulle's difficulties with his allies. For example, in December 1944, it was decided that strategic reasons demanded the temporary evacuation of Strasbourg, which had earlier been liberated. De Gaulle refused to accept this and showed that he was prepared to break with the allies on this question. He only got his way after a good deal of unpleasantness. There were long delays in the liberation of some areas (Saint-Servan and Saint-Nazaire, in Brittany, were only freed on 17 August 1944 and on 12 May 1945 respectively) but eventually victory was complete. The armistice with Germany was agreed on 8 May 1945.

It is difficult to give a picture of France at this time. There were areas where the Resistance had been particularly active, and where the process of liberation had been the work of the resistants them/ selves rather than the allied troops. In these areas de Gaulle's emissaries were not well received and it was difficult to enforce official decisions. Even where the Resistance had not been particu/ larly active and where de Gaulle's personnel had taken up their positions rapidly, difficulties arose as to where authority really lay. This was the time of the *épuration*, the long/awaited moment when those who had betrayed France by collaborating with the enemy or by attacking the Resistance were obliged to give account of them/ selves and be judged. Conditions varied greatly from one part of France to another; there were summary executions and humiliations in one place, a remarkable calm and continuity in another. In Paris there was no vast or prolonged wave of vengeance. In the south it was often different. So self/consciously revolutionary were some of the resistance leaders, that in Avignon, for example, a group of young men deliberately imitated the *sans-culottes* and installed them/ selves in a café, from where they directed operations which they thought were in the interests of justice.

It was a time of violence and of bitterness, in which thousands of Frenchmen were killed by other Frenchmen and some hundreds of thousands imprisoned. But this crisis was surmounted with surprising speed. Those who had been expected to be most rigorous in dispensing rapid justice (the communists) were usually less blood/ thirsty than those individuals or groups who saw things purely on a local plane.[2] In October 1945 de Gaulle decreed the dissolution of the armed units of the Resistance, and when the following month Maurice Thorez returned to France from Moscow, he urged his followers to accept this decision to assist in the return to normal life. At the end of April and at the beginning of May 1945, municipal elections were held in order to replace the emergency local authorities by others which would be more normally constituted.

For de Gaulle the re/establishment of the framework of govern/ ment within the frontiers of the State had been the essential task. He had prevented the Americans from setting up a provisional govern/

ment of their own. He had put an end to any idea of a negotiation with Vichy. He had succeeded in installing what he considered to be the legal government of France, that which he had established in London and Algiers, and in enforcing its authority. There were three other major considerations of policy as he saw them. The first was to create the role of France in the post-war world. The reluctance of the allies to accept de Gaulle or to consider France as one of the great powers, France's absence from the post-war summit confer-ences at Yalta (February 1945) and Potsdam (July–August 1945) caused de Gaulle to take every opportunity of asserting French claims. His visit to Moscow and the signing of the Franco-Soviet treaty in February 1945, and his refusal to be summoned to Algiers (which was French territory) by President Roosevelt, were attempts to demonstrate French liberty of action. The second consideration, closely linked to the first, was that of the French empire. De Gaulle was more conscious than most of the importance of French overseas possessions, since both in London and in Algiers he had been dependent upon the existence of a France outside Europe. He was particularly anxious to assert French rights in Indo-China, where the Japanese war had led both British and Chinese troops to invade different parts of the territory and where a nationalist movement was already asserting its rights. But above all de Gaulle's main concern was with the establishment of a permanent form of government in France.

It has often been said that once de Gaulle set foot in France, he became aware of the realities of the situation, and that this discovery changed his policies considerably. It has also been suggested that so far as the Resistance was concerned, de Gaulle had played the part of the sorcerer's apprentice, and that with his talk of insurrection he had helped to unleash forces which he could not control and which he completely disapproved of. It has also been said that he had simply made use of the Resistance, and that once he was success-fully installed in power then his attitude towards the ideals and the personnel of the Resistance changed. Naturally de Gaulle in Paris, faced with the realities of power, was different from the man in London or Algiers, who was only preparing for power. But none of these interpretations given is correct, because after 1944 there was no fundamental change in the attitude of de Gaulle. His profound aspiration was to be the leader of France. Once Vichy was eliminated, he could no longer consider himself as the leader of Free France, or of the Resistance. He was the leader of the whole of France, and the symbol of the unity of France. His first broadcast message, on his arrival in liberated Paris, had been to proclaim the unity of the French nation, who ('apart from certain traitors') must march together. He was haunted by the spectacle of Paris on the day of its liberation, when he had stood beneath the Arc de Triomphe and looked down the Champs-Elysées, black with people. All of France seemed to be there, all quarrels had been forgotten, France and the French were united around de Gaulle. This profound movement of national feeling was more than the victory of one set of individuals over another, and it had to be interpreted as such.

The first ministry that was formed in September 1944 was a sign of this preoccupation. It brought together the personnel of Gaullism, of the Resistance and of a number of the more respectable elements which had been in power before and after 1940. M. Jeanneney, for example, remained President of the Senate, and demonstrated the continuity of institutions. This ministry was not well received. It was a disappointment to those who had hoped for a great Ministry of Liberation, and it was said to resemble too many of the pre-war coalitions.

In practice this was inevitable. The Resistance movement was bound to break up once victory was won, and although there were certain new political formations, such as the Mouvement Républicain Populaire (MRP) or social Catholics, not everyone could join this. Therefore much of the energy and ambition of liberated France fell into the mould of all the old political parties, and de Gaulle became increasingly aware of their hostility to him.

It is true that within each of the parties new men moved rapidly into prominence, distinguished by their war or resistance records, but many of the old leaders remained. And they stayed faithful to their old ideologies, or subject to their former apprehensions. In many cases they had learned nothing and forgotten nothing. On the left

83

there was mistrust of de Gaulle, and suggestions that he was aiming at dictatorship. The communists were all the more intransigent because they could claim to have made up the major part of the Resistance and because they felt assured of commanding a large following. In the centre and moderate parties there was resentment at de Gaulle, an outsider in politics, who seemed ready to treat timeworn institutions and experienced politicians with disdain. In particular, relations were difficult between de Gaulle and Edouard Herriot, and de Gaulle was later to say that when he invited him to help in the reconstruction of France, Herriot replied that he was occupied with the reconstruction of the radical party. Among the more conservative there was alarm at some of de Gaulle's unconven/ tional ideas, and further to the right there was an unavowed nostalgia for the values of Vichyism.

De Gaulle became increasingly conscious of this hostility, but he did not choose to allay it by any policy of conciliation. His method was to turn to the country as a whole. He appealed to them by means of the policy of nationalizations (and fulfilled the promises made from London). The coal/mines, the Renault motor/works, the Gnome and Rhône aircraft factories, air transport were all nationalized. In October 1945 a programme of social security was established by decree. De Gaulle also appealed by a series of elec/ tions and referenda. He asked whether the Constituent Assembly which was to be elected should have unlimited powers to make a new constitution or whether certain principles should be asserted *ab initio*. In elections the vote was to be by proportional representa/ tion, organized departmentally, and for the first time women were to have the vote. De Gaulle visited different parts of the country, and attempted to organize a direct contact between himself and the populations. He tried to avoid direct antagonism by refusing to follow the policy of economic austerity and financial control urged by his Minister of the Economy, Pierre Mendès/France (who consequently resigned in April 1945), and by accepting the more liberal policies of René Pleven.

The referendum on the Constituent Assembly gave some satis/ faction to de Gaulle and in that assembly a large Communist,

Socialist and MRP majority was theoretically prepared to accept him. But de Gaulle knew that their reservations still existed. And he announced publicly that he was not prepared to give the Commu-nists the key ministerial posts which they claimed, since he did not consider them as fully French, in view of their liaison with a foreign power. When the Assembly began to deliberate he saw himself increasingly excluded, he saw the party frameworks asserting them-selves, he saw an end to the authoritarian and effective government in which he believed. His associates found him increasingly morose and pessimistic. His logical mind saw no future for him as things were going, but emotionally and intuitively he still had some hope. In January 1946 he appeared in uniform before his cabinet (less Georges Bidault, who was abroad) and brusquely announced his resignation.

There is some reason to think that he anticipated a more vigorous response to this resignation, whether amongst the politicians or amongst the population as a whole. Either to the one or to the other he might have appeared indispensable.[3] But the politicians were now caught up in the political game, and this was a game where de Gaulle had no obvious place; his resignation therefore simplified things. And there was another characteristic of pre-war France which had returned and which de Gaulle had underestimated: the aliena-tion of the mass of the people from the government. The enthusiasm that had existed for Pétain, and which had then been transferred to the Liberation and to de Gaulle, had been killed in the face of economic hardships and political intrigues. This was the period when only the black marketeers were successful. Malraux, when asked by de Gaulle what had most impressed him about this period, replied 'the lies'. Georges Bernanos, returning to France after a long exile, saw French society reduced to hands, hands that were grasping and demanding. In such an atmosphere the resignation of de Gaulle was only an event amongst others, to be greeted with ordinary cynicism.

This resignation virtually ended the period of provisional govern-ment, and with the adoption of the new constitution, ushers in the period of the Fourth Republic. This can be studied politically in three periods. The first lasted from January 1946 until the summer of 1953; the second, a short and in some ways parenthetic period, consisted essentially of the Mendès-France government, 17 June 1954 to 5 February 1955; the third ended with the final collapse of the Republic, the rising in Algiers (13 May 1958), the formation of the de Gaulle government (1 June 1958) and the adoption of the new Constitution, the Fifth Republic. The government of the Fourth Republic was based upon a constitution where the Chamber of Deputies predominated. The President of the Republic (elected by the lower and upper houses of Parliament, meeting together in an electoral college) had the right to dissolve the Chamber of Deputies, but only on certain special conditions. It was necessary that the Chamber should be eighteen months old, and that within a period of a further eighteen months there should be two occasions on which the government should be overthrown by a vote of confidence in the Chamber. This was only possible once, when the Chamber was dissolved on 2 December 1955. Therefore it was the Chamber which predominated, and whilst there were three different Chambers elected (1946, 1951 and 1956) there were twenty-one different governments between January 1947 and June 1958.

It seemed therefore that the hopes of 1944–1945 had been completely disappointed. So far was one from a new France, that at the beginning of 1947, when the new constitution was promulgated, one could not help but notice that the President of the Republic was Vincent Auriol (formerly Minister of Finance under Blum), the Prime Minister was Blum himself, the President of the Assembly Edouard Herriot and the President of the Senate (then called Council of the Republic) another figure of the Third Republic, Champetier de Ribes. Many of the most prominent politicians were men who had been known before 1940. Although de Gaulle's nationalizations had been followed in 1946 by the nationalization of gas, electricity and insurance, the movement of reform was soon spent.

And it was not only that the Fourth Republic looked increasingly like the Third. It seemed to share the same characteristics, principally the instability of governments, accompanied by the shuffling and re-shuffling of ministers, with the occasional desperate search for a

Prime Minister acceptable to the different groups. In 1952 the appointment of Antoine Pinay as Prime Minister was something of a surprise: its significance was that he had been a supporter of Marshal
Pétain and a member of the Vichy National Council. In 1953 the
appointment of Joseph Laniel was even more of a surprise. A prolonged crisis was solved by the nomination of a man who, as British
journalists pointed out, was not included in *Who's Who in France*.
The French *chansonniers*, describing how difficult it was to find a
Prime Minister, said that everyone had been desperately searching,
but they had found no one. '*Ils ont cherché, cherché, mais ils ne trou-
vaient personne.*' And nobody, '*personne*', was called Laniel.

This sort of hilarity with regard to the leading political figures of
the country seemed to have come to a climax with the Laniel
government, but there was another climax with the election of a
new President, after Vincent Auriol's retirement in 1954, when there
were thirteen ballots before the relatively unknown René Coty,
from Le Havre, was appointed. The multiplicity of parties persisted,
as did continued economic crisis, devaluation of the franc, social
disturbances and strikes, quarrels over Catholic schools. But there
were also a number of particular characteristics, many of which were
original to the Fourth Republic and which help to explain its
failure.

One was the particular nature of the French communist party.
There can be little doubt that the communists had distinguished
themselves in the Resistance; they were able to profit from this
record and to appear as the genuine party of the left. In the first
general election they became the largest single parliamentary party
and although the number of communist deputies was to vary (as
electoral laws, for example, changed), they nevertheless maintained a
solid and considerable block of votes. They could claim to be a
more national party than any other, since their strongholds were to
be found throughout France, spread over a wide social order, appeal-
ing to industrial workers, peasants and members of the middle
class (such as the state school-teachers). Their newspaper, *L'Humanité*, had been founded by Jaurès, and they also possessed a number of
publications which were aimed at particular sections of the commun-

ity, such as women, young people, intellectuals, former resistants and so on. The principal trade union, the *Confédération Générale du Travail*, was communist-controlled.

Above all, alone amongst political groups, the communists were disciplined in their organization. They had their internal quarrels, their expulsions, their dissidents, but none of these essentially affected the character of the party. Even when their leader Maurice Thorez was seriously ill and, typically, was absent in Moscow for medical treatment, his leadership was never seriously challenged. It seems an inescapable fact that during these years the French communist party represented a real and considerable force in French political life. And yet, from January 1947, when the communists resigned from the coalition government, they were excluded from any direct participation in affairs. All the non-communist parties and groups rejected the communists and refused to have them as allies. Whilst their votes counted in the overthrow of ministries or the rejection of laws, they were not allowed to take any constructive part in the process of government.

The reasons for this were apparently straightforward. The communists, as a party which believed in the class struggle and in the revolution, were theoretically prepared to act in the classical revolutionary manner. In 1944 some of their leaders were disappointed at the failure to be more revolutionary, but although they found that their action was weak, outside the party it was widely believed that it was impossible to co-operate with them. It seemed that any participation in bourgeois government by the communists could only be a manœuvre, a means of exploiting the situation in order to gain the realities of power. The more bourgeois the party the more it seemed that this was likely to be true. But the international situation gave a particular edge to this. As relations worsened between America and Soviet Russia, and as 'the cold war' intensified, the French communists found themselves in a special position. They had always followed the Moscow 'line' and their links with Soviet Russia were clear and never concealed. At a time when there seemed to be a danger of a Soviet attack on Germany, the communists appeared at best as committed to Soviet Russia, at worst as Soviet agents. It did not seem unreasonable to suppose that communist militants were prepared to sabotage the French economy in order to carry out a revolution which would be part of the Soviet conquest of Europe. The communists, therefore, could be accused of not being wholly French. *'Communistes, pas français'* was the remark of the German officer responsible for the execution of Resistance leaders at Chateau-briant, in Brittany. And communists, conscious of their patriotism during the war, believing that they alone supported the true interests of the working class, were resentful that their fellow-countrymen should think of them as a Nazi officer once thought of them. They were ready with their counter-accusations and an almost hysterical propaganda. It was their opponents who were not wholly French, since they allowed themselves to be bought by American aid and interests. If, amongst the communists, one could see 'l'œil de Moscou', amongst those in power 'l'œil de Chicago' was also visible.[4]

Another cause of the failure of the institution and of the society of the Fourth Republic was undoubtedly the role assumed by General de Gaulle. His resignation was not a retirement from public life. He kept a close watch on affairs, and from time to time he made appearances, and speeches, in which he took for granted that he had a special part to play in French public life. A group of French people remained loyal to him, and he maintained an organization. In April 1947 he decided to make this organization wider and more effective. He founded a new group, the Rally of the French People, or *Rassemblement du Peuple Français* (RPF). This group won a resounding victory in the municipal elections of October 1947, and in the legislative elections of 1951 it became the largest single party in the Chamber. The aim of the Rally was twofold. Most obviously it was anti-communist, but at the same time it always sought to establish a new constitution. De Gaulle was essentially calling for a complete break with the existing situation, and so the RPF, like the communists, were working from outside, anxious to destroy in order to reform. The RPF did not seek to co-operate, or at least, not until the formation of the Pinay government, when the fatigue of incessant opposition helped to convince some of them that here was a government which merited their support.

At this point de Gaulle, who must have been particularly irked that his supporters could become confused with the supporters of Vichy, realized that his attempt had failed. He had only succeeded in creating an ordinary, bourgeois party, like all the others, and although he had always refused to be a deputy, or to play the game from the inside, it seemed that he was, in fact, playing the very political game which he despised. It was easy to give his followers their freedom. It was dignified to retire to a country retreat, Colombey-les-deux-églises, and to write his memoirs. The episode of the RPF had created many enemies and had tarnished his reputation. But de Gaulle, in his aloofness, still continued to see various politicians and to concern himself with public affairs.[5]

However, although the dual opposition of communist and Gaullist tended to weaken the situation, neither was so important as the war in Indo-China. It was this, most of all and first of all, which suggested that the Fourth Republic could not solve the important problems which were placed, inescapably, before it. It is this, the so-called 'suicide' of the Fourth Republic. France had drifted into a war with the nationalist leader of northern Indo-China, Ho Chi Minh, whilst supporting a puppet régime in the south under the so-called Emperor Bao Dai. This war dragged on, in spite of successive statements by French leaders that it was about to end in victory. Both the Russians and, for a time at least, the Americans, disapproved of this. Within France itself it became a prime cause of bitter controversy. Communist mayors used to refer to the war as unjust and unworthy when attending the burial services of young men who had been killed in the fighting. Young people tried to prevent the unloading of American war material. There were everyday scenes which were ugly and tragic. The opposition (mainly communist) had no difficulty in pointing to the expense, the cost in men, the failure in military calculation, the uncertainty and the embarrassment. And it was less easy to reject the charge that French officialdom was corrupt. The accusations that France was fighting on behalf of the Bank of Indo-China, or that Frenchmen of all sorts were engaged in some bold conspiracy, were not easily refuted.[6]

It is not surprising that the Indo-Chinese war put considerable strain on the franc and on a situation of social unrest. When it was necessary for a government to face up to urgent problems, the constitution placed considerable obstacles in its way. The natural public response was indifference, or cynicism, or hostility. And in this atmosphere it was not realized that important changes were taking place. For example, the European policy of the Fourth Republic, especially of the MRP of Bidault and Schuman, was successful. The Schuman Plan of 1950, the Coal and Steel Community of 1951, the move to create a European army, all were projects dear to the heart of some very typical Fourth Republic statesmen.

There was something rather French about the idea of escaping from complete subservience to America and from the rearmament of Germany by means of the construction of Europe. Naturally this policy of building up European institutions was highly controversial and the project for a European army made difficult progress. The communists thought that the European ideal was an attempt to ensure the success of big capitalist companies and of American domination. The Gaullists objected on national grounds, since within an amalgam of Europe the true national identity of France might be lost. Politicians in the centre, radicals and socialists, found it difficult to agree on the details of such a policy.

At the same time as all this was under consideration, the foundations of the French plan for the economy were laid. The first plan covered the years from 1947 to 1952–53. A mixture of direction and liberalism was effected by a complex of consultations, and the plan as a whole was concerned with investment in power, transport, building materials and agriculture. A second plan, covering the years 1954 to 1957, concerned itself with the whole of the French economy. It was clear that many things were changing in French life, and although this caused certain politicians to be jubilant, generally speaking there was uncertainty.[7]

This preoccupation with economic growth coincided with, but can hardly be explained by, an important change in the demographic pattern of the country. It is possible that this change started about 1939, or about 1942, and that the war prevented the change from fulfilling itself. At all event, from 1946 onwards one can see that French women were bearing more children. Whether this was brought about by the existence of family allowances, first established in 1939, or whether one should look rather at the phenomenon of inflation, when it was easier to have a large family than it was to save money, there was a change in the attitude of young people. It could be that in France, as in other countries, the shock of war, defeat and occupation produced a change of values.[8]

There was one government which sought to overcome the causes of weakness in the country, and to reinforce what movement there was towards strength. This was the government of Pierre Mendès-France, from June 1954 to February 1955. Mendès-France, who had been one of the younger Radical deputies before 1939, who had served in the Popular Front and with General de Gaulle in London and Algiers, attempted to introduce a new atmosphere into politics. Showing a certain disregard for the routine methods of government and for the procedures of the political parties, he set out to govern by posing a succession of problems. If necessary, for each successive problem he would try to create a particular majority. He envisaged his government as introducing a sort of New Deal, and by frequent broadcasts of the 'fireside chat' variety, he sought to present himself and his policies as modern and dynamic. He encouraged people to write directly to him and assured them that all their letters would be read. There was something of a cult of the personality here, and with the support of a weekly newspaper, *L'Express*, and of the writer François Mauriac, the emphasis was placed on P.M.F. (as he was called) and on his ability to govern and to get things done.

His government addressed itself to four main sectors. The first was the colonial one. Mendès-France had shocked the Assembly into voting him into power, by his promise to end the Indo-Chinese war. This he did, negotiating the Geneva agreements whereby Indo-China was divided into two separate countries, North and South Vietnam. He negotiated an agreement whereby Tunisia was to become fully independent, and whilst insisting that Algeria (where fighting had broken out in November 1954) must remain French, he prepared a series of economic reforms for that country. The second sector was that of the economy (Mendès-France himself being an economic specialist). He asked for special powers whereby the economy could be directed towards greater growth and vitality, seeking to abolish the bottlenecks which only too frequently im-peded efficiency. The third sector was youth. He appointed a minister especially concerned with the problems of youth, and Mendès-France showed in his speeches that he was conscious of the impor-tance of the new generation.

Fourthly, with regard to European affairs, he brought the ques-tion of the European army out of the stalemate in which it had sombred, and allowed it to be defeated. He then attempted to negotiate a series of international agreements which would set up a European framework capable of accepting German re-armament. One of his hopes was to persuade Great Britain to enter the agree-ment, but he was only moderately successful. For all that the ageing Churchill professed admiration for the French Prime Minister, he was reluctant to accept that England was a part of Europe.

The result of all this activity was to bring up against Mendès-France a whole series of oppositions and hostilities. His colonial policy aroused the alarm of the powerful French interests in Algeria. His ending of the Indo-Chinese war was a public demonstration of French weakness, and it was not easy to forgive such realism. His economic policy smacked of *étatisme* and of technocratic inter-ventions in spheres which many preferred to see independent. He seemed more preoccupied with establishing economic efficiency than social justice. His European policy meant the end of a European dream (as it meant the end of the MRP monopoly in foreign affairs) and all forms of German re-armament were rejected by the com-munists. The cult of the *'mendésiste'* personality was found objection-able by many. It was suggested that he wanted to diminish the importance of Parliament and it was easy to be cynical about the performance of *'le superman'*. The fact that Mendès-France was Jewish added to this personal hostility, and gave an edge to accusa-tions that he had sold bits of France and to remarks about 'Monsieur Mendès, curiously surnamed France'.

One incident was typical. As part of his policy of improving the

health of the young, Mendès-France attempted to reduce the privileges of alcohol distillers and at the same time arranged for milk to
be drunk in state schools every morning. This brought against
him the powerful lobby of alcohol distillers, particularly important
in Normandy and Brittany; this earned him some resentment from
school-teachers who resented this interference and who suspected
that it would lead to an additional duty; this gained him a certain
amount of ridicule, as a purveyor of milk ('Mendès-Lolo'); and most
striking of all, it increased the indignation of those who claimed that
he was not patriotic, since he was far from being an advertisement for
French wines and alcohols.

It is not surprising then that an unholy alliance, notably including
the communists and the MRP, should have overthrown this government. Nor should it be forgotten that Mendès-France himself had
contributed to his failure. Apart from having a personality that too
easily aroused passions (and one could possibly apply to him Guizot's
remark about one of his contemporaries, Molé, *'cet homme aimable
n'avait pas d'amis'*), Mendès-France made no attempt to modify the
constitutional and political system which rendered him powerless.
He did not attempt to end the isolation of the communists, although
they had, at first, supported his government. He remained within
the framework of the Radical party, although his position there
was far from secure, and although he had little of the supple conciliatory skill which usually distinguished the radical politicians.

But the experience of the Mendès-France ministry was significant.
It illuminated many of the divisions of France. It suggested that a
change was taking place, and that there was a place for non-
traditional, technocratic government. It revealed that many
Frenchmen, even amongst their resentments, had developed a taste
for strong government.[9]

After 1955 the political confusion became considerable. Mendès-
France was succeeded by Edgar Faure, who had been his finance
minister and who was also a radical. Relations between them
deteriorated and Mendès-France was obliged to devote most of his
energies to attempting to win control of the radicals. At the close
of the year the Faure government was defeated and it was decided

to bring into force the dissolution clause of the constitution and to dissolve the Chamber. This was greeted in some circles as if it were purely an attempt to have elections before Mendès-France had had time to build up an organization. However, although Mendès-France attempted to organize a Republican Front, with the Socialists (under Mollet), the ex-Gaullists (under Chaban-Delmas) and other groups of moderates, it was typical of the fortunes of *Mendésisme* that the elections never lost their appearance of being something of a private feud amongst radicals, and that the man who was dependent upon public opinion should have opposed an appeal to the people.

The Chamber which was elected had all the appearance of being incapable of producing a stable government. The communists on the left were counter-balanced by a new and violent party, that of M. Pierre Poujade. Representing the small man, in all different types of commercial and business enterprises, this party was violent in its opposition to the existing state of affairs. It opposed modern technocracy, centralization, the importance of big business, the extent of state taxation and the parliamentary system. Its chief enemies were the communists and the *mendésistes*, since it was also nationalist. Provincial and traditionalist, nostalgic in its assessment of the past and violent in its attitude to the present, the episode of Poujadisme represents the uncertainties of the period. It appealed to many of the traditional right and to some of those who, impressed by their election victories, were normally moderate. It was a selfish and an egocentric party, with an improvised organization and a leader who had come unexpectedly into prominence.

The Republican Front formed a government with the socialist Guy Mollet at its head and Mendès-France as minister of state. In May Mendès-France resigned, being particularly disappointed in Mollet's attitude to the Algerian war. Mollet, having been rudely received by the French settlers in Algiers, only thought of a military solution and although he may have been tempted into one or two highly secret (and ineffective) conversations with the rebels, he refused any political consideration of the Algerian problem until military victory. More troops were sent to Algeria and the ramifications of the war were considerable. The French participation in the attack on

Suez in October 1956 was almost certainly caused by the belief that the defeat of Nasser would help the Algerian situation, as well as by Mollet's need to impress the Chamber with some signs of force if he were to remain in power.

It is true that the government pursued its negotiations towards European economic activity, and drove hard bargains with its associates. M. Gaston Defferre was also successful in establishing the framework necessary for French establishment in western and equa-torial Africa and Madagascar to proceed to forms of self-government. But in general terms the government only persisted because the com-munists were hesitant about overthrowing the socialists, and because groups in the centre approved of the European policy. When the Mollet government was eventually defeated over its financial policy in May 1957, the difficulty of forming any new government was immediately apparent. It was nearly three weeks before Bourgès-Maunoury formed a government which lasted for the summer holidays, then five weeks in between his defeat and the investiture of Félix Gaillard. During these periods France theoretically had no government and presented an unimpressive face to the world. The different parties of the centre became increasingly divided amongst personalities, and it was unthinkable that the left and the right oppositions could combine to form a government.

Everything that French governments touched seemed to turn to disaster. The lack of any determined fiscal policy threatened a finan-cial catastrophe. There were rumours and indications of military plots amongst the generals in Algeria; there were outcries against the use of torture by the army and protests became more vehement. Whilst groups of servicemen and Poujadists showed greater milit-ancy, there were signs that the police force in Paris was no longer completely reliable. It seemed that the French state was losing con-trol over its agents. In April 1958 the bombardment of a Tunisian village, Sakhiet, by units of the French air force (acting contrary to orders) created an international complication which brought the Gaillard government down. What was yet another ministerial crisis was to become a revolution.

8   The revolution of 1958

Si l'on faisait appel à un vieux pilote?   Chateaubriand

THE STORY OF THIS REVOLUTION is not unlike that of other revolutions. At the beginning of 1789, or 1848, where are the repub-licans to be found? In 1917, how many people in Russia were Bolsheviks and working for a communist revolution? It is almost an historical law that before a revolution it is difficult to find many revolutionaries. In 1958 there were conspiracies and plots, both within metropolitan France and in Algeria, both in the army and amongst civilians. These conspiracies usually had similar aims, to bring to an end the humiliating spectacle of French weakness which the parliamentary system was presenting to the world, and to win the war in Algeria by every means possible. But in spite of the simi-larity of these aims, there was nothing unified or co-ordinated about these various movements. They consisted of small groups ('group-uscules' as they could have been called) which involved various ex-servicemen's organizations and certain ex-generals, or which included some nostalgic evocations of the right-wing movements of the thirties, linked with a few adventurers and intellectuals. Their activities were not particularly secret and the government knew of their existence.[1]

In contrast to these groups there were three main sources of power. The first was the legally constituted power, the government which would have the support of Parliament. But with the resignation of the Gaillard government it seemed to be manifestly impossible for any new ministerial combination to emerge. The divisions between the centre parties, especially the MRP, the Radicals and the Inde-pendents, were so considerable as to prevent any leader from appearing. It was only after a month of negotiations and confusion that an MRP deputy from Alsace, Pierre Pflimlin, who had for some years been Minister of Agriculture, seemed to have brought together the sort of government likely to win enough votes in the Chamber. The second source of power was the army. Although the army contained a wide variety of opinions, the situation was such as to sharpen its political sense. As the normal source of political power, Parliament, became so loose as to lose all effectiveness, the tighter organization of the army emphasized its effectiveness; being in undisturbed control of Algeria, the distance between the army there and the authority of Paris became all the more marked, and the fear that the politicians in Paris would betray the army in Algeria was increased by rumours that M. Pflimlin had spoken in favour of negotiation with the rebels (and an article written by him in his own Strasbourg newspaper was quoted to this effect). Perhaps the most important point was that many army officers were convinced of the need for political leadership to win the Algerian war and they despaired of finding that leadership anywhere in the Chamber of Deputies.

The third source of power was the European population in Algeria. Ever since they had forced M. Guy Mollet to change his policy in 1956, they were conscious of their power. It seemed clear that no French government could do anything against the wishes of this population and through a number of deputies, businessmen and newspapers, the Algerian lobby was a powerful influence within metropolitan France. The fact that the Europeans were a very diverse population, with different social classes, political opinions and national origins, caused them to assert all the more strongly the one thing that united them: their determination to remain in Algeria and their insistence that the French government should support them. They too were particularly alarmed by the disintegration of the government in Paris and the rumours concerning M. Pflimlin.

Where, it must be asked, did General de Gaulle stand in all this? In one sense, he stood nowhere. The Gaullists were strictly speaking non-existent in the Chamber of Deputies. The General had severed his ties with them, and although Jacques Soustelle was known to remain a loyal friend, and although Chaban-Delmas had actually been a minister, there was no possibility of a Gaullist being chosen by the Chamber to be Prime Minister. In the army, de Gaulle's position was weak. Few amongst the hierarchy of officers had followed him to London and several had found themselves opposing the Free French forces, whether in Africa or the Middle East. There was a good deal of mistrust of de Gaulle amongst senior officers, whilst the younger officers thought that he was a back number. Amongst the French settlers in Algeria, de Gaulle's position was even weaker. He had not been popular with them in 1942, and there was nothing which suggested that he could possibly become their champion in 1958. But in another sense, the Gaullists were everywhere. It is as if there were a Gaullist thread running through every one of the conspiracies. This was always a question of personalities, since a number of loyal Gaullists, such as Soustelle, Michel Debré, Foccard, Frey, and others, had been watching events very closely and were involved in the majority of these movements. Certain individual officers, such as General Miquel, who was commanding the military region of Toulouse, had assured the Gaullists of his support. Chaban-Delmas had sent a representative, Léon Delbecque, to Algiers, to look after Gaullist interests there.

It is not clear, in our present state of knowledge, exactly how de Gaulle viewed these events. Some report him as having been extremely pessimistic. Other accounts suggest that he always expected that the inefficiencies of the Fourth Republic would bring him back to power.[2] At all events he was following the situation closely. He received many visitors at Colombey-les-deux-églises, and he went to Paris once a week. He must have been conscious of the fact that, for some time, there had been a greater awareness of crisis amongst the French public, and that a number of individuals had turned in his direction (often these had been *mendésistes*). President Coty had even, discreetly, enquired about the conditions in which he would accept a return to office. It is certain that he knew about the various plots and conspiracies, and that he knew how many of his supporters were involved. He neither encouraged nor discouraged them in this work. He seems to have allowed a very deliberate ambiguity to cover both his expectations and his policies.

However much plotting there had been, there was a certain spontaneity about the way in which events developed. It seems to have been agreed that there should be a manifestation in Algiers which would prevent M. Pflimlin's government from being invested. Some Gaullists appeared to have thought that such a manifestation would create a panic in Paris and would, in itself, create a movement in favour of the General. But when, on 13 May 1958, the Algiers crowd (led by students and the somewhat mature student, Pierre Lagaillarde) seized the official building of the Government-General and set up a Committee of Public Safety (falling back on the well-worn revolutionary vocabulary) there were a number of unexpected consequences. For one thing the rising took place whilst the Chamber in Paris was debating whether to accept the Pflimlin government or not. The resulting movement of opinion in the Chamber had the effect of confirming the Pflimlin government's majority. Then, the military leaders in Algiers were highly embarrassed by the rising and whilst unable to disavow the Committee of Public Safety they sought to come to some understanding with Paris. They realized that in every way they were dependent upon supplies and money reaching them from France, and since the government of Pflimlin also showed no desire to condemn the rising, there did seem a possibility that the crisis could be surmounted by some sort of accommodation. However, a further development was that a number of officers in contact with some of the military in France began to prepare for an invasion of France to be undertaken by parachutists. The consequences of such a move could obviously have been most serious and when rumours of such a possibility began to circulate in France, the inevitable reaction was the formation of groups to defend 'the Republic'. In a clash between Frenchmen, the fact that the communist party was the largest single political party and had the allegiance of many of the working class would have been of supreme importance. The threat of civil war seemed real.

In these circumstances General de Gaulle's position was a doubtful one. He himself seems to have been convinced that the Chamber of Deputies, the army and the leaders in Algiers were all united in not wishing for a Gaullist government. And so far as the opinion of the vast majority of French people was concerned, there was no means whereby this opinion could express itself. This was all the more difficult since, although the crisis was one which held the attention of the entire French population, ordinary life continued, French people still wanted their diversions, and they remained preoccupied with their weekends, especially the Whitsun weekend (Whit-Sunday was on 25 May). De Gaulle was determined on two things. First, that he would not become the head of government in the ordinary way. He was not going to succeed to Félix Gaillard as Gaillard had replaced Bourgès-Maunoury who had replaced Edgar Faure, etc. And the other was that he would not come to power as the prisoner of a group, or section, which would impose its ideas on him.

Given this difficulty de Gaulle made the revolution a very personal one by a remarkable display of political skill. He was determined to do everything he could to worsen the crisis, so that there would be no patched-up agreement, and at the same time he showed a remarkable sense of timing. The uncertainty as to what he would do, emphasized by the absence of any official policy statement by him and exploited by his frequent isolation at Colombey-les-deux-églises, meant that an increasing number of people looked to him as the *deux ex machina* who could resolve the crisis. On 15 May de Gaulle published a communiqué stating that he was ready to assume power in the republic. On the same day, General Salan, standing in front of the hysterically excited crowds of the Forum in Algiers, flung the name of General de Gaulle into the general enthusiasm. That this action was suggested to him by Delbecque who was standing immediately behind him makes this seem a very nicely judged affair, and although de Gaulle's name had been mentioned before, this was the first time that the crowds had had the opportunity to acclaim it. But it seems most likely that Salan's action was a sign of something which was to be very widely experienced: as the crisis worsened, men in positions of responsibility looked for means whereby they could shuffle off this responsibility and the figure of de Gaulle was most conveniently placed for this.

The arrival in Algiers of Jacques Soustelle (who escaped from police surveillance in Paris) on 17 May increased the pressure of those working in favour of de Gaulle.

De Gaulle's chief activity within France was to reassure the normal centre of power, that is to say Parliament. On 19 May (the delay meant that everyone waited to see what de Gaulle was going to do), he held a press conference which sought to show that he had no intention of setting up a dictatorship. His attitude towards the Committee of Public Safety in Algiers remained ambiguous, but his attitude towards one of the key figures in the Paris political scene was clear enough. He spoke with enthusiasm about his former friendship with Guy Mollet, recalling an incident in 1944 at Arras when they had appeared on a balcony together, a souvenir which was none the less remarkable because the incident had never, in fact, occurred. Clearly General de Gaulle wanted to reassure. And both M. Pinay, amongst the conservatives, and M. Mollet amongst the communist-fearing socialists, were reassured that a de Gaulle government would do little harm. But there did not seem to be any reason to move events forward until 24 May when parachutists from Algeria landed in Corsica and disarmed the police forces which had been sent to oppose them. The powerlessness of the state seemed only too obvious, and a parachute operation in France itself was organized for the night of 27 to 28 May. De Gaulle saw M. Pflimlin secretly during the night of 26 to 27 May, and after an inconclusive discussion he issued a communiqué stating that he had begun the normal process of forming a government. This statement astonished M. Pflimlin; it was totally unjustified; there was no constitutional reason why he should resign since he had the full confidence of the Chamber. But the publication of this communiqué caused the military leaders to put off the parachute operation. And since no one dared to deny that de Gaulle was forming a government, it demonstrated that effective authority had, in fact, passed into his hands, in a way that seemed both simple and natural. Pflimlin resigned and from then onwards the movement was in the hands of de Gaulle.

It is easy to insist on the fortuitous nature of all this. If M. Gaillard's government had not been brought down over relations with

Tunisia, if General Salan had not launched the de Gaulle candidature, if all the various activists had shown themselves to be more
audacious, then the story might have been very different. The French
revolution of 1958, like other revolutions, was an affair of an active
minority, all the more striking since many of this minority were not
in favour of de Gaulle. It appears essentially as a personal revolution,
a tribute to de Gaulle's skill and ability. It is difficult to see any
political principle involved except that of the need to instal a strong,
executive government. And the final scenes, whereby de Gaulle
won over the recalcitrant socialists by agreeing to speak in the Chamber (an experience which he liked, all the more since he realized
how excellent his performance would be), emphasize that this might
have been a 'confiscated revolution' (as Victor Hugo said about
1830) but that it was always a personal one. As de Gaulle sat alone
on the government front bench, deputy after deputy went up to him
and shook him by the hand. There were no more negotiations.
It was the same in 1814, when the members of the Napoleonic
Senate had wished to accept Louis XVIII only on certain conditions.
But as the king landed in France and journeyed in slow solemnity
towards his capital, one by one the senators left Paris to go north-
wards and pay homage to the king.

Two things must be emphasized. The first is that de Gaulle was
accepted because he would not lead a revolution. The *opération
séduction* which followed the *opération sédition* (the phrase is almost
certainly M. Bidault's) was meant to reassure. And although the
starting point of the events was the Algiers rising and although the
nub of the crisis was the situation in Algeria, negotiations between
the French politicians and de Gaulle were hardly centred on the
subject of Algeria. De Gaulle actually came to power without
announcing what his Algerian policy would be. There are accounts
that, here and there, he gave assurances that Algeria would remain
French; here and there too there were men who claimed to have
reason to recall that de Gaulle's record in colonial affairs was a liberal
one. Everyone had his own idea of what de Gaulle would do, and
it varied from those who thought that he would support the settlers
to those who thought that he would use his prestige among the

Moslems to make peace. So the revolution of 1958 was in one sense an insurance against revolution, in another a complete uncertainty.[3]

In these circumstances de Gaulle's choice was to emphasize continuity. He excluded the communists from all his negotiations; Socialists, MRP, Independents, Radicals and Gaullists were each given three posts; he took as his ministers some of the most prominent politicians of the Fourth Republic, Mollet and Pflimlin being ministers of State and Pinay minister of Finance. A number of civil servants were brought in to the government, the most prominent being Couve de Murville, who became minister for Foreign Affairs. De Gaulle's personal ally, André Malraux, also became a minister. Perhaps the only unusual appointment was that of Michel Debré as minister for Justice. All the more unusual since Debré, a fiery Gaullist who had had contact with more than one of the conspiracies, was given the special mission of drawing up a new constitution. It was planned that this constitution should be presented to the population by means of a referendum in September, and if it were accepted it would be followed by legislative elections in November and by a Presidential election in December. France thus entered a prolonged period of electoral activity, in which it was popularly assumed that the referendum would be approved, the legislative elections would be favourable to de Gaulle and that de Gaulle would be elected President. But the overwhelming nature of the response was surprising and many political commentators were proved wrong. The majority in favour of the constitution totalled four-fifths of those who voted. In the elections, which were held in single-member constituencies with a double ballot, the opposition, consisting of communists and the democratic left (mainly *mendésistes*) were almost eliminated. The new *Union pour la République* (UNR), which was avowedly Gaullist, although it did not have the open support of de Gaulle who considered himself to be above parties, was the dominant party with 200 out of 465 metropolitan seats. When the specially designed electoral college, consisting of deputies, senators, mayors and other local government representatives, met to elect the President of the Republic, de Gaulle received 78.5% of the votes cast. The Fifth Republic began when President de Gaulle appointed Debré to be his Prime Minister (using the term *Premier Ministre*, rather than the traditional term, *Président du Conseil*).

Thus if, in May and June 1958, de Gaulle had been at pains to show that he would preserve continuity, within a very short space of time this continuity had been broken. A new constitution would be worked out by new men. Not only had a number of the leading politicians been ousted in the elections (Mendès-France, Edgar Faure and Gaston Defferre were the most notable examples) but three-quarters of the new Assembly had not sat in the Assembly elected in 1956. The old political grouping, Communists, Radicals, MRP (not to mention Poujadists) had suffered devastating losses, and new men, often insisting simply on the fact of being new, some-times claiming to have no political ideas at all apart from their loyalty to de Gaulle and their hostility to the Fourth Republic, dominated the scene. The Prime Minister was a man who, prior to June 1958, had never been a minister and who had not been a mem-ber of the Assembly (but a senator). When he formed his govern-ment the Socialists, led by Guy Mollet, refused to take part and yet another break with continuity was effected.

It is, of course, true that this break can be exaggerated. The method of voting being different, the results of the elections were different. This did not mean that the political complexion of the country had changed completely. The communists, for example, maintained their vote, and about one Frenchman in five who voted voted communist. Had there been a system of proportional repre-sentation, the communists would have had something like 87 seats; but the double ballot system was unfavourable to the communists who found it impossible to organize an agreement with other left-wing parties, and in their isolation could only get 10 deputies elected. The socialists and radicals also suffered from the double ballot, and would have had more seats from proportional representation, whilst the independents and the UNR profited from the new system and would have had many fewer deputies.

In this sense, the break in continuity was less remarkable than it appeared to be. In another sense the election of 1958 put the 1956 election in proper perspective. The ex-Gaullists had done very poorly in 1956 because they were Gaullists without de Gaulle, in contrast to their position in the 1951 election; the Poujadists had sprung up sensationally in 1956 only as part of a movement of frustration, and they could not be expected to be a permanent political force; an individual such as Mendès-France had had a personal success in 1956 which was bound to slump with the dis-appointment of his ineffectiveness.

If one wished to be cynical one could proceed by saying that in 1958 the French population emphasized continuity by demon-strating a quality that had often been seen before. France is not the home of lost causes; when a régime collapses no one will fight for it. Napoleon found this in 1814, the Bourbons in 1815 and again in 1830, Louis-Philippe in 1848 ('comme Charles X, comme Charles X' he is thought to have murmured as he fled), Napoleon III in 1870, Pétain in 1944, possibly de Gaulle himself in 1946. The readiness to abandon a régime is usually a demonstration of its weakness, and implies that people have become alienated from it, that there is no great social interest which is committed to its support. At the most one could hope for a gesture of loyalty, but no more. And in 1958 a massive demonstration was organized in Paris to defend the Republic. An impressive number of people marched through the streets and shouted slogans, but afterwards they went home to bed. There was no violence, a threatened strike never materialized and it is permitted to wonder if all the demonstrators even voted against de Gaulle. It was only a gesture. Why should a communist strive to defend a system of government which had excluded him from power? Why should a young man wish to defend a régime which condemned young men to endless fighting in Al-geria, or why should an old man be anxious to see prolonged a system which seemed unable to halt the rise of prices and the in-creasing difficulties of living? The bourgeoisie, as a whole, had every-thing to lose by fighting for the Fourth Republic. Only those (mainly *mendésistes*) who believed that the Fifth Republic was marked by the original sin of its birth, and that however carefully de Gaulle might have proceeded along the constitutional path of the vote in the Chamber, and then referendum and election, nevertheless he owed his power to an illegal rising in Algiers, could remain clear in their opposition. They were the legitimists of 1958, like those who, in 1830, could not accept Louis-Philippe's Bourbon blood as compensation for the rising of the people which had really brought him to power.[4]

In 1958 there were new elements. There was the Algerian affair, which had assumed such proportions that normal political life could only continue with great difficulty. It was essential to discover some means out of the impasse. But this suggested that the coming to power of de Gaulle was far from being a revolution, it was only the appointment of a man with a special mission. Once this mission was accomplished, then there would be no further need for him, as Mendès-France had been necessary only to bring about peace in Indo-China. This was to assume, too, that there were no fundamental differences among French people, and that the threat of some sort of civil war during May 1958 had been merely a manifestation of the Algerian war, a falsification of reality. On the other hand it could have been that the Algerian war had illuminated rather than created these differences amongst the French. If so, it would be necessary for some means to be found whereby communists, and the left wing in general, could exist within the same framework of social and political existence as those who had voted Poujadist in 1956 or those who had favoured the movements which led to 13 May. In which case the mission of Gaullism might extend beyond a solution to the Algerian problem.

The crisis of 1958 also saw a personalization of politics. The political mobilization of society was in terms of one individual. To some extent this had already happened with Marshal Pétain, who had, in his own words, made a gift of his person to France in 1940. To a section of the population the possibility had, for a moment, existed, of Mendès-France personifying the energies and efforts of society. It could be argued that this is nothing new. Both Louis XIV and Napoleon are only the most conspicuous examples of individuals who personify the State, and there is a long tradition of the political-cum-religious leader in most developed societies. But in modern times, the role of the leader has become fuller. In western

European countries the democratic process has obliged everyone to have some involvement in politics, however theoretical or super-ficial this involvement is. As the processes of all modern government become increasingly technical this involvement becomes more complicated, and consequently it is more difficult for the population to understand what is going on. There is, in consequence, a desire to simplify matters and to see government in terms of individuals, since an individual is more easy to observe, to imagine and to com-prehend, than the remote, impersonal forces of the State. This desire is rendered practical and feasible by the development of modern methods of communication, such as the press, the radio, the cinema and television, which familiarize the whole population with the existence and the nature of particular individuals, and which allow these individuals a direct contact with the populations. There is thus created an actor-audience relationship which seems to permit both participation and understanding.

In France the need for the personalization of power was associated with the realization that the State was disintegrating before the enormity of the problems which it faced. And in this need for an actor-audience relationship which would replace the sense of being abandoned, de Gaulle played his role. He appeared as a solitary fig-ure, one who had had no contact with the existing system. In his first press conference, widely heard on the radio, he described himself as being a man who belonged to no one, and who therefore belonged to everyone. In his first statement during the crisis he recalled that once before, from the depths of the abyss, France had turned to him for salvation and he had responded; once again he held himself in readiness. His press conference had ended with the words, 'now I shall return to my village and I will wait to see if I can serve France.' This reference to his village, his frequent returns there, all empha-sized his independence and even suggested a sort of virtuous simplicity. Against a backcloth of dissentient politicians and threat-ening civil war, he was able to go through the dramaturgical process of establishing himself as a leader, all the more dramatic because there were obstacles in the way of his success. In a letter to the former President of the Republic, Vincent Auriol, de Gaulle referred to the sectarianism, which he could not understand, of those who wanted to prevent him from saving France and said that if they succeeded all that would be left for him would be to stay, until his death, with his grief. No one suggested that de Gaulle was particularly clever, and that he had the requisite political intelligence to succeed. His virtue was his patriotism, his prestige, his own un-questioning belief that he was fitted to lead France. The audience saw an actor who was lost in his role; within the drama of their country they saw the drama of an individual. And it was in this way that the situation developed whereby, as one observer put it, if political authority was in Paris and military authority in Algiers, moral authority was in Colombey-les-deux-églises.[5]

Naturally, not everyone thought in this way. There were those who could not think of de Gaulle being above party since they remembered him as the leader of the RPF. They would not think of him as being for nothing in the crisis of the Fourth Republic since he had presented it, at its birth, with two formidable legacies, financial inflation and the war in Indo-China. Nor did they see him as the peaceful villager, patiently waiting to be called upon. His involve-ment in the conspiracies and his knowledge of how to manipulate the political machinery necessary to establish himself made him unfitted for any Cincinnatus role. And most important of all, there were those who rejected the whole process whereby power could be personalized in this way. They believed that the link between leader and masses was the link between feudal lord and vassal. They refused to accept that the destiny of France could be identified with the destiny of one man.

But it seems that in 1958 the mass of the population was anxious to identify themselves with one man. And perhaps this readiness corresponded to a deeper alienation which the students and activists of Algiers had underlined. The political ideologies and energies of the Fourth Republic no longer corresponded to France. The Fourth Republic had been, in many respects, a repetition of the Third Republic. The same type of ideological quarrels over matters of the Church and education persisted, only being joined by quarrels over the Resistance movement and collaboration, new versions of the

Dreyfus affair. The same type of politicians had come to the fore, who excelled in the game of politics as played in the small town and the backward rural community. This was a political system which was suitable for a country with a declining population, dominated by a small-scale, static economy and by the issues of the past. But this system no longer corresponded to French society because French society was changing. The population was growing, communications were being revolutionized, the countryside was changing, industry and commerce were unleashing new and dynamic forces well beyond the routine of the small family firms. In these circumstances the politicians of the Fourth Republic appeared to be increasingly irrelevant, and there was enthusiasm for those who tried to break out into something new, as there had been for the social Catholics in their early days, for the policy of constructing Europe, or for the personal dynamism of Mendès-France. But these had all proved disappointments. In 1958 de Gaulle offered another opportunity for change. In that sense one can talk of the revolution of 1958.

9   The Man

This strange, attractive and yet impossible character.
Half revolutionary and half reactionary ...   Harold Macmillan

WHEN ONE RECOUNTS the history of France both before and
after 1789, one is obliged to consider a multiplicity of detail concerning administration, finance, the economy, the movement of
ideas, social classes, diplomacy and so on. But after 1799 there are
some historians for whom this ceases. Henceforth everything is
subsumed in the personality and action of Bonaparte. Not until 1814
or 1815 do these historians return to the themes and subjects which
constitute a state and a society, abandoning their preoccupation with
the intelligence or the caprices of one man. It is interesting to reflect
that this has only partially happened since 1958. The problems of
France have never been lost sight of and it seems unlikely that historians will forget them whilst they expatiate on the nature of General
de Gaulle. This is not only because historians have become wiser; it
is also a commentary on the way in which Gaullism is a discussion
of issues rather than the presentation of an ego. But any consideration
of contemporary France must move into the realm of Gaullology
(which has almost become an independent branch of political
science) and consider the personality and the ideas of this inescapable
figure.

Charles-André-Marie-Joseph de Gaulle was born on 22 November 1890, at Lille. His father, Henri de Gaulle, worked in the pre-
fecture of the Seine before becoming a teacher in a Catholic school
in Paris, with a particular interest in history. The Gaulle family
was aware of its long ancestry and considered itself to be of the
petite noblesse, a minor aristocratic family with strong bourgeois
connections but with little money. Both the father and the mother

(who was *née* Jeanne Maillot) were Catholics and royalists, but when the Dreyfus affair was at its height, in the late 1890's, Henri de Gaulle quarrelled with most of his royalist friends because he did not believe in Dreyfus's guilt and because he could not accept an injustice.

It is easy to suggest that this background explains much of Charles de Gaulle. Coming from the north of France he had a certain cold-ness in his temperament, perhaps a touch of melancholy, as well as a disposition to work hard. Conscious of his ancestors, and through his father's teaching, he developed a sense of history which was never to leave him. Not being wealthy and living in Paris (his first memo-ries are of Paris) he also had the sentiment of belonging to the people. From his father's ideals and actions he derived a combination of certain traditional values and the need for individual judgement. Such a picture seems convincing but one has no means of knowing whether or not it is true. It is not clear at what point he developed his remarkable patriotism or at what moment he began to believe that he himself was destined to play an important role in the history of France. But his formative years coincided with a revival of French self-confidence, when France was 'herself again' as one writer put it[1] and when much of the bitterness which had accompanied the Dreyfus affair began to die away. The fact that after attending Catholic colleges de Gaulle chose a military career, entering the army in 1909 and becoming a cadet at the officers' training college of Saint Cyr the following year, could only have emphasized this conviction, and might have created the belief that his destiny and that of France were linked.

If one was a young officer in 1914, provided that one was not killed (which was to be the fate of most of de Gaulle's contemporaries) then the future seemed reasonably bright. De Gaulle distinguished himself, being cited for bravery; wounded three times, he became a prisoner, and in spite of several attempts at escape, he remained in Germany until the armistice. It was probably during this period of captivity that he began to read widely and to develop a literary and philosophical culture which was more considerable than that of most other young officers. After the war he served in Poland

and in the Middle East, before becoming a lecturer at the Ecole de Guerre, specializing in military history. He began to write and to publish and his name became quite widely known. He seems to have earned a great deal of admiration for his efficiency and he impressed many by his intelligence and culture. But by 1939 he was only a colonel. For him, as for others, promotion was slow; there was little that was particularly distinguished in his career.[2]

This can be explained. Although de Gaulle was able to impress people (as he impressed Marshal Pétain), he did not always succeed in making himself liked. His successes were invariably accompanied by setbacks, and beside those who esteemed him there were those who distrusted him. He easily made enemies; his self-confidence could seem like arrogance and his devotion to duty revealed his ambition. He showed many signs of having difficulty in fitting in to the exact-ing complications of the army as an institution, and early photo-graphs suggest a man somewhat apart from his times, an almost Proustian figure of the past.[3] And then he became that most difficult of things, an intellectual among soldiers, a man who intervened both by the written and the spoken word in certain of the issues of the time. In particular he became a partisan of new methods of warfare. This emphasized the possibilities of war as movement, ideas at variance with the official doctrines of providing France with prepared places of defence. But the importance of de Gaulle's contribution was not a matter of originality, since there were other theoreticians of this type of warfare who could claim to have pre-ceded him and since it seems that de Gaulle did not realize the importance of air power.

The significant feature of de Gaulle's conception of warfare lay in his manner of presentation and in its implications. His was not a straightforward, technical argument. It tended to be philosophical, to consider the role of the army within the State, to depict the sort of ruler that was necessary for France. And the political undertones of all this were confirmed by de Gaulle's contacts with certain groups and individuals. He attended meetings of a Maurrassien group; he had dealings with a number of progressive Catholics; he laid siege to a number of leading politicians (including Léon Blum) although he only succeeded in gaining the real attention of one of them, Paul Reynaud—appropriately, perhaps, one of the least assimilated to any party. These political activities were ambiguous and it must have been difficult to classify de Gaulle. However much a certain ambiguity may have served him in later years, it only made him distrusted prior to 1939. And the failure of his career is underlined by the fact that by 1939 he was at odds with Pétain, for both personal and professional reasons (since they disagreed as to the authorship of a history of the French army), he was regarded as a nuisance by the Minister for Defence, Daladier (who was also the Premier), and the type of military strategy in which he believed had been decisively rejected by the French command.

From 1940 the story moves quickly. After commanding his forces in a moderately successful tank operation in eastern France, General de Gaulle was summoned by Paul Reynaud to the Under-Secretary-ship of State at the War Ministry. This was probably a measure of desperation. De Gaulle therefore had only a few days of govern-mental experience before he went to London and announced his refusal to accept the armistice and his determination to resist the Germans. In London he gathered around him an almost Falstaffian collection of fighting men. He had no arms and no money. When he wanted to send two telegrams it was only because one of his staff had ten shillings that they could be sent. When his famous radio speech of the 1st June had to be typed, it was thanks to his chief aide, Geoffroy de Courcel, having a relative in London who could type, that this was done. He himself was disobeying orders and was always conscious of this. Dependent upon the British for money, equipment, and the use of the radio, he had nevertheless to demon-strate that his was an independent government, unlike that of Mar-shal Pétain. To assert this independence he had only his pride and his obstinacy.

It was not long before he had made himself disliked and both the British and the American governments came to wonder whether his contribution to the war effort justified the difficulties of dealing with him. He seems to have aroused an almost pathological hostility on the part of Roosevelt and to have angered Churchill in a way which has rarely been equalled. The imbroglio in North Africa after the allied landings in November 1942 illustrates his position very clearly. He was excluded from the confidence of the allies, and other leaders, whether from Vichy or especially created (like General Giraud) were preferred to him. When the allies landed in Normandy in June 1944, de Gaulle was only informed at the last minute, and plans were made to deal with France as a conquered country, a treatment which was not considered for other countries, since the governments in exile were recognized as the legal governments. In a moment of folly, Churchill even considered having him arrested, so determined was he to do without him. Yet it was de Gaulle who triumphed and however long the British and the Americans took to recognize his provisional government, they were obliged to do so in the end.

As has been shown, 1958 represents a not dissimilar Gaullist success. Starting from a position where there was not a single important or influential group which wanted to see him return to power, and many that were determined to prevent him, the situation developed into one where it seemed inevitable that only de Gaulle could take charge of affairs.

Since the period before 1939 is a period of failure, and since the period afterwards is a period of success, there is a danger of forgetting the pre-war officer. There is a danger of seeing de Gaulle's victories in terms of pure tactical skill, a tribute to his patience, determination and sense of timing. We know that de Gaulle has the ability to wear out an adversary by a constant reiteration of the same point. We have been told how he could make the most of his own techniques and ill-humour, particularly exploiting the English officers' dislike of such displays, and following up outbursts of temper with perform-ances of great charm. He has always been a superb actor. He showed, from 1940 onwards, skill in manoeuvring, keeping together his followers in London, out-playing Giraud in Algiers, coming to agreements with the Resistance in France. But behind all this there still remained much of the writer and thinker of pre-war, the man who discussed the practical issues of a mechanized army within the framework of philosophy. Even during the difficult years of London and Algiers, when more than once he thought of resigning, de Gaulle remained reflective and meditative, attempting to see his actions within some intellectual framework.[4]

This of course has been denied. De Gaulle has been described alternatively as opportunist, ready to do whatever seems advisable, or as realist, adapting himself with varying degrees of cynicism to the prevailing conditions. 'Things being what they are' (*'les choses étant ce qu'elles sont'*) is one of his favourite phrases. One could also claim that there is a great deal of illusion about de Gaulle, and it is not for nothing that he has been seen as a Walter Mitty figure, a man who believes in a strength that he does not possess, but who behaves with such conviction as to persuade others that this power exists in reality. De Gaulle had some cruel words to say about Albert Lebrun, the last President of the Third Republic, saying that he lacked only the two qualities of being a head of state, that of being a leader and that of having a state.[5] But one might well ask, where was the state that de Gaulle ruled in 1940? It is reasonable to suggest that the stiff-backed two-star general, whose unyielding intransigence impressed as it aggravated, created a mythical state out of the table and four chairs which were his only real possessions. After the liberation, with France in ruins, de Gaulle behaved in international diplomacy as if he were the head of a powerful state. This is the de Gaulle of illusions and de Gaulle the illusionist. But even so this cannot be a complete story. All his life de Gaulle has been a teacher, and when, in one of his press conferences, he leant back in his chair and said, 'Let us talk about China, this old country older than history itself' one sees an essential de Gaulle, the man who might have been a Sorbonne professor. In his early days he was a lecturer, a writer, an active member of discussion groups. In London and Algiers, he broadcast. Later, after his 1946 resignation, as leader of the RPF he became an itinerant orator. In solitude he wrote the memoirs which, from 1954 onwards, marked the recovery of his reputation. Since 1958, the press conference and the televised talk have become the most redoubtable weapons of the régime. Gaullism means words, and words mean ideas and principles.

*

The first principle of Gaullism is that it is the nation-state which is the most important feature of political and social life. For de Gaulle the nation-state of France is the essential reality of modern French life. In the past, men might have felt loyalty towards a local seigneur or towards a particular province; there might have been a time when their loyalty was directed towards a religion; there was a time too, when people thought to identify themselves with their social class, or with some ideology, such as communism, or with some international organization such as the League of Nations or the United Nations. But for de Gaulle these varied loyalties were ephemeral. Basically, there is only the force of national patriotism. 'All my life', he writes in the first page of his Memoirs, 'I have had a certain idea of France.' And this idea of France, unlike other so-called nationalisms, is by no means exclusive. There is no concentration on a France which vanished in 1789; there is a France which reached its height in Louis XIV, in the Committee of Public Safety, in Clemenceau. De Gaulle is struck by the majesty both of Notre Dame and of the Arc de Triomphe, by the whole of French history.

It is sometimes said that there is something mystical about this conception of the nation. There is a whole tradition of the post-1918 world (which remains strong in England) condemning nationalism and rejecting it as out of date. It is commonly said that the nation-state is irrelevant and unable to exist economically, militarily or culturally. Nations have to come together if they are to have some success in ordering their affairs, and to pose the idea of the nation-state as the essential political principle is, allegedly, to be dangerously anachronistic. It is true that there is an element of mysticism in de Gaulle's thinking, his conception of France being the apprehension of something which is alive and real. It is true, too, that his view of the nation-state is not unlike the view taken by French historians writing at the end of the nineteenth century, such as Sorel and Lavisse (except that de Gaulle is sometimes a bit vague in his historical thinking, referring to Germany and Italy as if they had existed as states for thousands of years). But this exaltation of the nation-state is at the same time both a precise and an apt calculation. It is precise because it has a particular significance for the French. If they can forget that they are Catholic or anti-clerical, bourgeois or communist, in a Parisian bureau or on a Breton farm, and if they can remember only that they are French, and if they can see themselves as only the children of France, then the greatest difficulty of governing France is over. It is appropriate because modern times see the reinforcement rather than the disappearance of nationalist sentiment. The emergence of new nations, the development of the USA and the USSR (which de Gaulle always refers to as *la Russie*), the decline of ideologies which might have abolished frontiers, such as international communism, all suggest the strengthening of nationalism. And whilst this has been happening, the individual within modern mass society seeks to identify himself with something, seeks to escape from his isolation, and can only do so by identifying himself with his nation and by recognizing his role within the nation-state. One realizes this now, and it is striking to see how de Gaulle spoke in one of his early writings of this need for individual men to accept the collectivity (although he expresses it non-critically).[6]

For all these reasons, it is hardly just to reject de Gaulle's concept of the nation-state and of nationalism, out of hand, as many (non-French) commentators have done. It must be emphasized that this is very different from the nationalism of someone such as Maurras, or the nationalism of some of the French during the Indo-Chinese and Algerian wars. Theirs was a nationalism based on hatred and resentment, aspiring after conquest and domination, accepting the one nationhood but rejecting the nationhood of others. It was often a nationalism that was fixed and static, refusing to accept change. For de Gaulle, although the nation-state is a fundamental reality, within it there is bound to be evolution and development, and it has often been noticed that de Gaulle has assimilated much of the thought of Bergson, emphasizing perpetual change.

After the nation-state, the second principle of Gaullism stems from another fundamental notion, that the world is a dangerous place, that life, whether for a man or for a nation, is a perpetual struggle. This being so, the state must be organized to meet this danger and de Gaulle is convinced that a parliamentary system is not the best way of doing this. Parliaments exist for discussions, but there has to be a leader who will take the decisions and who will assume the responsibility of directing the state. This being so, the state must be strong and this means that the state has to look to its position in the world, its 'rank' as de Gaulle put it in his Memoirs (*le rang*).

From this principle stems a whole series of Gaullist preoccupations: the need to sustain France's national interests and France's power in the world at large (made all the more important because of his conviction that geographically, historically and morally, France is a country with a particular role to play in world civilization); the need to define the nature of the leader and how he should acquire the necessary prestige within the state (this is discussed in *Le Fil de l'Epée*, first published in 1932); the need to equip the state with an effective military force which it controls itself; the need to have a machinery whereby the state can be ruled and emergencies met. In all these considerations it is the practical rather than the theoretical that counts; technicians and administrators promote change, such methods as nationalization or economic planning are accepted, and all, irrespective of theories or conceptions of justice, because such methods make government more effective.

The third principle of Gaullism involves the people. The nation-state, the leader and the people; these are the three focal points which have to be brought together. And they are brought together essentially through the power of the people. De Gaulle believes in the existence of the nation as a reality; he cannot imagine any political power which does not derive its existence from the people. Political control rests with the population as a whole. But this popular control must take on a particular form. The form is that by which the leader is placed in direct contact with the people. It is the system of direct democracy (possibly deriving from Rousseau, and possibly as expressed in the practice of Bonapartism) as contrasted to the system of parliamentary democracy (as practised by the Third and the Fourth Republics for example). There must be no intermediaries, no series of *élites* which can stand in the way of communication between the leader and the people. And, on the great issues, the population has to be consulted, the population alone can take the great decisions of principle as the leader alone can take the great decisions of action.

Within that situation the various institutions of the state—the army, the political parties, the trade unions, the universities, the Church, the Academies—all play their role. But it is within that situation, and by maintaining a basic harmony. If one of these institutions assumes too large an influence within the state, then the state is bound to collapse or to disintegrate. And essential to the harmony is that the authentic communication between leader and people has to exist and flourish.

All these principles have been illustrated by de Gaulle's practical experience. In international affairs he found that it was always the national interest which predominated. When he arrived in London in 1940 there was a moment of euphoria, as enthusiasms and emotions ran high. But this did not persist. Within a short time the British government was considering British interests, and in his contact with Churchill de Gaulle noted how, once Churchill saw before him the incarnation of an ambitious nation, he felt the shadow of Pitt stir within him. In particular de Gaulle became aware of British interest in the Middle East. With Roosevelt, de Gaulle saw that behind the veneer of idealism there was a statesman following his idea of the interests of his country and determined (so de Gaulle believed) to establish some sort of authority in France. With Stalin, de Gaulle saw the ambitions of eternal Russia. And in each case de Gaulle thought it was natural that this should be so.

In French history he found endless examples of the weakness of the state and of the inability of parliamentary government to produce leadership. The experience of 1940 was essential. When de Gaulle attended (as a visitor) the debate in the Chamber which replaced Daladier by Reynaud, he saw a debate from which France was excluded. When France was militarily defeated some weeks later, there was no leader who could carry on the fight, no apparatus whereby the emergency might be met. There was only a handful of parliamentarians who could not take decisions, who did not represent France and who thought only of themselves. For the third principle too the experiences of 1940–44 were all important. In 1940, when he set out on his adventure, who came to support him? It was not the *élites*. It was the ordinary people, *le petit peuple*, who rallied to him. And in 1944, when de Gaulle at last returned to France it was not to any agreement with any power or group of representatives that he owed his success. As he walked, with untypical hesitation, towards the first Frenchman whom he saw, he was before the test of his own principle. But he was recognized and acclaimed; the contact between the leader and the people had been made, and it continued until the day of the Liberation when he saw the people of Paris standing before him in the Champs-Elysées and realized that the people were united in him. Subsequently, the deputies and the political parties succeeded in interposing themselves between him and the population.

And because of these principles certain actions seem logical enough. If one believes in the reality of the nation-state, and if one accepts that there is perpetual change and evolution, then a colonial empire is not a permanent reality. It is possible to envisage the evolution of new nation-states. In the same way, if one accepts the essential existence of the nation-state, then ideologies are of secondary import-ance. One does not object to communists because they have the ideology of communism, any more than one would try to isolate Soviet Russia merely because her government is communist. But one will oppose communists when their loyalty to Soviet Russia seems to replace their loyalty to France. Therefore in the days of the provisional government de Gaulle always refused to give any of the key posts to communists, and in the days of the RPF he always attacked them as '*séparatistes*'. He has never been anti-Semitic, but his attitude to the Jews became critical when he suspected that, at the time of the Arab-Israel war in 1967, certain French Jews were showing more loyalty towards Israel than towards France. So far as the need for a strong state was concerned all his constitutional ideas (as expressed say, in his speech at Bayeux in June 1946, or in his earlier attempts to influence the form of government) stem from this principle. As do a whole host of minor actions. When, in 1944, he entered liberated Paris, he did not go at once to meet the Resistance leaders at the Hôtel de Ville. He went first of all to the rue Saint-Dominique, the War Ministry which he had left in 1940, because he had to show that first of all it was the state that was being re-established.[7] The next day, when he led the parade down the Champs Elysées, de Gaulle is said to have watched meticulously over the way in which the procession was organized, seeing the symbols of the state in such questions of precedence.[8] Finally, de Gaulle has always used every method whereby his contact with the people can be direct and unimpeded. The radio, the television, the referendum, are the most obvious. But the most typical is the tour of the provinces, the habit of plunging personally into the crowd and shaking hands. For him this is not a mere exchange of enthusiastic banalities; it is not the traditional hand-pumping of the vote-seeking politician; it is the ritual enactment of a fundamental principle.

Therefore Gaullism is something that has been worked out intellectually, experienced personally, and expressed practically. It is because of this that Gaullism has a style. De Gaulle has the supreme self-confidence of one who knows that he stands for a body of principles and coherent doctrine. He knows that its appeal is universal. He is the symbol of an old France and of traditional values. His patriotism, his culture, his name (and appearance) recall this old France. But he also stands for the rejection of the collapse of France, for resistance and insurrection, for the new France that emerged from the catastrophes of the 1940's. He is a conservative figure who has always emphasized modernity, a soldier who has flouted military principles, a Catholic who makes his religion a private matter, an authoritarian who seeks public approbation. All his life he has explained his position, but he has always been secretive; he has always been passionately devoted to certain causes, but he remains cynical; he seeks to rise above political parties, but he remains a politician whose skill is remarkable. He is egocentric, arrogant and ruthless; yet he is patient, liberal and jovial; he is difficult, yet he has inspired the greatest devotion; he is pessimistic, yet he has shown the greatest self-confidence.

It must always be remembered that Gaullism is a living thing. The Gaullism of the 1940's is not necessarily the same as that of the RPF, or that of the epoch prior to 1962, or that of the period post-1968. But in all these different circumstances de Gaulle has always been conscious of himself and of his destiny. He has all the romantic-ism of a figure that is severely classical. Perhaps he sees his life as Chateaubriand saw his, as a moment between two epochs; perhaps he sees himself as one of the characters of Madame de Staël, who, abandoned on a desert island, carves on a rock the messages which will be useful for those who follow him on the island. But at all events Gaullism is an epoch in the history of contemporary France. Of all twentieth-century Frenchmen it is General de Gaulle who throws the longest shadow.

10   President and parliament

Voilà le roi qu'il nous fallait. C'est la meilleure des républiques.   Lafayette

THE MOST URGENT PROBLEM facing the French government in June 1958 was Algeria. General de Gaulle recognized this by going to Algiers immediately after the voting in the Chamber was finished. But it was typical of de Gaulle that he should have placed the Algerian question alongside that of France's new institutions. When he began his speech to the massed crowds in the Forum of Algiers, with the dramatic words *'Je vous ai compris'*, he did not specify what it was that he had understood. He went on to speak of the Algerian people having opened the way towards a new France. Obviously there was a tactical reason for this, since the Algerian impasse was one where de Gaulle had to walk warily, and he had every advantage in manoeuvring himself out of the constrictions of this affair into the wider avenue of reforming France. But there was a doctrinal reason too. It was essential that the French state should equip itself with the appropriate institutional strength if it was to govern. When, in the course of 1958, de Gaulle found himself in disagreement with Guy Mollet over the budget, he would not permit him to resign until the new institutions were in place. The budget, he said, was a matter of circumstance; to reconstruct the Republic was a matter of principle. It seems likely that for de Gaulle, Algeria too, however imperative and menacing, was a matter of circumstance.

But de Gaulle did not have a ready-made constitution in his pocket, as he did not have a ready-made list of ministers. And the need to devise a constitution rapidly, at a time when de Gaulle and his ministers had a great deal of urgent business, was complicated by the circumstances. The new constitution not only had to be acceptable to the lawyers, but it had to be both acceptable to the different party leaders who were represented in the government and approved by the electorate. There were times when the procedure threatened to be laborious, and there were also a number of changing conditions, particularly after de Gaulle's visits to the French territories of Africa and Madagascar in August.

The key figure was Michel Debré, the minister for Justice, who had been in charge of administrative reform during 1945 and who had been interested in constitutional questions since that time. During June and July he was chairman of a small working party which was in touch with a committee of the Cabinet, presided over by de Gaulle. When this procedure seemed slow, Debré, at de Gaulle's request, isolated himself during the 14 July celebrations and completed the first draft. This was discussed by the Cabinet and was then put before a Constitutional Consultative Committee, an *ad hoc* body consisting of persons nominated both by the government and by Parliament. It was presided over by Paul Reynaud, whose personal assistant Debré had been in 1938, and who thereby accomplished his transition from the Third to the Fifth Republic. After a good deal of discussion and amendment, it was examined by the Council of State, the supreme administrative body. The final draft was presented to the electorate at a large meeting, symbolically held in the Place de la République on 4 September 1958 (the anniversary of the proclamation of the Third Republic) and introduced by an excited and mystical speech from André Malraux. (The referendum was held on 28 September.)

It is not surprising therefore that this constitution should have contained many obscurities and inconsistencies. They were the result of haste and improvisation, the effect of compromise and the reflection of uncertainty. To some extent the views of de Gaulle are faithfully expressed (and he was always a little contemptuous of the details of constitutional arrangements). Debré's own ideas, put forward during the days when he was active in the Resistance or as a Gaullist propagandist, found their places in the text. There is more than an echo of various critics of the Third Republic, such as the conservative politician André Tardieu, and two constitutional specialists, René Capitant (who joined de Gaulle in London) and Joseph Barthélemy (who advised Pétain). Its intellectual origins are therefore varied, and not conspicuously modern.

But there was a common ground of agreement amongst all those who could claim to have influenced the new constitution. This was the conviction that the republican institutions had declined and were declining, and that the nature of this decline meant that the executive government was being dominated by a divided and self-perpetuating legislature. In other words the governments were not strong enough to deal with the problems that faced them. The remedy was clear enough. It was to give more power to the executive and to restrict the power of the legislature. This is one of the basic principles of Gaullism: the state has to be endowed with a strong government. But the other principles are not forgotten: namely, that there is a French nation which possesses an essential unity which has to be discerned and animated, and that power can only come from the people. Given these circumstances and these principles, it was inevitable that there should be two pillars to the new constitution, Parliament and the President.

Parliament continues to exist in its two chambers, the Senate and the National Assembly (or Chamber of Deputies). General de Gaulle did have certain ideas for a profound reform of the Senate, which would have meant changing it into a specially contrived corporatist body, but in 1958 he found it politic to abandon these ideas and the Senate remained a Chamber to be chosen by the representatives of local authorities, and to be renewed partially (rather than as a whole) every three years. The Chamber of Deputies was to be chosen by universal suffrage (voting directly) and should not last longer than five years. The function of Parliament is to pass laws, and in that sense Parliament exercises a control over all government, but this constitution took great care to enumerate and to limit these powers of control. The political power of the Assembly was weakened in a number of specific ways. For one thing it was decided that the function of cabinet minister was incompatible with the exercise of a parliamentary mandate. Any member of

Parliament who becomes a minister must automatically abandon his seat (within a month of being appointed, and he cannot vote during that month). At the moment of his election, a member of Parliament is obliged to name a *suppléant* who will automatically replace him should he become a minister. Then the amount of time for which Parliament is normally in session is reduced, the constitution fixing two sessions, from October to December, and for a further period of not more than three months in the spring. The Assembly can be dissolved at any time (except in the year which follows its election). The President of each Chamber is no longer to be elected annually, but in the case of the National Assembly for the duration of the legislature, in the case of the Senate after each partial renewal. This means that the authority of each President is increased, that of the ordinary deputy or senator correspondingly diminished.

The two most striking methods of limiting the power of the Assembly concerned the means of overthrowing governments and the legislative process itself. Under the Fourth Republic the governments had been continuously obliged to stake their existence on questions of confidence in order to proceed with the legislation that they considered necessary. Under the 1958 constitution the demand for a question of confidence comes from the Assembly, and has to take the form of a motion of censure. Such a motion has to have the signed support of one-tenth of the deputies; to be passed it has to have an absolute majority, and only those deputies who vote for the motion of censure are counted, absentees or abstentionalists counting as having voted against the motion. Should a motion of censure be rejected, then its signatories cannot put forward a new censure motion in the same session of Parliament; an interval of forty-eight hours must occur between the tabling of the motion and the debate and vote. It is possible for the government to put the procedure into motion, since it can stake its existence on the acceptance of a law, or part of a law, by the Assembly. But when the government poses the question of confidence, this must be followed within twenty-four hours by the deposition of a motion of censure. In the absence of such a motion, or if such a motion should be defeated (in the conditions described above), then the law is considered to have passed, notwithstanding the fact that there might not be an actual majority in its favour.

The power of Parliament to legislate is curtailed by a series of innovations. Hitherto the French Parliament, like the British Parliament but unlike the American, could pass laws on any subject; but the constitution now distinguished between the domain of legislation which belongs to Parliament, and the domain of legislation that is the prerogative of the government. The latter is described as the *domaine réglementaire*, that of administrative regulation. That is to say that there are some matters on which Parliament can continue to legislate fully. These have been specified as civil rights, the fundamental guarantees of public liberties, the obligations of the citizen for purposes of national defence, nationality, marriage and inheritance, the definition of crimes and penalties, judicial and criminal procedures, taxation, the electoral system, the rights of state employees, nationalizations and denationalizations. On other matters, Parliament can only define the fundamental principles which shall apply, that is to say on questions of national defence, local government, education, social security, the law of property and commercial law, labour and trade-union laws. A further area of laws, defined as organic, and applying to items such as the budget or the detailed regulations of the various constitutional bodies, have to follow a particular procedure as they pass through Parliament. On subjects which are not specifically allocated to the domain of the law, Parliament cannot legislate at all. And even within the domain of the law it is possible for Parliament to delegate its powers, for a stated period, to the government.

The procedural provisions are all in favour of greater governmental control. In particular, the government was anxious to dominate the committee system which traditionally gave great advantages to parliamentary critics. The committees were usually composed of experts and their scrutiny of governmental texts had often led to profound modification of a bill. Under the new constitution the number of standing committees was limited to six in each chamber (with the hope that these committees would become larger and less expert). When a bill was submitted to Parliament it was to be the government's text which would be discussed, and not any counter-text submitted by any committee. No new amendments could be brought forward at the last minute and only those amendments which had already been brought forward in committees could be discussed in the whole House, so that there was little prospect of surprising the government or bringing about delay by having to refer the matter back to the committee. The government could request each chamber to vote by a single vote on the text under discussion, thus effectively having with this vote (the *vote bloqué*) a means of closing debate. So far as the budget is concerned a special procedure was devised. The government can send it on to the Senate if the Assembly has not voted the first reading within forty days, and if Parliament has not come to a decision within seventy days, then the government can impose the budget by ordinance. Individual members cannot propose bills or amendments which would increase public expenditure or reduce public financial resources. In all matters of determining the agenda of both Houses, or of settling a deadlock between the two Houses, it is the government which has the initiative.

Thus it can be seen that the constitutional engineering of 1958 was aimed at reducing the power and influence of Parliament, whilst retaining the Parliamentary system. It went further than most of the would-be reformers of the Fourth Republic had dared to consider. It sought to abolish parliamentary sovereignty, whilst retaining a parliamentary régime. But the biggest blow to parliamentary prestige was undoubtedly the principle that henceforward the President of the Republic, the head of the executive, would be elected from outside Parliament, and not by Parliament meeting together in an electoral college as had been done under the Third and the Fourth Republics. The 1958 constitution laid it down that the President was to be elected by an electoral college of some 80,000 people, composed mainly of the *notabilités*, that is to say the deputies, senators, mayors and a portion of the municipal councillors (designated according to the population of the commune). Thus the electorate for choosing the President was not unlike that for choosing the

Senate. The procedure was to be by two ballots, unless the first yielded an absolute majority (which de Gaulle won in 1958). In October 1962 this system was changed, and the President was to be elected (again with a two-ballot system) by universal suffrage. This early reform of the 1958 system clearly accentuated the distinction between the institution of Parliament and the institution of the Presidency.

Traditionally, the powers of the President of the Republic were always considerable, and the constitution of the Fifth Republic enumerates many of the functions which were those of the President under the Third and the Fourth Republics. He appoints the Prime Minister and he accepts his resignation; he presides over the Council of Ministers; he appoints and dismisses ministers at the request of the Prime Minister; he negotiates and ratifies treaties; he promulgates laws and can send them back to Parliament for reconsideration; he has the right of appointing to many offices and he also has the right of pardon. These were the powers of other Presidents. They too were the heads of the executive, the first citizens of the state, the heads of the armed forces and the protectors of the constitution, however they chose to interpret their roles. But the President of the Fifth Republic was given certain additional attributions. He has the right to accept or refuse the request for a referendum to be held concerning certain specific questions; he can dissolve the National Assembly if it is more than a year old; and in an emergency, that is to say in a situation which the President of the Republic judges to be an emergency, he can govern by decree (but he cannot, in these circumstances, dissolve the Assembly or prevent it from sitting).

It is clear that there is a basic contradiction between the position of Parliament and that of the President. However much the powers of Parliament may be curtailed, no government can normally exist if a majority in the legislature is hostile to it. But the President has considerable authority, and since 1962, he too can claim to be the people's choice. What if there is a conflict between the President and the Assembly? Clearly it is basic to General de Gaulle's thought that such a conflict would be resolved by a decision of the people, but the manner in which the decision would be taken would necessarily vary according to circumstance. It can be suggested that this dilemma is an essential part of Gaullism, since Gaullism believes in the existence of an agreement amongst the French whilst at the same time believing that France is a divided country. It is possible that the office of Prime Minister was devised in order to bring about a *rapprochement* between the Presidency and Parliament.

By the constitution, the head of State and the head of the Government are distinct from one another. The Prime Minister chooses those who are to form his government; he is responsible to Parliament; it is he who faces the deputies and senators; it is he who is obliged to explain and to justify policy. He therefore has to have the confidence of the Assembly, and therefore it could reasonably be expected that he would be a go-between, bringing the policies and attitudes of the two institutions into line with one another. If this was the intention of the constitution, it does not seem to have worked out in that way. It was on 5 January 1959 that General de Gaulle assumed his function as President of the Republic. A communiqué, issued that evening, announced that M. Michel Debré had been summoned to the Elysée Palace. General de Gaulle asked M. Debré to make suggestions concerning the composition of a government. 'At half-past seven', the communiqué went on, 'M. Michel Debré was again received at the Elysée. He submitted the general principles of his policy for the approbation of General de Gaulle, and the names of those who would be members of his government should he form one. The President of the Republic appointed M. Michel Debré Prime Minister; at the proposal of the Prime Minister he appointed the members of the government.' This is clear enough. General de Gaulle did not appoint as Prime Minister the man who represented the majority in the Assembly. (It can be argued that had he done this he would probably have appointed M. Jacques Soustelle.) Of the 27 ministers who formed Debré's government only 8 belonged to the UNR, his own party and the largest party in the Assembly. Nor did de Gaulle choose the man who would be most successful in the art of parliamentary management. (It can be argued that had he done this he would never have appointed Debré who had no experience of the Assembly and who was sometimes more irritable and impatient with Parliament than was wise.) De Gaulle chose a Prime Minister whose ideas were the same as his own, and he deliberately announced this. In other words, the Prime Minister is the expression of the President's power, not that of Parliament. The 1958 constitution therefore consists effectively of two institutions: President and Parliament.[1]

Every constitution has to be seen in practice rather than in theory. It was not long before many of those who had helped to make the constitution of 1958 began to complain that things were happening that had not been intended. In particular it was claimed that the Presidency had been envisaged as an arbitrator, an office above the ordinary day-to-day business of politics, a means of ensuring that the institutions worked and the difficulties were overcome. Some socialists protested that they had never wished to create a monarch. Others expressed surprise that the Prime Minister should be so effaced ('*Monsieur Debré existe-t-il?*' asked one constitutional expert, whilst others chose to call him Fidel Castrato). There were many doubts concerning the exact meaning of certain of the clauses of the constitution (such as the delimitation of the legislative domain). There were many apprehensions as to how General de Gaulle intended to use his emergency powers. There was no lack of historical examples, and a good many were invoked in order to understand the nature of the régime. It was variously compared to the governments of the Ancien Régime, of Louis-Philippe, of Napoleon III and, outside France, to the government of the Weimar Republic. There were many who thought that it could only be a transitional régime, either because it was said to be based on military power, and therefore it would inevitably be replaced by a direct military régime (the parachutists were said to compare de Gaulle's role to that of General Neguib in Egypt, who was the precursor to Colonel Nasser), or because it only existed in order to solve one specific problem, that of Algeria. There were also many who believed that there was very little that had been changed. The condemnation of the Fourth Republic by Mollet, Pflimlin, Pinay, Bidault etc. was greeted with some cynicism, and the re-appearance of Paul

Reynaud was seen as a sign of the continuity of French politics. Knowing foreign observers were prodigal in their use of the phrase *'plus ça change . . .'*

The immediate working of the constitution was affected by the Algerian affair and by the circumstances connected with it. It was not that General de Gaulle enjoyed the unbounded confidence of the whole population; on the contrary there was considerable distrust of him from the start, and there was bewilderment as well as disap, pointment as his proposals began to emerge. But the complications of the Algerian situation were so considerable, the practical diffi, culties of framing any alternative policy to that of de Gaulle were so great, and the refusal of anyone else to assume responsibility for Algeria was so total, that everything centred increasingly on the person of de Gaulle. The personalization of power became even greater than in the days of May 1958, and it was enhanced by the deliberate mystification which covered de Gaulle's ideas. As late as August 1959 the editor of *Le Monde*, trying to see what the government would do, was forced to make an exegetical analysis of de Gaulle's utter, ances on Algeria from 1955 onwards. In these circumstances the constitution appeared of minor importance, compared to de Gaulle. This gave the General the opportunity of asserting his position as President.

He had written before the war that great leaders 'have always stage,managed their effects', and if his Presidency is to be compared to the court of Louis XIV (as the satirical journal *Le Canard Enchaîné* was quick to do), it ought to be in terms of the almost ritualistic devotion of the ruler. Periods of silence and isolation alternate with periods of direct contact with the population. During the periods of isolation (and de Gaulle had written that 'nothing enhances authority more than silence') there are no public appear, ances and no discussions with political leaders, within the framework of a Parliament, a party congress or a regular television programme. If he has to appear, there is no communication, no interviews in airports, no kerb,side conversations. The weekends at Colombey, les,deux,églises are strictly private. There are no constituents to look after, and no obligation to explain policy as it is being formulated.

In all this there is a deliberate cultivation of the isolation of an *homme secret* (*Le Monde*, 11 November 1959). But at carefully calcu-lated moments this isolation ceases and then the greatest attention is paid to protocol and etiquette. It is then, too, at a reception or garden party, that with apparent informality the General will put forward some opinion, or hint at some attitude, or speak at unusual length with some politician, so that all his words and actions have to be carefully scrutinized if his policy is to be divined. But the great moments of contact are the provincial tours and the official speeches and press conferences. During his first year of office, apart from his visits to Africa and Madagascar, de Gaulle carried out six tours of various provinces and in his first three years of office it was estimated that he visited fifty-nine different departments and made literally hundreds of speeches, whether in towns or small hamlets. Invariably the same pattern was followed: the General would plunge into the crowds and shake hands with those around him. During his television addresses he would speak directly to the audience, often referring to himself in the third person, insisting on the decisions which he had taken and usually excluding references to the government. He would dramatize the situation in the most personal way, speaking of his old country and himself being face to face with each other once again, calling upon the French to help him in his task, and occasionally enlivening his performance with the unusually recondite word or the unattributed quotation which would subsequently lead to discussion and explanation in the newspapers.

The press conferences, beginning in March 1959, have been called the 'ultimate weapon' of the régime and have invariably made a considerable impact. Never held more than twice a year, they have been eagerly awaited and preceded by great speculation. They have often contained surprising and dramatic announcements, but they have always been a wide-ranging one-man commentary on the world scene played out before a large audience in the Elysée palace and before the even larger audience of the television public. Their form has scarcely varied, and as early as November 1959 *Le Monde* referred to the rites of this ceremonial as '*un mystère de gaullisme*'. Sitting on a raised stage, backed by curtains through which he has just made his entrance, with his ministers sitting to one side and the Elysée secretariat sitting on the other, it is a twentieth-century version of the monarchy as Bagehot saw it, 'the attention of the nation is concentrated on one person doing interesting things'. In 1958 television was still a luxury in France, with only half a million sets, but the number of sets grew rapidly and with the press and the radio it was possible to rivet public attention on the actions of one man in an unprecedented manner.[2]

De Gaulle asserted his authority with regard to Parliament, making it clear in a declaration of 30 January 1959 that he would not hesitate to use his power of dissolution should it prove necessary. And he equally asserted his authority over the Cabinet. It seems that the Prime Minister did once call a meeting of the Cabinet without the President (a *conseil de cabinet* rather than a *conseil des ministres*) but this only happened once and it is as if he had been called to order. The only cabinet meetings were those presided over by de Gaulle. They were not often held (there were forty-five in 1959, and forty-six in 1960), nor were they prolonged. Ministers were encouraged to direct their attentions to the affairs of their ministries and they could be asked to make a report at a cabinet meeting. There was rarely a general discussion, and when in September 1959, prior to visiting Algeria, de Gaulle consulted his ministers about Algeria, it was clear that this was unusual. More common was the announcement that de Gaulle had given advance information to the Cabinet of the public statement that he was to make on Algeria. The Cabinet therefore was not a political body, discussing policy; it was not even a body taking a collective decision. It was a group of administrators reporting to their chief.[3]

The constitutional consequences of this were not slow to appear. The President of the Assembly (Chaban-Delmas), speaking in Bordeaux in 1959, distinguished between two sectors of government. The one was 'Presidential', and comprised Algeria, the French territories overseas, foreign affairs and defence; the other was 'open' and comprised the remaining affairs (which, as was pointed out, were considerable). In the Presidential sector, the government carried out the President's decisions; in the open sector the government elaborated policy (or as Chaban-Delmas put it, *'dans le premier secteur le gouvernement exécute, dans le second il conçoit'*).

This declaration, which was an implicit rejection of the written constitution, aroused surprisingly little comment. This was partly because those who rejected the idea of the 'Presidential sector' were thought to be in opposition to Algerian policy, and not many politicians wished to be associated with them in this matter. But it was also because Chaban-Delmas's statement appeared to be little more than an appreciation of the situation as everyone understood it. No one really doubted that de Gaulle was effectively the sole authority on the subjects specified. And, in time, it was suggested that this 'Presidential sector' could be extended so as to cover any subject or any matter.[4] The administrative services attached to the Presidency of the Republic increased enormously in the course of 1959, and this increase was a sure testimony to the activity of this institution.[5] And it was not only that the President could take advice on any matter and could establish committees, perhaps with one or two ministers present, under his chairmanship. It was not merely his personal decision to pardon Gaston Dominici, the old farmer from Lurs who was serving a life sentence for having murdered a British family, the Drummonds, or his intervention in the affairs of the Académie Française, when he asked for a candidature to be withdrawn. Such actions illustrate the interfering powers of the Presidency. But in the course of 1960, de Gaulle radically altered the nature of the constitution. He stated, on 4 November 1960, that he could, if he wished, consult the country directly by means of a referendum. Constitutional appearances were to some extent preserved, since the Prime Minister went through the form of requesting a referendum. But no one could have any doubt that the President had attributed to himself a new power. And the body which was supposedly the supervisory institution, overlooking the constitution and acting as a sort of Supreme Court, the Constitutional Council, was unable to stop this. In these circumstances it could be said of General de Gaulle, *'l'Etat, c'est lui'*.[6]

But was this so? Was General de Gaulle so powerful as compared to other leaders in other countries? It is true that other leaders had to contend with the constricting powers of a federal constitution, say, or a political organization to which they owed their supremacy. De Gaulle had none of these things, and it is tempting to think that the government of France was now locked within the brain of one strong personality. It is not clear to what extent this was the case. But it is certain that de Gaulle, utilizing an extraordinarily efficient civil service, was to some extent its prisoner. There is some reason to believe that de Gaulle was not at all clear what he should do in Algeria. It was to his officials that he turned, many of them young men, many of them trained in the Ecole Nationale d'Administration. The policies which followed were the result of official soundings and investigations, official experiments and tests. One has always to ask the question, to what extent was de Gaulle as important as he appeared to be? The left wing in France used to suggest that de Gaulle was a prisoner of reactionaries. Nothing suggests that this was true, but it is more than likely that one has exaggerated the freedom of de Gaulle to determine his own policy. The fact that he returned to power, after a long period of isolation, and found himself surrounded by a host of problems which were severely technical, emphasizes this probability.

And undoubtedly an element which played an important part in the establishment of de Gaulle's supremacy was the UNR. This political party was founded in October 1958 and represented various forms of Gaullism. It brought together the old faithfuls of 1940, the old supporters of the RPF, and certain of the groups which had been most active in 1958. The party was formed in order to fight the elections, and although de Gaulle claimed that he was not taking part in what he called 'the competition' of the elections, he agreed that he could not prevent candidates from proclaiming their support for him. Although it is not sure what role he played in the formation of the UNR, nevertheless his political associates at this time, men such as Debré, Soustelle, Chaban-Delmas, Frey, Delbecque, and so on, became members. In the eyes of the electorate support for the UNR was support for de Gaulle and no effort was made to disabuse them.

In the course of 1959 difficulties began to arise. There were some UNR deputies who were solidly supported by particular regions. The influence of Chaban-Delmas in the Bordeaux region, of Soustelle in Lyons and of Delbecque in the north was such that these were their personal fiefs. But other UNR deputies failed to have this assurance. They were particularly susceptible to various economic and social grievances, and complained that they had little influence on social and economic policy. They were worried about the gap which they said existed between the rank-and-file members, and the executive committee in the Assembly. Above all, the Algerian question proved decisive. Under the leadership of Soustelle, a member of the government, many deputies insisted that the party should proclaim its attachment to the cause of French Algeria (which they had frequently supported during their election campaigns). But others, including Chalandon, the secretary-general of the UNR, insisted that their duty was to trust General de Gaulle. The parliamentary group, in October 1959, nearly voted a motion in favour of '*Algérie française*', but this was prevented by the adjournment of the meeting. In November 1959 there was a clash at the party assizes, held in Bordeaux.

Fidelity to de Gaulle and recognition of the gravity of the Algerian situation held the party together, but there were other, more normal political methods being used. General de Gaulle personally intervened on many occasions. He prevented the UNR from having a President (who might have been Soustelle); he stopped the organization of an '*Algérie française*' alliance; at a private reception he seems to have used his considerable powers of persuasion on a number of carefully selected UNR personalities, persuading them not to come to a decision at Bordeaux which would have limited his freedom of action over Algeria; when a new secretary-general was chosen in November 1959, it was Jacques Richard, who had been a member of de Gaulle's private secretariat from June 1958; both the Prime Minister and the Minister for Information, Roger Frey, acted as intermediaries between de Gaulle and the UNR. The result of all this action was that the UNR became a governmental party. As M. Michel Habib-Deloncle put it in November 1959,

138

whilst there would be criticisms of the government, they would find expression through the internal means of communication of the party. The UNR had to be the government party.

This was of considerable value to de Gaulle. Without it, it is doubtful if he could have pursued his Algerian policy. He might well have failed to weather the first parliamentary crisis of the régime, when a vote of censure was organized by the left wing, in co-operation with some independents, over war pensions. The UNR voted solidly for the government. But in doing so it was affirming the importance of parliament. Some thought that, paradoxically, the UNR was both strengthening the government and saving parliamentary government in France.[7] De Gaulle could be contemptuous of political parties, but he found the UNR very useful and he was ready to devote time to it, a sign that he accepted its importance. On all sides there was the hope of making this Assembly something better than its predecessors, and when M. Vincent Auriol was reported as saying that without political crises there was no political liberty, he found little support. It was reminiscent of the remark made during the 1789 revolution by a lady in Brussels to whom an emigré had said that he regretted the Ancien Régime, 'except, of course, for the abuses'. 'But the abuses,' she replied, 'they were the best part of it.'

11   Algeria

Une France: de Dunkerque à Tamanrasset.

BY THE TIME of the establishment of the Fifth Republic, the French Empire (which the Fourth Republic had preferred to call the French Union) was changing considerably. Indo-China had ceased to be French since the Geneva agreements; Tunisia and Morocco had asserted their independence (which theoretically they had never lost since they had been protectorates); the French-African territories had received a certain amount of money by the *loi-cadre* of 1956, and the conference of African states which had met in Bamako in September 1957 had discussed the possibility of further independence. But since de Gaulle believed in the greatness of France, it seemed possible that he would want to stop this progress.

Two African leaders also seemed ready to envisage new arrangements. Houphouet-Boigny of the Ivory Coast, a member of the National Assembly and frequently a minister in Fourth Republic governments, suggested that independence was a word which was in danger of becoming out of date. Both he and the leading politician of Madagascar, Tsiranana, preferred to think of some sort of Community of Franco-African states, and this was set up in the vaguest terms by the constitution of 1958. The President of the Republic was also to be the President of the Community, and within that community each country would elect its own government and its own Prime Minister, although France would continue to supervise its foreign and defence policies. De Gaulle foresaw himself on future 14 July celebrations, presiding over a dinner-table of thirteen or fourteen different Prime Ministers, that of France and those of the Community. He showed the importance that he attached to this by his extensive tour of African territories in August 1958 and his ready confrontation with a more vociferous opposition than that to which he was accustomed. It could be that he thought of Algeria one day fitting in to this system, although he never said so.

But de Gaulle was also prudent. During his African tour he was adamant that if some French territory voted against the referendum, then this was a vote for independence and that independence would become an immediate reality. 'If you want independence, take it!' he shouted to African demonstrators. Only one state, Guinea, voted against the referendum and it became independent automatically.

It seemed that the Franco-African Community was going to be a great success and it is surprising to find de Gaulle showing a lack of enthusiasm. Little effort was made to organize the institutions of the Community, and once Mali (the temporary federation of Senegal and the French Sudan) and Madagascar started to request a more complete independence and membership of the UN, de Gaulle made no attempt to dissuade them. Houphouet-Boigny, disappointed at the lack of a positive response from de Gaulle ('I waited at the church, alone, with my flowers in my hand,' he said) also moved for full independence. By the summer of 1960 French ministers were attend- ing tribal dances in celebration of the various independences that meant an end of the Community. It all worked very smoothly and by 1960 it was clear that the French empire would consist of only Guadeloupe and Martinique in the West Indies, Guiana in Central America, Djibouti and French Somaliland in Africa, and the establishments in Oceania, as well as Réunion and those in India (which were eventually integrated into India).

There was also Algeria. Most French people were agreed that there was little truth in comparing Algeria to territories such as the Ivory Coast, or to foreign examples such as India. (Ireland perhaps was a better analogy.) Algeria had occupied a special position in colonial mythology, and had always seemed to be particularly closely linked to France. In 1930 when extensive celebrations had marked the centenary of French conquest, nothing seemed more certain than the continued French domination of this territory. The disagreements that existed were between the French in Algeria and the French in France. No one believed that there was an Algerian nation which was

Arab and Berber, Moslem and non-French. Even when metropolitan France was spectacularly defeated in 1940 there was no nationalist revolt against the French, and the 1945 rising at Sétif (which was brutally crushed) seemed the outcome of local conditions rather than the prelude to any large-scale agitation. During the post-war years it was in Morocco and in Tunisia, rather than in Algeria, that the most important nationalist, and anti-French, developments were to be noted. Yet after a rising that had begun on a small scale in 1954, the crisis of the French in Algeria was as deep as it could be.

By 1959 the European, or non-Moslem, population numbered 1,075,000. This was an increase of 8 or 9 per cent from what it had been in 1954. Nevertheless, in spite of this manifestation of demo-graphic strength, this community had no sense of security without the continued guarantee of a French presence. By 1959 the Moslem population was nearly 9,000,000, a rapid population increase which was particularly felt in towns which were growing at a dangerous speed (Algiers, Oran, Constantine and Bône, for example, had seen their populations rise by 35 per cent in five years). There were over-whelming problems of food, housing and employment, which would have existed even without a war. It was impossible to estimate the strength of the Algerian rebels, their armies being camouflaged amongst the local populations, withdrawn into the mountains or installed in the training camps of Tunisia and Morocco. It was impossible to estimate the unity of the Moslem populations, with the traditional division of Arab and Berber being overlaid by differences of tactics, and by the differing nature of Tunisian, Moroccan, Egyptian and non-Moslem influences. The fact that the titular head of the rebellion, Ben Bella, and other leaders, had been prisoners in French hands since 1956, and the presence of more than 300,000 Algerian workers in metropolitan France, showing divided political influences, were further complicating factors. There were notabilities who professed undying loyalty to France (the 'Beni-Oui-Oui' they were called by their enemies). There were some 50,000 Moslems who were serving in the French army. And there were Moslems who wished to be associated neither with the rebels nor with the 'Beni-Oui-Oui'.[1]

Within France itself, opinions were confused. Parties which one would have expected to show sympathy with the Algerian nationalists were sometimes reluctant to express this sympathy. The Communists, for example, had hesitations about a revolutionary movement which they had not inspired and which they were not directing. They feared that an independent Algeria might fall under the control of the USA, and whilst rejecting the rights of the wealthy settlers or of banking interests, they had sympathy for the civil servants, shop-keepers, peasants and workers who made up much of the European population. The Communists were French nationalists, and they were as nostalgic as any in their appreciation of France. Individuals who were often liberal in their appreciation of various political and social problems, such as M. Bidault, were none the less intransigent in their hostility to any surrender or negotiation over Algeria. And in a country with a centralized educational system, where generations had learned from the text-books that Algeria was a prolongation of France, there were those—in Brittany, for example—who felt little enthusiasm for the continual spending of money on the far side of the Mediterranean when their own region was in urgent need of investment. Some businessmen pointed to the wealth of the Sahara in oil and gas, which was just being discovered, and asserted that any political concessions in Algeria were acceptable if these resources could be developed by them. Intellectuals tended to concentrate their attention on the stories of the tortures which some sections of the French army found it necessary to inflict on Algerian rebels. Some, with a social conscience, emphasized the human problems present amongst this teeming population. And there were many who dreamt dreams: that there would be a complete military victory (and the Governor-General up to 1958, Lacoste, had often spoken of the struggle being almost won, *le dernier quart d'heure*); that Ben Bella would, Nkrumah-like, leave his prison and become Prime Minister of an Algerian Dominion within *un vrai Commonwealth*.

And what did de Gaulle think? It was said that in September 1957 he had recalled Napoleon's attitude towards the opponents of the Revolution in Vendée (the *chouans*) and his order that the killings must stop. But it was also said that he had complimented Lacoste on the work that had been done, and that he frequently alluded to the French mission in Algeria. If one tries to fathom what was in his mind, and leaves on one side all these totally contradictory rumours, one must take into account what one knows of his doctrine and principles. Believing in the nation-state, he must have been cynical about the claim that Algeria was French, with one-tenth of the population of mixed European descent and the remainder being Arab or Berber. Believing that France must have a strong state, he must have been concerned that France was so susceptible to pressure from Algiers and from Algerian groups. A prolonged colonial war was a bad influence on the army, since it encouraged traditional methods of fighting and organization, and since it deflected the army from its real vocation, which was that of defending France. Furthermore, if either the army or the Algerian settlers were to play too large a role, they would upset the harmony of the state. If France were to occupy her rank in world affairs, then she would have to solve this problem which was absorbing her energies, but this would have to be done without the humiliation of defeat.

Such principles must have been in de Gaulle's mind from the beginning. But to what extent he had a considered policy is by no means sure. Uncertainty was one of his tactical assets, but it may have represented the real state of his mind. Perhaps the truest anecdote concerning what he thought he would do about Algeria in May 1958, is that which makes him say, simply, 'I shall go and see for myself.' In 1958 he visited Algeria five times, visiting the towns and villages much as he did in France, touring the military units and camps, shaking innumerable hands and making a great many speeches, the wording of which was carefully adapted to the particular circumstances of each occasion. This was the first phase of his Algerian policy. It was one of investigation and experiment, during which he shrugged off the occasional flouting of his orders and avoided any direct clash.

During this period a number of firm principles gradually emerged. One was his determination to remove from Algeria those closely connected with 13 May. He got rid of the Committees of Public Safety and asserted his authority over General Salan, replacing him

in December 1958 by M. Delouvrier, a high-ranking French admini-
strator, and by a new Commander-in-Chief, General Challe, an
air force general who had turned to Mollet during the May crisis.
Challe launched a series of new offensives from the beginning of
1959, which were in contrast to the former strategy. Making
more use of aircraft, Challe sought to clean up rebel strongholds
and to destroy rebel strength. Whilst supporting this vigorous
military action de Gaulle also returned to a somewhat *mendésiste*
approach, with the idea that it was through economic policy that a
satisfactory solution of the affair would be reached. A speech in
Constantine in October 1958 announced a massive programme of
investments and deliberately disdained to outline any political plans.
This gave point to his conviction, which he was at pains to stress,
that Algeria was in process of changing considerably. '*L'Algérie de
papa est morte*', he was reputed to have said in Oran, and he rejected
any settler dream of a return to the certitudes of 1930. In all this, he
was relying on his own prestige. Just as he had rallied all Frenchmen,
could he not rally all Algeria? Like Napoleon he called on the
rebels to accept *la paix des braves*. Like earlier observers (Senator
Maspétiol for example) he believed that a large and influential
section of the Algerian population could be won over to some sort
of co-operation with France. *Le plan de Constantine, le plan Challe*
and the prestige of General de Gaulle: these were the three fixed
points of policy.

This policy reached its logical conclusion in a declaration made
on 16 September 1959, carefully timed so as to take the wind out of
the sails of France's critics at the forthcoming meeting of the UN.
He envisaged three possibilities for Algeria: there was complete
independence; there was complete '*francisation*' or integration with
France; or there was the government of Algeria by the Algerians
in close union with France and receiving aid and help from France.
The choice between the three would be made by the population of
Algeria in a referendum which would take place once a cease-fire
had been established and normal conditions restored. De Gaulle
was still cautious. He took care to reject independence as a solution,
saying that it could only lead to chaos, but he did not offer any clear

indication of his attitude towards the other two, so that the possibility of *'francisation'* or integration persisted. For Soustelle this was still *'la solution la plus française'* and since it remained a possibility, he felt able to stay in the government. A number of UNR deputies, however, thought that even to talk of an Algeria governed by Algerians was going too far, and they resigned. It was noticed that both M. Delouvrier in Algiers and M. Chalandon, the secretary of the UNR, spoke with approval of this third solution, and it was widely believed that this was the solution which de Gaulle preferred. But were this so, there was very little response from Algerian leaders. The rebels insisted that discussions should be held with Ben Bella, and no important Algerians announced their adhesion to this policy. Amongst the settlers and the army there was complete disapproval. French public opinion was disappointed. Things had not progressed: one was virtually still with Guy Mollet and the need for an armistice before negotiations could begin.

But the next phase of the Algerian imbroglio changed all this. General Massu, the prefect and military commander of Algiers, who was reputedly responsible for imposing authority on the Arab quarter of the capital and who had been closely associated with the Committee of Public Safety, gave an interview to a German newspaper in which he insisted that Algeria could only be French. This was clearly a challenge to the authority of de Gaulle. He was recalled and dismissed. The response of certain of the Algerian leaders was to try and organize a repeat performance of 13 May. On 24 January 1960 the university building of Algiers was occupied and legitimate authority defied. But this defiance was to last only a week. In spite of the excitement and of a momentary panic in the political milieux of Paris, this was only a gesture. De Gaulle affirmed that his policy would not change and the rebels had little option but to give up. The army had been hesitant but not joined them; the vulnerability of the settler position had been illuminated.

This episode strengthened de Gaulle. He was voted special powers by Parliament and he received the support of the trade unions. He felt strong enough to dismiss Soustelle and to affirm that Algerian policy was in his hands. After another visit to the army, during which on the 4 March he for the first time spoke about '*l'Algérie algérienne*', he began a tentative series of negotiations with some rebel leaders, both in secret and at Melun. His representatives con⁄tinually insisted that there should be a cease⁄fire before any further progress could be made or considered. The new military pressure, which was now being organized by General Crespin (who replaced Challe in March 1960) sought to destroy rebel centres, to seal off the rebels in Morocco and Tunisia, and by a policy of moving popula⁄tions ('re⁄settlement' as it was called) to destroy rebel organization. The objective of this intensified campaign was not a complete military victory, but to force nationalist elements to opt for an armis⁄tice and for some sort of co⁄operation with France. But the Melun talks, and the policy as a whole, hung fire. Exasperation grew in Algeria, and in France there was an increasing volume of protest from intellectual and religious leaders at the continuation of the war.

On 4 November 1960 de Gaulle took a new initiative. He an⁄nounced that the French population would be consulted by referen⁄dum on Algeria's future and he spoke of 'the Algerian republic which will some day exist'. He denounced both those who favoured abandonment and those who wanted 'a sterile immobilism'. He made no mention of military victory. The appointment of M. Joxe, a former ambassador to Moscow, as minister for Algerian affairs suggested that further developments were on the way, although it is not clear what was intended. The situation was publicly trans⁄formed during de Gaulle's visit to Algeria in December. The hostile manifestations of the settlers came as a surprise to no one. But for the first time (except for a demonstration by Moslem students in Algiers the preceding month), on 10 and 11 December Moslems in Oran and Algiers demonstrated in favour of the Algerian republic, of the National Liberation Front and of de Gaulle. This has been termed the Dien Bien Phu of official propaganda and the turning⁄point of the war. 'The abscess that has lasted for six years is beginning to burst' was the comment of a French officer. The idea that there was a mass of uncommitted opinion hostile to the rebellion and ready to be won over to France was now difficult to sustain.

Outwardly de Gaulle remained serene and saw no reason to change his policy. Opening the referendum campaign he spoke of the necessity of the two communities working together and of the role which France still had to play in Algeria. Debré declared that nothing healthy would be accomplished without France. But privately he was said to have told army officers that he foresaw the outcome, that he foresaw it without pleasure but that he was resigned to the inevitable.[2] Many of the Algerian settlers certainly drew their own conclusions. The result of the referendum in January 1961 showed only 18 per cent of those voting as opposed to de Gaulle's policy, and this was an unnatural alliance of the extreme right, who accused de Gaulle of wishing to abandon Algeria, and of the communists, who refused to believe that de Gaulle wished for a peaceful solution. It seemed clear enough that the French population were not interested in supporting the settler cause, and many began to join in the formation of a secret army, the OAS (*Organisation armée secrète*), which would overthrow de Gaulle. An attempt had already been made to assassinate him in September 1960, and more attempts were to come.

Certain of the military also drew their conclusions. On 22 April 1961 four generals, including Generals Challe and Salan, seized power in Algiers and proclaimed their opposition to de Gaulle amongst an ecstatic population. This took everyone by surprise in Paris and the rumour that the parachutists were about to drop on the capital caused a moment of panic. De Gaulle, wearing uniform, invoked his emergency powers and denounced the *'pronunciamento'*, as he called it. Exploiting television to the full, he dramatized and personalized the issue. *'Françaises, Français, aidezmoi'* was his appeal. Everywhere in France there seems to have been a unified rejection of the generals' action. In Algeria the national servicemen did not want to get caught up in some endless adventure a long way from home and they preferred to obey the orders of the President (whom they heard on their portable radios, thus creating what some called a *gouvernement républicain transistoir*). Young officers showed little enthusiasm for a rising led by elderly men, and the political organizations of the settlers found themselves ignored by the generals. On the evening of 25 April Challe realized that his attempt to create a 13 May had also failed and he surrendered (whilst his companions went into hiding).

From this time onward the Algerian settlers could only act secretly and through individual acts of terrorism. From this time too all the energies of the French government were concentrated on negotiations. Major military operations were abandoned although there were a great many punitive operations against local rebels. But the uncertainties remained considerable. The idea of some sort of partition of Algeria was floated, perhaps as a threat. The suggestion was put forward that the Sahara should be excluded from the negotiations, since its mineral wealth was entirely a French creation. There was the constant hope of being able to find some negotiating partner other than the FLN. De Gaulle had at all costs to avoid presenting a spectacle of French weakness to the French. He had to find a solution which would be acceptable to the French electorate. Therefore he had to negotiate with all the toughness and laborious patience for which he was renowned.

But he could not allow the negotiations to become bogged down. There was the fear that there might be further defections amongst the army, or that the OAS would succeed in provoking the Moslems so that the army would have to defend the Europeans and confidence would be destroyed. There was the very real apprehension that his Algerian interlocutors would be disavowed by the rebels themselves. There was the constant pressure from other countries, and whilst grumbling and discontent at home were not in themselves dangerous, perhaps the biggest fear of all was that the differences amongst Frenchmen over Algeria could become more serious and violent. Therefore from time to time de Gaulle revived the negotiations by brusque declarations. On 5 September 1961 he announced that the Sahara was an integral part of Algeria and could not be separated from it. On 31 December he spoke of the coming disengagement of France from Algeria and of bringing two divisions back to Europe. He allowed demonstrations against the OAS, and by himself attacking this terrorist organization he gave the impression that it was the OAS, rather than the nationalists, that was the enemy.

When negotiations began in earnest, in the Jura mountains in February 1962, it is interesting to see that de Gaulle was careful to ensure that M. Joxe was accompanied by two other ministers, M. Buron, a Social Catholic, and M. de Broglie, an Independent. He thereby associated the political parties with the outcome of the talks.

The period between January 1961 and March 1962 must have been one of the most difficult for de Gaulle, but it came to an end with the Evian agreements of 18 March 1962, and the cease-fire of the following day. Provisional institutions were set up in Algeria, and a prominent Algerian personality, Abderrahman Farès, was released from prison in Paris and placed at the head of a provisional executive. Ben Bella and the other imprisoned leaders were also released. By the terms of the agreements France was allowed to retain the naval base of Mers-el-Kebir and in the Sahara the French Army was given certain rights for three years. French settlers were to be allowed to stay on and to be given certain privileges; if their lands and possessions were nationalized they were to receive compensation.

The news of this agreement caused consternation in Algeria. The OAS intensified its desperate campaign and used every method to prevent the agreements from coming into effect. In France it was responsible for many violent incidents, mostly unco-ordinated, and the actions of the OAS tended to consolidate support for the referendum. In the political discussions, particularly in the special debate in the Chamber (a debate which concluded without a vote) attention was focused on the idea that France would continue to be important in Algeria. Madame Devaud, a UNR deputy whose family lived in Algeria, expressed the opinion that '*l'Algérie algérienne*' would always remain '*l'Algérie française*'. In these circumstances there was little sympathy for the Europeans, and comparison between them and those of Alsace-Lorraine in 1871 did not have much effect. The violence of the OAS (which began to attack the army) and the violent language of those who attacked the agreements ('*l'Algérie de papa*' had disappeared, remarked M. Biaggi, but one now had '*L'Algérie de Bazaine et de Judas*'),[3] succeeded in alienating support. On 5 April 1962 the referendum showed a solid vote in

150

favour of the government. Although there were many abstentions (nearly 25 per cent), almost 65 per cent of the population voted for the government. That is to say that of those who voted, about 90 per cent voted in support. General de Gaulle had won the support of a whole spectrum of political opinion, going from the communists to the right wing. Only the extreme right voted against the government. Out of a situation where the spectre of civil war had occasionally raised its head, a form of national unity had been created after all.

The war had lasted for seven and a half years. In terms of lives some 12,000 regular French troops had been killed and some authorities speak of 150,000 of the rebel army. Amongst civilians some 10,000 Europeans had been killed or wounded and for the Moslem population the figure was about 45,000. Many Europeans and many more Moslems were missing. More than a million Moslems had been uprooted in the course of military operations, and after the Evian agreements it was the European community that had to move. During May a special air-lift system had to be organized in order to meet the demands of those who wanted to leave, and by the end of the year only about one-eighth of the European population and a mere handful of Jews remained in Algeria. The evolution of Algerian politics was soon to discourage these too. No one can estimate, with any conviction, the total cost of the war, with its inflationary pressures and its effect on foreign reserves. The final financial cost was the influx of this European population into metropolitan France, many of whom were far from rich, many of whom were exacting in their demands that the French government should compensate them for their loss of situation and domicile, all of whom were embittered and disillusioned as they experienced the shattering of a dream-world.

Admirers of de Gaulle have pointed to his handling of this Algerian issue as a masterly exercise in political skill. His critics and detractors have seen it as a monument of duplicity and weakness which culminated in the betrayal of French citizens. Both admirers and critics exaggerate, but both are right. The greatest success for

de Gaulle was that the war was finished and disengagement accomp
lished, all in a general climate of French agreement and without
any civil strife within France. Like the decolonization of the French
African territories, the procedure was, in the last resort, smooth and
simple. And it must be said, there was no great scar on French self
consciousness. It was astonishing to realize how easy an armistice
and evacuation were. The greatest criticism was that there had been
a great deal of deception. For all his ostentatious assurance de Gaulle
had abandoned a position which he had earlier announced as
firm, and there was a brutality about his eventual abandonment
of Algeria which must have been particularly unpleasant to those
who had committed themselves to defend those positions which he
had earlier indicated as being essential. The editor of *Le Monde*,
BeuveMéry, was a supporter of the Evian agreements, but he asked
if it had been necessary to have had so many contradictory gestures
and declarations, if it would not have been possible to have avoided
a situation where honest men considered themselves betrayed and
dishonoured. Possibly he exaggerated the effects of the Evian agree
ments.[4]

It is tempting to think that de Gaulle viewed the Algerian situa
tion in two fairly distinct ways. In the short term he had to deal with
the situation which he had inherited and he had to deal with a variety
of interests and confusions. He had here to be secretive, experimental
and ambiguous. He had to move with events. But it was the long
term which concerned him most. Here he realized that considerable
changes were inevitable. He did not foresee them all, but his historical
sense was realistic. And it was here that he was determined that the
life of the French people and the destiny of France itself should not
be chronically disturbed by the crisis of the French in Algeria.
As he told his television audience on the night of 26 March 1962,
the Algerian affair was but one amongst many.

And there is a further point. It is important to realize that de Gaulle,
in a constitutional, political and moral position of power, without
rival or alternative policies, was nevertheless unable to move as he
wished. The constraints on de Gaulle were considerable. They came
from officials; they were associated with indispensable political

colleagues; they arose from a number of pressures, sometimes from powerful organizations such as the banks, sometimes from the deliberations of the UN. De Gaulle was never free to do just what he wanted, and this is one of the least appreciated circumstances of the Fifth Republic.

12   Europe and the world

By unanimous consentment of all peoples, the kingdom of France has always been recognized as the first and most excellent kingdom in Christianity, as much for its dignity and power as for the absolute authority of him who governs it.   The Venetian ambassador to Paris, 1562

AFTER THE REFERENDUM of 11 April 1962, in order to mark the end of one period of Gaullism and the beginning of another, General de Gaulle asked for the resignation of the Prime Minister, Debré. (It could be that he had seen Debré as useful in the context of Algeria, because of his contacts with many of those who had been most determined to keep Algeria French, but this is probably too limited a point of view.) In his place he appointed Georges Pompidou. Pompidou had been a schoolmaster, and subsequently he had been Director-General of the Rothschild Bank. He had been associated with de Gaulle for a number of years and had performed a number of confidential missions for him as well as concerning himself with certain family affairs. But Pompidou had never been a member either of the Assembly or of the Senate. Nevertheless he decided to go before the Assembly and seek its approval, although it was not necessary to do this in terms of the constitution. In this debate M. Pompidou was greeted with a certain coolness, if not hostility, on the part both of the Independents and of the Social Catholics, and although he was given a majority there were a disquieting number of abstentions. It was in this debate, too, that a change of orientation was to be noted. There were a good many deputies who still wanted to speak about Algeria (where much was happening), and there were others who were chiefly preoccupied with possible constitutional reforms, but the main concern common to all was Europe. How should the organization of Europe continue, what was to be the role of France in shaping the political future of Europe: these were the main questions. More than one journalist noted that the question of Algeria had been replaced by the question of Europe.[1]

On 15 May this was confirmed by General de Gaulle's press conference, which was largely devoted to European problems. De Gaulle's definition of Europe as he saw it greatly displeased the Social Catholic ministers within the Pompidou government (who appeared to have had no foreknowledge of what the General would say), and they resigned almost immediately. Although the government was quickly reconstituted, to consist only of UNR and Independents (notably Valéry Giscard d'Estaing, Minister of Finance since January 1962) amongst the political parties, it was clear that European affairs could create a crisis for the Fifth Republic.

There were two organizations which specifically claimed to act as the promoters of Western European unification. The one was the North Atlantic Treaty Organization (NATO), which was the military framework created to meet an expected Soviet attack during the period of the so-called cold war. This originated between France, Britain, Belgium, Holland and Luxembourg in 1948 and became complete in 1949 with the association of the USA, Canada and other European countries. During 1950 attempts were made to include West Germany, and the then French Prime Minister (Pleven) attempted to make some measure of German re-armament acceptable by making it part of a European army, called the European Defence Community (EDC). From this time onwards this issue became one of the most difficult in French politics, cutting across party division and complicating political life. On many occasions governments shrank from bringing it before the Assembly, and eventually it was Mendès-France who insisted that a decision must be reached. On 30 August 1954, after M. Herriot had temporarily vacated his presidential seat to urge the Assembly to reject it, the EDC was defeated. As was immediately pointed out, Mendès-

France now had to reconstitute a defence policy, and in 1955, by a new agreement, West Germany did in fact enter NATO.

The other organization which promoted Western European unity was the Common Market, the European Economic Community (EEC). Originating as the plan for a Coal and Steel Pool in Western Europe, it had been put forward by the MRP Foreign Minister Robert Schuman in 1950, and it had been elaborated by M. Jean Monnet. By 1954 it was thought advisable that the economic agreement which had been established in the Coal and Steel Community should be extended to the entire economies of the six European countries concerned: France, West Germany, Belgium, Holland, Luxembourg and Italy. After a great many negotiations, in which Great Britain did not join, and which lasted for about two years, the Treaty of Rome was signed on 25 March 1957 and was due to come into operation on 1 January 1959. The negotiations might have dragged on for much longer had it not been for the determination of a number of individuals (notably M. Spaak of Belgium, Dr Adenauer of West Germany and M. Mollet, then the French Prime Minister) to push the agreement through; it seems likely that it was because of their hope that economic agreement would lead to some form of political agreement that they were so inclined. M. Jean Monnet had formed a pressure group in favour of a 'United States of Europe', and the Suez and Hungarian affairs of 1956 had confirmed the need for Western Europe to unite if it wished to be an effective force. The great fear had always been that the French Assembly would reject this treaty, as it had EDC, and it is sometimes suggested that the British government, which was proposing a European Free Trade Area rather than a European Community, expected this rejection until quite late in the day. It was to prevent such a rejection that a whole series of concessions were made to the French, notably in the field of agriculture and also by allowing decision-making to be concentrated in the EEC Council of Ministers. Eventually the treaty was debated during a heat-wave in an ill-attended Assembly, and was ratified without much enthusiasm.[2]

It is necessary to stress, therefore, that both instruments for European union owed their origin to the French, and that the severest opponents of these European arrangements were also French. Even when Frenchmen were in favour of the European Economic Community they would remain basically protectionist, and it was for this reason that they rejected the Free Trade Area (and possibly because of this British initiative were all the more ready to accept the Treaty of Rome). The coming of General de Gaulle to power in 1958 therefore seemed a particularly critical event for the organization of Europe, and speculation as to de Gaulle's attitude towards NATO and towards the Treaty of Rome was all the sharper because at first he made few revelations. He had been sharply hostile to the Fourth Republic's European policies. He had dismissed the Coal and Steel Pool as *'un mélimélo'*, he had denounced a supranational Europe as a monstrosity and he had bitterly opposed any limitation on France's control of her own defence.

It came therefore as a surprise when he announced his acceptance of the Treaty of Rome. At first this appeared to be a sign of French weakness during the Algerian war. France, already isolated at the United Nations when the Algerian affair was discussed, could not face further isolation in Europe. But it does not seem that this can be an adequate explanation. In spite of the preoccupation of the Algerian affair, de Gaulle formulated a European policy which he was to follow with great fidelity in the years to come. Put very simply, the principles of this policy were that in matters of defence France would not accept any interference with her independence, but in matters of Europe France was prepared to accept a community which would be useful to French interests and which would consist of six sovereign states cooperating together.[3]

So far as NATO was concerned de Gaulle believed that the organization should be fundamentally revised. If this did not take place then it would become increasingly less important, France would depend less upon it and would derive less benefit from it. The faults of NATO were often explained by de Gaulle. NATO owed its origins to the days when the Western European states were weak and when they had been apparently faced by the possibility of Soviet aggression. American power was then considerable and it was natural that America should appear as the protector of Europe.

But since then the American predominance had been affected by other developments. America had not succeeded in establishing a complete domination and de Gaulle began to believe that Russia was less to be feared than hitherto. Western Europe was recovering her strength and it was conceivable that eastern Europe was also beginning to recover her nationalist identities. Therefore NATO was an organization which depended too much on America. America was not a country which could be trusted with the safety of Europe, since American interests did not coincide with European interests. Ever since Roosevelt and Stalin had met at Yalta in 1945, and had supposedly divided the world between them, de Gaulle had been suspicious of American intentions. American criticisms of France's policy in Algeria did not decrease de Gaulle's conviction that French (and European) interests did not always coincide with American interests.

It so happened that in the late 1950's and 1960's NATO was faced with a number of technical problems. Should the role of NATO be augmented making NATO a nuclear force in its own right, or should the increasing power of the European states reduce the role of NATO? What was the most effective form of nuclear deterrent? What would be the role of tactical nuclear weapons? Against what objectives would the nuclear weapons be launched?

De Gaulle seems first of all to have considered a reform of NATO. A letter, written in September 1958, suggested that NATO should be reorganized so as to become an equal partnership between America, England and France. This received no support, either from the Americans or from the British. It seems possible that, towards the end of 1962, de Gaulle also envisaged some sort of Anglo-French co-operation which would replace NATO, but once again there was no support from Great Britain.

Apart from these two ventures (which remain somewhat shadowy)[4] de Gaulle seems to have adhered to the policy that France insisted upon a completely independent control of her weapons, especially nuclear. It was on 13 February 1960 that France exploded her first atomic bomb in the Sahara, and one began to understand the Gaullist belief that the nuclear weapon was the great leveller amongst powers. A state such as America, or Russia, could be infinitely more powerful than a state such as France. But if France was able to equip herself with a sufficient nuclear strength as to be able to inflict extensive damage to an aggressor, this disparity of strength would not matter. No country would dare to attack France if faced by such a response. All this was dependent upon France having nuclear weapons and being able to deliver them; it was based on the assumption that in any future conflict nuclear weapons would be used (and it advertised the fact that France would use them); and it was based upon the idea that nuclear weapons would not be used against enemy forces, but that they would be used to destroy enemy cities and to inflict the maximum amount of destruction on an enemy society. There was no place for integration in this policy, and although France remained a member of NATO, de Gaulle consistently criticized NATO and advertised his indifference to it by a series of minor, but calculated, measures, such as the refusal to store American nuclear warheads and the withdrawal of the French Mediterranean fleet from NATO command.

This policy did not imply any rejection of the American alliance. De Gaulle always insisted that this was necessary to France, although regarding it as an ordinary alliance, not one which would involve putting French forces under a non-French command or making the security of France dependent upon decisions which were taken by individuals not under French control. France preserves her liberty of action, but preserves the alliance. This emphasis made de Gaulle's policy more palatable to many, who regarded the presence of American troops in Europe as a better guarantee of French security than the French nuclear deterrent. And criticism of Gaullist policy has tended to be confined to a fairly technical field. It has been claimed that as methods of warfare develop, France will inevitably be left with out-of-date and ineffective weapons, *'une bombette'*, which the French might not even be able to deliver. It is said that some sort of a unified command is essential if western forces are to have any effectiveness at all. And there has been continued complaint about the cost of this nuclear policy. But most people assumed that France had to equip itself with such weapons. Not to do so would be a disadvantage for the uncertain future; it would underline not so much a failure of French greatness in any mystical sense, but an inadequacy of the French technological performance; no one was prepared to advocate being dependent on America. It must be remembered that French nuclear policy did not originate with de Gaulle, although he profited from earlier work and gave far more emphasis to it. The determination to produce a modern, efficient and independent army was a policy which appealed to many officers who were otherwise hostile to de Gaulle as his Algerian policies became clearer.

De Gaulle's acceptance of the Treaty of Rome as an arrangement which would be beneficial for France meant that the Common Market would have to be sufficiently tightly organized to provide the specific advantages whilst at the same time being a sufficiently loose organization to allow national identities to persist. It was not easy to maintain these dual aims. Nevertheless this was precisely what de Gaulle set out to do. And he attempted to do this by making the running in a number of ways. In accordance with the terms of the treaty it was the French who were the most insistent on keeping to the timetable and introducing the progressive economic adjustments which made the Community a reality. De Gaulle also took the initiative in launching proposals for some sort of political union. After consultation with the separate states (a form of procedure which he always followed since the governments involved were the only 'realities', as he said), in September 1960 he spoke of establishing a machinery for periodic inter-governmental meetings, and he even envisaged the eventual signing of a treaty which would be approved by a European referendum. In March 1961 a committee, headed by a leading French Gaullist, Christian Fouchet, was set up to consider these proposals, and in the course of the year the different governments of the Community made further suggestions. In the course of 1961 and in January 1962 the Fouchet Committee produced a number of plans and although there was a distinct divergence between France and her five partners, since they wished to make the institutions for co-operation more important and powerful, further discussions in the spring of 1962 seemed to reduce the area of disagreement. But the question of Great Britain's possible entry into the Common Market came to complicate the affair, since it was suggested that Great Britain ought to be consulted on the machinery for political union, and that a political agreement should only be concluded after Great Britain's entry.[5]

De Gaulle could either accept Great Britain's entry, and thereby find an ally in rejecting any close political union with important political institutions, or he could reject Great Britain's entry and preserve French pre-eminence within the Community by accepting a greater measure of political unity. It was a measure of his self-confidence that he decided to do both. He did revive the Fouchet proposals. In September 1962 he visted Germany and showed that both Chancellor Adenauer and himself were anxious to establish on a bilateral basis what had not been attainable by the six countries together. At his press conference of 14 January 1963 he announced two things: that the French and German governments had agreed to consult together at regular intervals and to embody this consultation in terms of a treaty; that he did not consider Great Britain yet ready to become a member of the Community and he put an end to the negotiations then being held in Brussels between the British government and the Six. (He was entitled to do this since the Treaty of Rome permitted one country to veto the admission of another.)

This press conference represented the summit of de Gaulle's European policy. France, more than any other country, had the initiative within Europe. In the negotiations it had been the Dutch who were isolated more than the French and there was no united front against France. De Gaulle had shown his loyalty towards the American alliance during the Cuba crisis (October–November 1962) whilst emphasizing his rejection of American influence in Europe. (It was widely suggested that England had been thought of as 'a Trojan horse', which would have brought America into the Community.) He had ridiculed the idea of a united Europe taking the place of individual national states. ('Dante, Goethe, Chateaubriand', he said in May 1962, 'belong to Europe in the degree to which they were respectively and eminently Italian, German and French. They would not have been of use to Europe had they been stateless and had they thought and written in some integrated Esperanto or Volapuk.') But he had also defended the importance of Europe at a time when people thought that Europe was in decline, when the loss of European colonial empires seemed to symbolize that decline. De Gaulle affirmed the potential value and strength of a Europe which stretched from the Atlantic to the Urals. Even western Europe took her place alongside America, Russia and the developing countries of the Third World, as one of the great forces in existence. For all these reasons, Gaullist policies triumphed. There was much resentment in other European countries at the brutal and egocentric manner in which French policy decisions were announced and there were many idealists who regretted the re-affirmation of national values. But within France it was important that within a few months of the Evian agreements which recorded the end of an empire, the French public could see, on television, their President dismiss Great Britain and speak as if he stood for all Europe. However great was the admiration and affection which many French people felt for Great Britain, or however much they resented the costs of the nuclear programme, in the circumstances de Gaulle's actions struck a responsive chord and gave satisfaction to many.

De Gaulle's conduct of foreign affairs has been compared to that of Bismarck,[6] and there are certain resemblances. Both men have shown a passionate devotion to diplomacy, and their concern with the machinery of negotiation is derived from their view of the world as a collection of national powers seeking for some sort of equilibrium. For de Gaulle as for Bismarck, there are always a good many irons in the fire and a reversal of alliances is always possible.[7] One can never divorce his foreign diplomacy from his domestic preoccupations. Nor should one try to separate his policies in western Europe from his attitude towards Soviet Russia and the countries of eastern Europe. In a sense his European policy can be seen as a modified version of his predecessors' policies, but his approach towards the communist countries of Europe is totally different. The most fervent supporters of the idea of Europe, usually Catholics or Socialists, were also devoutly anti-communist. Their very sense of Europe was sometimes a derivative of their fear of Soviet aggression. But de Gaulle, on the other hand, has constantly sought to further diplomatic, economic and cultural collaboration with Soviet Russia and the other states of eastern Europe.

As with Bismarck, the explanations for de Gaulle's policy can be multiple, and it is difficult to classify them in any order of priority. Obviously de Gaulle, the champion of the nation-state, is a cynic with regard to ideologies; he is not prepared to reject a country (or an individual) because of some political creed. Behind the proclaimed political doctrine de Gaulle always thought that he could see the persistence of the national process, with its historical ambitions and aspirations. For him, Stalin was essentially the champion of a Russia on fire with a national ambition that was mightier and more durable than any theory, any régime. The aims of Stalin were simply the dreams of 'Mother Russia', and de Gaulle invariably referred to *la Russie* rather than to *l'Union Soviétique*, thus emphasizing eternal Russia, the state rather than the system. Equally, in eastern Europe, de Gaulle expected that the national interests of Poland, Czechoslovakia, Yugoslavia, Romania, Hungary and so on, would eventually triumph over any international ideology or conspiracy. This is not to say that de Gaulle has not, on many occasions, expressed his distaste for the communist system and 'its character of intense oppression' as he has called it. But his hostility towards the French communists in the post-war years came from the fact that they appeared to serve the interests of another country, that is to say Soviet Russia, rather than their own. In a letter to the writer and resistance hero Vercors, written in 1956, he puts his attitude to the communists very clearly. Whereas he, de Gaulle, had tried to serve France only, they had served France, but they had also served another country. And they had served this other country before France. He expressed indifference to their social ideals, but wished that they would be loyal to *la chose nationale*.[8] In other words, the question of communism was always subordinated to national interests.

But these personal calculations have to be seen in the light of more general considerations. In France there was a long tradition of friendship with Russia. The Franco-Russian alliances of the 1890's and the 1930's had been important moments in this tradition. De

Gaulle himelf had gone to Moscow with all possible haste after the Liberation. If the Franco-German alliance was to be hailed because it went against three centuries of history, then Franco-Russian friendship was something that was natural enough. It was even, in the words of the Soviet ambassador speaking in 1965, 'an unavoidable process'. In general terms it could be argued that the French experience of revolution made them less susceptible than the Anglo-Saxons to the brutalities and crudities of the communist revolution. More specifically it should be remembered that the French communist party had for years stressed the achievements of Soviet Russia in peace and in war, and although there had always been a counter-propaganda to this, there were very many Frenchmen disposed to co-operate with the communist world. The fact that the communists themselves, normally his opponents, would welcome this policy, must have provided de Gaulle with still further encouragement.

At all events, 1958 was not a bad moment for a re-assessment of the French attitude towards eastern Europe. Events in Hungary and Poland seemed to have shaken the system of Stalinist control; the growing disagreement between Soviet and Chinese communism completed the destruction of monolithic communism. De Gaulle believed that France should take the initiative and should be seen to do so. Therefore France welcomed the evolution of national communisms, and sought to strengthen what was thought to be their tendencies towards greater independence. In 1961 de Gaulle stressed the importance of having an understanding, then a co-operation, and finally an 'osmosis', between the countries that had created civilization and that continue to create it. In 1962 he spoke of a real, and 'even a sincere', détente in Europe. It is true that there were moments of difficulty. During the crucial periods of crisis de Gaulle maintained his loyalty to the American alliance. His alliance with Western Germany (which was dependent upon the American alliance) meant that he had to be particularly firm over Berlin and at times almost violent in his denunciation of East Germany. Soviet newspapers denounced French imperialism in Algeria and elsewhere in Africa, and when Mr Khrushchev visited France in 1960 (to be greeted somewhat sardonically by the General, 'vous voici enfin,

Monsieur Khrushchev'), the French Prime Minister complained of the Soviet propaganda that had accompanied the visit. But the main lines of the policy remained firm. De Gaulle believed in co-operation with the communist countries, and he increased his diplomatic repre- sentation in eastern Europe; he sent out a whole series of trading and cultural missions (which often established further working parties and commissions) and as time went by he became increasingly insistent upon this process, possibly as he became aware of the limita- tions of the Franco-German alliance.

One of the reasons why de Gaulle was so anxious to maintain an understanding with Russia was because of his fear that without such an agreement linking Europe to Russia, then the USA and the USSR would simply come to a direct understanding. One of the memories which continued to haunt him was that of Yalta; one of his most fundamental beliefs was that the two great powers would decide the world between them, and this could only be to the dis- advantage of a country such as France. This is an important element in de Gaulle's anti-Americanism.

To explain Gaullist anti-Americanism much importance has been given to de Gaulle's own wartime experiences. From Americans, such as Roosevelt, he met little sympathy and less understanding (Churchill's insistence on Great Britain's special relationship with the USA must have contributed to his belief that he was dealing with 'the Anglo-Saxons'), and this must have influenced de Gaulle in these, his crisis years. It has also been suggested that America, with its amalgam of different populations, offends de Gaulle's sense of the nation-state. From time to time de Gaulle has spoken cynically of the American civil war 'which still continues', although, like many Frenchmen, his knowledge of the United States does not seem to be extensive.

However, the essential nature of de Gaulle's attitude towards the United States turns around two elements. The one is American size and power. The vastness and the ambition of the United States, in military, diplomatic, economic (and probably cultural) matters, is so considerable that, over the years, this is the one power capable of depriving France of its independence. Within the military framework of an organization like NATO, France was only a sub-ordinate power dominated by the USA. Within a world economy where all economic calculation was based upon the dollar, decisions which vitally affected France could be taken in Washington. For de Gaulle this was unacceptable. And it was all the more unacceptable when Europe was strong and when America appeared to be over-extended and over-committed, with a dollar that was to be shown to be increasingly susceptible to attack.

The second element involved the American understanding of the world. De Gaulle was convinced that he understood the great changes of the moment, but that the American comprehension was necessarily limited. Without experience of revolution, American statesmen thought only in terms of preserving the status quo. They saw everything as a struggle between the American way of life and a communist conspiracy. They did not understand why changes were taking place, and dominating such organizations as the United Nations (one which de Gaulle instinctively distrusted), they intervened foolishly and dangerously in different parts of the world, often disregarding or misunderstanding the interests and the opinions of their supposed allies. De Gaulle wondered what it was that America could offer, other than a continuation of the cold war and a resistance to change.

The Gaullist method was not to try and influence American statesmen. This was the method that Churchill had preferred (and which de Gaulle had dismissed as 'formulae of empiricism and compromise').[9] De Gaulle preferred to attack American supremacy and American policies wherever possible. And he sought to challenge the American presence, especially in the countries of the Third World (sometimes called, after America, Russia, Europe and China, the Fifth World). This was not merely a question of arranging financial aid for those countries which are poor. It involved visits to foreign countries, with the ritual of a few words spoken in the relevant language and the reception of the great acclamations which almost inevitably greet the most famous of all Europeans. The tours of Latin America in 1964 were typical of this policy. They increased the prestige of France, and they contributed to the anti-American feelings which were already there. For de Gaulle therefore, they were worth while.

The French recognition of Communist China in January 1964 and the exchange of ambassadors that followed is an outstanding example of Gaullist diplomacy. A series of possible motives can be invoked. In personal terms de Gaulle was impressed by China, by the weight of her history and culture. He was always anxious to show himself on the side of change and progress, and he demonstrated his sense of reality by accepting the new China as a powerful agent of the present and of the future. Anxious too to show that he saw events in their true perspective, he demonstrated his personal pre-occupation with world problems by singling out the Chinese ambassador for particular attention at receptions (in November 1966 for example). But beyond this personal attitude, there was the diplo-matic calculation that there could be no settlement in the Far East without China, and that France ought to play a part in that settle-ment, not only for reasons of prestige, but also because France, like all countries, is bound to be affected by the affairs of the Far East. The recognition of Communist China would be a means whereby France could insinuate herself into this sphere. A Franco-Chinese understanding would create a possible means of pressure on Soviet Russia, whilst recognition of Communist China and rejection of the Formosan régime would run counter to American interests in the area (although it is possible that de Gaulle did not originally intend to break with Formosa, but would have liked to keep this extra iron in the fire).[10] Finally it is possible that de Gaulle wished to emphasize a certain similarity between France and China: both powers were opposed to the twin hegemony of Russia and of America, and both were independent.

There was always something incongruous about de Gaulle, on one of his provincial tours, addressing a small audience of peasants, and speaking to them almost entirely about foreign affairs and about France's role in the world. But it was not entirely foolish. It was in this field that de Gaulle could best exploit his reputation and his experi-ence; it was here that the successes were most apparent; it was on this subject that Frenchmen would forget their sectarianism and remember that they were French. And since, for de Gaulle, the world is a dangerous place and to live in it is to take part in a struggle, then foreign affairs and the international scene are inescapable realities for France. Of course it has often been argued that de Gaulle's successes are not real. The essence of power remains in the hands of America and Russia, and de Gaulle cannot change this. All he can do is to pretend that he has changed it, and to live a Walter Mitty-like existence of self-delusion. If one defines influence as the ability to persuade some state to adopt a policy which it does not wish to adopt, then French influence is not considerable.[11]

This is not altogether just. De Gaulle realized that his period in office coincided with a moment when America was afraid of being over-committed, and when Russia was in favour of *détente*. He was the first to say things which many others were later to say. He was one of those who increased the number of options open to world statesmen. He was imaginative and daring. And doubtless it gave him some satisfaction to see that in terms of French politics there was a certain *élite* which found his policy unacceptable. His view of Europe was intolerable; his nationalism was narrow; his hostility to the USA and his friendliness to Russia were dangerous; his diplomatic method would only make enemies unnecessarily. But in France in 1964, nearly 50 per cent of the population expressed satisfaction with this foreign policy. Gaullism was once again established amongst the people, though reviled by their representatives.

14   Marshal Pétain, the hero of Verdun, who, on the 17th June 1940, told the French people that he had asked for an armistice. ('With a breaking heart I tell you today that we must give up the fight.') Here he is seen at his trial for treason in July 1945, when he refused to recognize the authority of the court and remained silent. He was condemned to death but this sentence was commuted by General de Gaulle into life imprisonment. He died and was buried at his place of exile on the Ile d'Yeu.

15   Charles de Gaulle as a young officer, when he chose to serve in Pétain's regiment, the 33rd Régiment d'Infanterie.

16 De Gaulle, leader of the Free French in London. It was from London, on 18th June 1940, that he broadcast his famous message to the French nation ('Come what may, the flame of our resistance must not and shall not die') which rejected Pétain's acceptance of defeat. This marked the birth of Gaullism.

17 On 25th August 1944 de Gaulle strode in triumph down the Champs Elysées. It was a great day in the history of France, and for de Gaulle it was more than a personal triumph. He thought that he saw the French people united in their enthusiasm for him. On his right is Georges Bidault, who was to become his Foreign Minister, but who was also to become, after 1958, one of his bitterest enemies, accusing him of betraying France by abandoning Algeria.

18 De Gaulle at Sir Winston Churchill's funeral, 30th January 1965. Among the visiting royalty de Gaulle stood out as one who had worked with Churchill during the war years. Their quarrels were famous, Churchill being impatient with de Gaulle's pretensions and de Gaulle being determined to look after French interests. But there were many similarities between the two men.

19 Two figures of *après-Gaullisme*? Pompidou, Prime Minister 1962–68, leaves the Elysée Palace (centre) after one of the Wednesday morning cabinet meetings. For long he was seen as the most likely successor to de Gaulle. On his left is Couve de Murville, Foreign Minister from 1958 to 1968, a longer period than any other French minister.

20 The Paris–Toulouse super-express, the *Capitole*, covers the 443 miles in 6 hours, at an average speed of 74 m.p.h., with a 40-mile stretch at 125 m.p.h. One of the technical achievements of post-war France has been the speed and efficiency of the State-controlled railways.

21 Below: the toll bridge over the Seine at Tancarville, not far from Le Havre. Like certain other projects, the bridge was inaugurated under the Fifth Republic and contributed to its prestige, but it had been started before 1958.

22 The nuclear power station at Chinon (opposite).

23 The tidal barrage over the river Rance in Brittany (opposite, below). This barrage, which also serves as a road bridge, was opened in 1966. It harnesses the 38-foot rise and fall of the tides to provide 240 megawatts of electric power. Beyond it lies Saint-Servan-sur-Mer and the promontory of the Cité d'Aleth, a Roman site.

24   The church at Ronchamp, built in 1950–55, is one of the most striking
designs of the Swiss architect Le Corbusier, much of whose work can be seen in
France.

25   André Gide (above right) was perhaps the most famous French writer
between the two world wars. His anxious preoccupation with himself was not
unlike that of the French nation during those years.

26   Jean-Paul Sartre (below right) emerged as the most considerable literary figure
after 1945. A novelist, dramatist and philosopher, he has become increasingly
concerned with politics. During *les événements* of May–June 1968 his relevance was
to some extent re-affirmed when he spoke to the students occupying the Sorbonne.

27 France has always been famous for atrocious housing conditions. This, the rue Galande, near Saint Séverin, is in the Latin Quarter not far from Notre Dame.

28 A terrace café on the Champs Elysées. Behind, the Arc de Triomphe.

13   The evolution of the régime

Le coup d'état permanent.   François Mitterrand

THE YEAR 1962 SAW the successful conclusion of the Algerian
phase of the Fifth Republic; 1963 and 1964 saw one of the triumphs
of foreign policies; in the third phase of Gaullist government the
emphasis was placed on the permanence of new institutions and on
prosperity. The constitutional reform was sprung unexpectedly on
the political world in the autumn of 1962. This reform stated that the
President of the Republic, instead of being elected by a collection of
notables, as laid down in the constitution of 1958, should be elected
by universal suffrage. This reform was to be approved (or rejected)
by referendum, and it was this which aroused the most immediate
opposition. Constitutionally speaking it was doubtful whether
General de Gaulle was acting correctly by using the procedure of the
referendum, since any revision of the constitution had to be discussed
by Parliament. There was almost unanimous hostility to the proposal amongst the non-Gaullist political parties, since they believed
that it would be dangerous to have a President elected by universal
suffrage. Such a reform would increase Presidential powers whilst
decreasing the powers of Parliament, and their hope was to return
to a normal world of pre-crisis politics now that the Algerian war
was over. But de Gaulle was determined to affirm the position of
the President and to do so institutionally; this would make him the
keystone of the constitution. The doctrine of the reform was the
purest of Gaullisms: an appeal to the people over the head of the
élites of deputies and senators. An attempted assassination of de Gaulle
by the OAS in September 1962 emphasized the need for speedy
action and provided the needed psychological atmosphere.

In October 1962 a motion of censure was passed in the Assembly, censuring the government for the illegality of its proposed constitutional reform. The President immediately exercised his right to dissolve the Assembly and the French electorate were faced with three votes in fairly rapid succession. On 28 October there was the referendum to approve or reject the proposal to elect the President by universal suffrage; on 18 and 25 November, there were the two ballots of the general election. At the first, of those who voted, 62 per cent approved and voted *oui*; at the general elections, a UNR majority emerged. The absolute majority of the Assembly being 242, the UNR had 233, whilst a new formation of Independent Republicans, that is of independent Gaullists, led by Valéry Giscard d'Estaing, gained 35 seats. Together with certain individual supporters, M. Pompidou could count on something over 270 votes. The socialists and communists came to a working agreement that they would not oppose each other at the second ballot, and they managed to increase the number of their deputies, the socialists from 43 to 66 and the communists from 10 to 41 (without having any substantial increase in their overall vote). But this did not alter the situation that for the first time the Gaullists had the overall majority in Parliament and could look forward to five years' rule, together with a President who would be elected by the population as a whole. The climax of this phase of Gaullism could be said to come with the press conference of 31 January 1964, which stated that the President alone can hold or delegate the authority of the state.[1]

It was in his television speech of 16 April 1964 that one saw General de Gaulle pay particular attention to the economy, forcing his way through a thicket of statistics in his demonstration of French prosperity. Perhaps it was this prosperity which surprised and impressed foreign observers, even more than the political stability. They had become accustomed to thinking of France as the sick man of Europe and to asking undergraduates why France had never had an industrial revolution. The French economy had such a reputation for defying modernization and resisting improvement that the revelation of new dynamic forces seemed so remarkable as to merit the term of *le miracle français* (and it was all the more impressive to British observers since it coincided with an awareness of British economic stagnation). The contrast between the Fourth and the Fifth Republics politically, which was so frequently drawn by the President, seemed less impressive than the contrast between them in terms of economic growth and prosperity.

The economic history of the Fourth Republic has invariably been presented as a series of attempts to maintain prices and wages in some sort of rough correlation, accompanied by a disastrous number of unbalanced budgets and devaluations. The methods used by different administrations varied (and not always with the political ideology of the minister concerned), so that one saw attempts to control prices by forcible control, by improving the circuits of distri-bution, by reducing state expenditure, by subsidies and tax remissions, or by cutting the rate of growth and investment. Observers differ as to the success of these various policies. M. Pinay's reputation, for example, depended upon the apparent price stability that he suc-ceeded in imposing for a time in 1952; there are economists who pre-fer M. Edgar Faure's period in office, whilst others believe that right at the end of the Fourth Republic, M. Félix Gaillard provided his successors with a successful financial operation.[2] But one has the impression that whatever success any one of these attempts may have had, in general they failed to give any coherence to the economy or to impel it forward with any success.

This is only partially true. A number of actions were taken which permanently affected the French economy. To begin with, there were the post-war nationalizations which gave the government control of important sectors of the economy. The establishment of planning soon went beyond the significance of the first Plan, which applied only to limited sectors of the French economy, and the Plan covering the years 1954 to 1957 was an attempt to establish a whole pattern of development. Along with more specific and limited plans (devised, for example, by Mendès-France or Edgar Faure), it served as a guide to policy and it was the prelude to the important scheme of indicative planning which came into operation in 1958.[3] Another permanent arrangement affecting the French economy as a whole was the Treaty of Rome, which meant the opening up of

French markets to competition, as well as the possibility of French industry and agriculture finding increased outlets in Europe. In France as everywhere the whole period of the late 1950's was a period of expansion, with sustained demand, organizational reform, and a high rate of investment. Throughout the Fourth Republic there was a general increase of the gross national product, at a general rate of about 5 per cent a year, which was sustained even at the end of the period of immediate post-war expansion.

In these circumstances the contrast between the supposed stagnation of the Fourth Republic and the dynamism of the Fifth is far less than is often suggested. The Gaullist government inherited the European Economic Community, a group which was already expanding, and the creation of which meant further expansion.[4] The economic planners were already at work advising on a whole series of measures to promote efficiency and coherence, and the government had all the powers necessary to control or to influence most sectors of the economy. Therefore it would be true to say that a shake-up had already taken place. Naturally the crisis of 1958 and the imminence of the Common Market did create a new sense of urgency; the coming to office of such a technocrat as Michel Debré was an encouragement to the personnel of economic planning, many of whom were young and ambitious, and it underlined what one might call the mystique of planning. But 1958 is less of a break in economic than in constitutional terms.

In December 1958 de Gaulle's government devalued the franc by about 15 per cent and accompanied this with a deflationary policy which sought to limit both current and capital expenditure, to increase the prices of public utilities and to control wages. A new franc was introduced which was meant to affirm the new solidity of French money and since it was one hundred of the existing francs, it was intended to be psychologically reassuring. Payments would be made in a few coins instead of many notes, an only too visible sign of devaluing currency. The old days of the early Third Republic would be recalled, days when the franc was secure. (In fact the change-over took longer than was expected, and French people found it difficult to count in hundreds rather than thousands.)

Whether France was then lucky in terms of the booming world trade figures of 1959, or whether these governmental measures were in themselves adequate to restore competition is uncertain. France did have a natural 'built-in' protection against foreign incursions, being traditionally a country of low imports, and because a combination of conservative buying and high retail pricing prevented non-French goods from being too successful on the French market when the Common Market came into force. At all events French exports soared and it was an expanding economy that was able to absorb the tariff cuts of the Treaty of Rome (and the shock of 750,000 settlers returning from Algeria). The fact that the French planners and technocrats were surprised by the extent of the French export boom and by the relative stagnation of imports was in itself notable.[5] It seemed that politically and economically Gaullist France was riding the crest of a wave and if (as we are told) 'charisma' was the O.K. word for 1963, then General de Gaulle must have made his own contribution to that phenomenon.[6]

But it was not all plane sailing. Difficulties arose which could be treated with various degrees of seriousness. First of all there were a number of social problems. They had not disappeared with the disappearance of the Fourth Republic. There remained areas of France which were dynamic, and areas which were stagnant. There were classes and groups of the population which seemed to profit from the expansion, and other classes which suffered. There were areas which were more affected than others, or more apprehensive than others, as the Treaty of Rome took shape and became a reality. The agricultural sector was the most evident. Agricultural workers and farmers were leaving the land and going to work in the towns, or in those few industries which were being established in the countryside. But those who remained were all the more conscious both of their grievances (their long hours of work for relatively low returns, and the uncertainty of being able to get an economic return for a crop) and of their strength (they still represented an important part of the population, and psychologically, they felt that they could touch a responsive chord in the hearts of many Frenchmen and most

French deputies). In 1960 they asked for a special session of the Chamber to discuss their problems, and this demand was repeated subsequently, but was always rejected. They requested a special meeting with de Gaulle; they inspired an unsuccessful motion of censure in the Assembly in 1964; they demonstrated, blocked roads and railways, burned their surplus produce in public places, threatened or subjected to ridicule the representatives of the state. And in return for all these agitations, various concessions were granted them of one sort and another, but which left them still hostile and uneasy, frequently on the verge of violence.

In industry there was also discontent. Prices rose and profits rose, but wages did not keep pace with this movement (which was to some extent controversial, the government always claiming that the rise of prices was much less than various opponents suggested). There was an important and dramatic strike of miners in 1963. There had earlier been strikes in particular regions, especially where pits had been closed, but this was a general strike of miners. The government was determined to show that it was not going to be treated as if it were an ordinary government of the Third or Fourth Republic. It was anxious to demonstrate its authority and it took special powers to requisition the mines. But in practice it did not dare use them. The strike lasted for some six weeks and was widely supported. The government remained silent and showed no disposition to act as a strong state.

Economically speaking, by the end of 1963, the government became uneasy about the extent of the expansion and the inflationary tendencies that were being unloosed. There was therefore a reinforcement of economic orthodoxy. In September 1963 a stabilizing plan was introduced which blocked credits and sought to pin down prices. Arrangements were started to provide for a balanced budget. And the French government began to buy gold, and to advise holders of foreign currencies (especially dollars) to turn them into gold. The climax of this policy came in February 1965 when the President's press conference contained a vigorous recommendation of gold as the world's basic currency. The tendency of all these moves was obviously to restrain the rhythm of economic expansion. It was

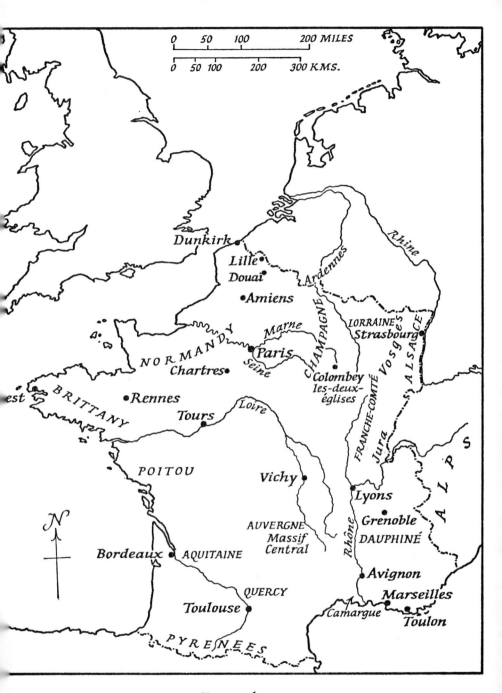

France today

true that these policies, whether of price controls or of budgetary limitations, were often relaxed in practice. It is also true that by the autumn of 1963 there was a slowing-down of consumption which was probably beginning to affect production. But the fact remains that the French government was opting for stability rather than for expansion, and was placing a great emphasis on the strength of the franc. It could be argued that there was little value to an economy in having wealth stored in vaults (and the Bank of France began to acquire so much gold that it was obliged to build extensions to its storage space), rather than circulating freely. The real aim of the policy was so to increase the value of the franc, and to vaunt the prestige of gold, that eventually the dollar would no longer be accepted as the prime international currency. This, it was said, was to choose *le franc* rather than *les français*, and the slowing down of French expansion permitted sections of the economy to be neglected and underpaid, whilst other areas were developing slowly and deriving a relatively small benefit from *le miracle français*.

Politically speaking, the great problem was the Presidential elec-tions which were due to be held in 1965. At first it seemed that de Gaulle had outplayed his rivals. He had not let it be known whether or not he would himself be a candidate. His age (he was 75 when the elections were held) encouraged a good many rumours that he would not stand, and it was remembered how, when speak-ing about Marshal Pétain, he had written in his *Mémoires de guerre* of old age being a shipwreck. Surely then, it was said, he would not wish to be in office for another seven years? It was not until the last possible moment, in November 1965, that he announced his candidature. In this uncertainty, and faced with the problem of a new type of election, the different oppositions were undecided how they should proceed. This was all the more unfortunate because when municipal elections were held in February 1965, although they had been prepared with great care by the government of Pompidou, they were not a Gaullist success. Although there was no fundamental swing of opinion, the big towns voted for opponents of Gaullism. Lyons, Marseilles, Nice, Grenoble, Tou-louse, Toulon, Lille, Arras, Rennes: they all voted anti-Gaullist, whether to support a mayor who claimed to be a political (as in Lyons) or a representative of a new, non-traditional political formation (as in Grenoble), or simply one of the traditional opponents of the régime.

Therefore there seemed to be an anti-Gaullist movement in the air and the left-wing parties were especially conscious of the need to capture it. But in spite of having a candidate who was an impressive and able man, the mayor of Marseilles, Gaston Defferre, the left could not bring itself to unite under his leadership. Eventually it was M. Mitterrand, a former minister of Mendès-France, who was accepted as the candidate who would receive the votes of the left, communists, socialists and independent socialists. But M. Lecanuet decided to stand on behalf of the centre, especially the MRP, so it was clear that the opposition was divided. And psychologically speaking, General de Gaulle had a great advantage because he believed in the Presidential system. All the opposing parties were opposed to it; but they were nevertheless playing its game by being candidates (Mendès-France, for example, refused to be a candidate because he was opposed to the system). This meant that Mitterrand was not an enthusiastic candidate. During his campaign he announced that if he were elected, he would dissolve Parliament and have general elections. This was to suggest that general elections were more important. But the mass of the French population was by now passionately attached to the idea of Presidential elections, and was confirming de Gaulle's belief that such a system was thoroughly democratic, republican and French.

For all these reasons it did not seem that de Gaulle could lose. Yet the campaign began to take on an unexpected vigour. As the opposition candidates journeyed across France, some of them succeeded in creating a considerable response. The extreme right-wing candidate, Tixier-Vignancour, was the first to have an American-style perambulation. During the summer his caravans and tents visited the beaches 'from Dunkirk to Menton', and his eye-catching symbol, TV, was soon placarded throughout the country. Mitterrand had not been a popular choice, and certain trade-union leaders, for example, had said that they could not urge their members to vote for him. But he ended his campaign with a gigantic meeting in Toulouse which had an atmosphere of *kermesse* and triumph. M. Lecanuet presented himself as a young, Kennedy-style candidate, and he too evoked response from crowds which went well beyond the usual *clientèle* of the MRP. The other opposition candidates were less adventurous: M. Marcilhacy, the independent senator who stood for the local *notabilités*, and Barbu, a sentimental eccentric who claimed to represent *les chiens battus* and the common man, were more restrained. Indeed, the latter hardly fought a campaign at all.

And from this world of excited meetings, whistle-stop tours and helicopter journeys, with Lecanuet and Mitterrand even distributing key-rings (a favourite salesman's gimmick of the time), de Gaulle held aloof. He did not even propose to use all his allotted television time, so determined was he to show that he was above such mani-festations and secure in his confidence of victory. But the growth of enthusiasm amongst the opposition, and the extraordinary interest in the television appearances of his rivals (especially Lecanuet) caused him to revise this opinion. Possibly this change of mind came too late. It was said that if he had allowed himself to be tele-vised in an interview, before the first ballot, then he would have had sufficient support.[7] But as it was he failed to gain the absolute majority on the first ballot, winning only 43.7 per cent of the metro-politan votes. Mitterrand got slightly more than 32 per cent and Lecanuet nearly 16 per cent.

Thus a majority of French citizens were anti-Gaullist. The shock to the General's pride was probably much less than was suggested, and the belief that he would withdraw and would refuse to be a candidate at the second ballot was probably completely without foundation. Both the General and the Gaullists fought fiercely in the second round, where their only opponent was Mitterrand (the 1962 law laying down that only two candidates should take part in the second round). Both contestants attempted to win as wide a support as possible. Mitterrand denied having any intention to proceed to socialism; the Gaullists denied that there was any question of a confrontation between right and left, between a *Bloc National* and a *Front Populaire*. Finally, on 19 December, after a heavy poll, de Gaulle gained 54.5 per cent of metropolitan votes and Mitterrand 45.4 per cent. De Gaulle was therefore elected for a further seven years.

Obviously such an election was notable in France. Not everyone cared for the American-style campaigning, and it was not only the austere Mendès-France who complained that one was trying to sell a President in the same way as one sold tooth-paste. There was a certain amount of misunderstanding and exaggeration about the effects of television. When the analysis of the votes began to come in, it was seen that the man who appeared to have made the biggest impact on the television audiences owed his chief support to Catholic regions in the west which contained the lowest numbers of television licence-holders. In spite of his successful publicity and his skill in posing as the opponent of injustice, Tixier-Vignancour was only able to rally a small number of votes (5 per cent on the first ballot). That is to say that the traditional voting patterns in France were not upset by the new system. It seems likely that some communists may have voted for de Gaulle (out of nationalism); that some of the traditional right might have voted for Mitterrand (out of protest). But de Gaulle, in spite of his efforts, was to appear increasingly as a right-wing leader. His warnings about the dangers of party politics, of returning to the confusion and weaknesses of the Third and Fourth Republics, were not heeded by nearly half the population.

And psychologically speaking there was a great change. Prior to these elections, there were some who thought that the great danger in de Gaulle's hold over France lay precisely in this dominating position. It was feared that the death or the resignation of de Gaulle would have a traumatic effect on France. December 1965 suggested that a great many Frenchmen envisaged a change of President with a calm, if not cheerful, equanimity.[8] Subsequent reflection and further political activity served to confirm these impressions. It was clear that de Gaulle could no longer be thought of as a supreme arbitrator, above the ordinary rough and tumble of politics. It was all the more striking because during the campaign he had endeavoured to maintain that appearance. Only with the realization that all was not going well did de Gaulle accept to be a candidate like any other, and thereby abandon one of the most important aspects of Gaullism. Furthermore, the constitutional implications of this form of Presidential election seemed far from clear. It seemed that parliamentary elections would become a sort of third ballot of the Presidential elections, and that a conflict between an Assembly and a President, both elected by universal suffrage, would be ex-tremely complicated.

The fact that since M. Pompidou had become Prime Minister, the functions of that office had become increasingly subservient to the Presidency increased the confusion. The notion that there was a *domaine* reserved for the President and that there was another *domaine* for the government was completely abandoned and out of date. By his speeches and by reports of his activities it was clear that he was intervening in every aspect of governmental life. The function of the Prime Minister seemed to be one of preparing the dossiers which were then sent on to the President. It was in the Presidency, with the advisers of the Presidency, or in meetings (whether of the Cabinet or of *ad hoc* committees) presided over by the President, that the decisions were taken. During the Presidential elections, although the policies of the government were under discussion, it was as if M. Pompidou had disappeared from sight. In all these circumstances what was the role of Parliament? More than one member of the UNR was anxious about this, and Valéry Giscard d'Estaing spoke of the need to give a coherent and liberal meaning to the institutions of the Fifth Republic. Even amongst Gaullists, the constitutional future of the Fifth Republic had become uncertain.[9]

Everything confirmed the idea that there was going to be a polar-ization of French politics, intensified by the prospect of general elections, which had to be held in 1967 if not before. The Gaullists endeavoured to enlarge their hold on the right and the centre and tried to bring both individuals and groups into the general framework of a *Comité d'Action pour la Cinquième République*, presided over by M. Pompidou. The Pompidou government was reconstituted, Edgar Faure and de Chambrun, who belonged to central groups, became ministers, whilst M. Debré (who had become deputy for Réunion in 1963, having lost his seat in 1962) replaced Giscard d'Estaing with the mission of re-invigorating the economy. The idea that ministers were technicians and apart from politics was abandoned, and in 1966 it was known that even those ministers who had not previously been deputies or senators (such as Pompidou and Couve de Murville) would have to confront the electors. Thus the whole of Gaullism was becoming more political.

Meanwhile, on the left, prolonged conversations between the communists (Waldeck Rochet) and M. Mitterrand on behalf of the socialist and radical federation, in which the independent socialists (led by Roccard, and including Mendès-France) joined, succeeded in establishing and making arrangements for the elections, and even went some of the way to establishing a joint programme. Fears that General de Gaulle might bring the date of the election forward caused the communists to designate their candidates earlier than had been agreed, and the hope (which had never been very great) that there would be only one left-wing candidate at the first ballot had been abandoned. The interpretation of the elections as a left- and right-wing confrontation had to be modified by M. Lecanuet and his Catholic centre supporters, who hoped to manoeuvre themselves into a dominating position in the Assembly.

It was therefore in a tense and excited atmosphere that the elections of 1967 were held. There were many rumours of what would happen if there were not a Gaullist majority in the Assembly, and certain Gaullists were reported as using threatening language. There was talk of the President having recourse to emergency powers and of reforming the constitution by means of a referendum. There were suggestions of even stronger methods and the Ben Barka affair (the kidnapping in the centre of Paris of the leading opponent of the Moroccan government, with the help of French government secret service agents) gave weight to the suggestion that there were some men in the government entourage who would stop at nothing. De Gaulle himself was not supposed to take part in these elections, but in a television appearance made before the campaign was opened, and in another made on the eve of the first poll of 5 March (which was said to be unconstitutional) he left no doubt as to how he wanted people to vote.[10] It was his face that was on the 'Vème République' posters and no one could have any doubt as to the 'politicization' of the Presidency. The Prime Minister took a prominent part in the campaign, with two important public debates, the one with M. Mitterrand at Nevers, the other with Mendès-France at Grenoble. It was noticeable that the Prime Minister sought to draw the discussion away from social and economic affairs, towards a discussion of institutions. The Gaullist argument was always that the opposition would bring France back to the incoherence and the divisions of earlier times; the opposition stressed social injustice and the dictatorial nature of the régime. 'You are definitively a man of the Fourth Republic,' said Pompidou to Mendès-France, in the early hours of the morning, after a prodigious debate. 'And you a man of the Second Empire' was the reply.

The first ballot suggested that there was not going to be any fundamental change in the composition of the Assembly, in spite of all the rumours and excitement. The communists and socialists increased their votes very slightly, the Gaullists slightly more. The centre parties lost votes. But in spite of a heavy poll, it was striking to see how the first ballot in 1967 resembled the second ballot in 1962. It seemed that an absolute majority for the Gaullists was certain. But the second ballot was a considerable surprise. The final result was that out of the 470 metropolitan seats the Gaullists, or Fifth Republic groups, gained 233 seats, whilst the non-Gaullists gained 237.

This was not a positive defeat for the government since the non-Gaullists did not form a unity. The communists, members of the Federation, and independent socialists, who might have been considered to form a relatively united anti-de Gaulle and left-wing group, gained 193 seats. In any case the government's situation was retrieved by the votes of the overseas territories (that is to say New Caledonia, the Wallis Islands, Futuna, Polynesia, the Comores and St Pierre and Miquelon) where the Gaullists gained most of the seats, and in the entire Assembly of 487, the Gaullists could be said to have 247 seats, against a non-Gaullist 240. But this calculation was a generous one (since it includes amongst the Gaullists two deputies whose adherence was not altogether certain) and it was not immediately available since the second ballot in Polynesia was only held on 29 March. In any case, the majority being dependent upon a deputy from Oceania was reminiscent of one of the worst features of pre-1958 times.

There was therefore jubilation on the left ('The Left must be prepared to assume office', said Mendès-France; 'this can happen sooner than we think'), disappointment and recriminations amongst the Gaullists. For some the mistake had been not to pursue a policy which was more resolutely social. Left-wing Gaullists were particu-larly severe on the conservative nature of the policies followed,[11] and a sudden wave of social unrest seemed to confirm their suggestion that there was a very real social malaise which explained the govern-ment's relative failure. (Workers temporarily took over the Berliet works near Lyons, there was a strike at the Rhodiaceta works at Lyons and Besançon, a strike amongst metallurgical workers at Saint-Nazaire, bus drivers in Paris, etc. There were also some violent manifestations amongst wine-growers in the south, sixty people were injured at Carcassonne, and so on.) The analysis of political experts brought out the fact that what had really happened during the second ballot was an unexpected movement of votes towards the left. In particular those who had voted for an extreme-right or a centre candidate (such as M. Lecanuet's Centre Démocratique) who did not stand at the second ballot (to do so he needed to have gained 10 per cent of the possible vote) either abstained or voted for the left-wing opposition, even if it were communist. This is to say that a good part of the moderate opinion in the country was pre-pared to do almost anything except vote Gaullist. And this central group was one which had firmly supported de Gaulle from 1958 to 1962.[12]

This sort of analysis did suggest that in the first election which was being held in absolutely normal conditions (both 1958 and 1962 had been affected by Algerian affairs), one can register a decline of Gaullism, and the outlines of a crisis of the Gaullist state. It is true that the victory of the Left was a myth; it was not a victory at all and it was legitimate to suggest that the Left seemed destined to be constantly in a minority. It is true too that M. Pompidou showed himself adroit at managing the Assembly, and that the government did not hesitate to introduce unpopular measures, such as a reform of social security which meant a reduction of benefits, and an increase in public transport costs. But the mythology of Gaullism seemed to be bruised (hardly according with the spectacle of de Gaulle as the first of the electioneering gentlemen of France) and the style of the régime had made enemies.

Abroad, too, de Gaulle had his successes which sometimes had the air of failures. Within the Common Market France seemed more than ever to be in the centre of disputes, and at times de Gaulle used language which was brutally clear. He insisted, for example, that the Common Market had to include a common agricultural policy, which would enable French agriculture to get rid of its surpluses. 'Failing which', de Gaulle added, once an agreement had been reached in December 1963, 'we would have been compelled to resume our freedom in all respects and there would have been no Common Market' (31 January 1964). It is true that the great crisis of the summer of 1965 was not of de Gaulle's choosing. It was the EEC Commission (a body to which de Gaulle was naturally hostile, since he thought that executive power should belong to governments only) that launched the affair, more or less demanding from France acceptance of the role of supranationality, in return for concessions on agricultural policy. When this proposal came before the Council of Ministers of the EEC, it was clear that it was being sympathetically considered by all the ministers present, but not by the French. De Gaulle then withdrew the French representatives from Brussels, thus in a sense breaking off diplomatic relations. Once again it seemed that there was a threat to the whole existence of the Common Market, since it was clear that de Gaulle was not only rejecting the proposals of the Commission, he was also asking for a fundamental revision of the Treaty of Rome. It could be that France's partners in the Common Market had somewhat lost sight of their conception of Europe, since they had become increasingly anxious to thwart French policies. The problems of Europe, like politics in France, had become highly personalized.

It is true that this aspect of dealing with international problems was exhilarating, and that many individuals enjoyed the excitement and the personalized form of nationalism which they involved. But responsible organizations showed their anxiety. The possibility of severe agricultural and industrial losses was held up by many as the immediate outcome of the crisis. Doubtless this had its effect on the Presidential elections, and contributed to the relative popularity of the European-minded Lecanuet. Undoubtedly the unity of the Five was also impressive. It could not be broken by a number of French attempts to bring about bilateral agreements. When the alternatives to the Common Market were explored, they seemed to suggest that they would be less advantageous to France.

It was not until January 1966 that official and full-scale negotiations were taken up again, and Couve de Murville was ambitious enough to present the Five in Luxembourg with a detailed time-table of how Europe should proceed. The final outcome was a compromise in every sense of the word. France conceded nothing, and the Five conceded nothing. In the sense that there was no real move to supranationality, and in the sense that the common agricultural policy was pursued, one could talk about a French success. But quite apart from a number of detailed, technical concessions that the French were forced to make, there was a blow struck at the spirit of Europe. From this time a great pessimism begins to grow about Europe. Whilst economic interests in France experienced unease about the lengths to which their President was prepared to go, convinced Europeans became conscious of the fact that they were now only limping forward. Europe, far from being the dream of centuries and a consensus of values, was merely a device, a form of inter-governmental co-operation, within which there was one partner who was totally egocentric. It did not seem to matter that de Gaulle had legalistically been right on the details of the issue (the Commission's proposals were put forward in a highly irregular way, for example). What did matter was that de Gaulle was increasingly seen as the enemy of Europe in many quarters. Again, his continued refusal in 1967 to countenance British entry into Europe seemed all the less surprising because the British economy was only too obviously in crisis. But it confirmed the impression that nothing further could be done in Europe whilst de Gaulle was still President of France.

The victory of Gaullism was thus the victory of the forces of inertia.[13]

Within the Brussels crisis there were obviously other considerations. For a long time de Gaulle had been disappointed in the Franco-German treaty. In 1963 he had compared the treaty to young girls and roses, which do not last for long, and he had quoted Victor Hugo, 'Alas, I have seen young girls dying'. In 1964 he expressed even more clearly his regret that Franco-German co-operation was not working as well as it might, and in an obvious move to press the West Germans, he showed signs of looking towards Eastern Germany. He could not accept that Germany for obvious reasons wished to stay aligned to NATO and to the American alliance; he could not, for equally obvious reasons, make any move towards equipping West Germany with nuclear weapons or bringing about her unification. Time therefore showed up the weaknesses in his policy.

In February 1966 de Gaulle announced that France would begin to withdraw from NATO. But he also stated that France would remain loyal to the Atlantic alliance. Such a policy aroused some alarm, since for technical reasons it seemed that the French action would only reduce the efficiency of the defence of France without giving any corresponding advantages. The fact that none of France's partners sought to follow her in leaving NATO emphasized the loneliness of the French gesture. Equally, the attempts to come to a meaningful understanding with Russia never seemed to get any-where. French trade with eastern Europe increased, but it did not increase significantly, nor did it increase more than that of other countries, nor did it prevent the Russians from having direct discussions with the Americans when it suited them.

This is not to say that the French policy did not have its attractions. There was no movement in France, or in any other country, in favour of the supranationalist institutions of Europe. There was no important movement of French opinion in favour of the British entry into Europe. There was a feeling that national aspirations were normal and respectable, that the national state was the repository of values and the means of identification. There was general agreement that France should come to an agreement with eastern Europe and there was a vague approval of anti-Americanism. De Gaulle's policies were always imaginative, clearly explained and logically presented. Foreign affairs were interesting and exciting. But a feeling of unease grew all the same.

Perhaps this feeling was most clearly brought out by two typically Gaullist adventures. The one was his famous utterance amongst the French-Canadians, '*Vive le Québec libre*', on 24 July 1967. Perhaps this slap in the face to the Americans gave a momentary, and secret, satisfaction. But (however mistakenly) it also seemed to be an un-warranted and useless intrusion into another country's affairs. There seemed to be an element of vulgarity about de Gaulle here. And then, after the Arab-Jewish war, there was the criticism of the Jews. It was logical within the framework of Gaullist thought. He dis-approved of French Jews who felt loyalty towards Israel rather than France. He wondered if Israel was a national, historical reality as compared to the Arabs. He disapproved of this victorious representa-tive of American interests in the Mediterranean and Middle East. But whilst recognizing the logic, many felt that this policy was in-humane. This sort of Gaullist success did not improve the standing of Gaullism.

Internationally, even when de Gaulle was right, there were over-tones which damaged the logic of his policies. Had he only wished to see the French Canadians have a more powerful voice in their own future, then his remarks would have been acceptable; but *vive le Québec libre* was to proceed by *électro-choc* and it was thought frightening. When he claimed that in international monetary matters there was no shortage of international liquidity, when he criticized the move to create special drawing rights, and when he asked for a new conference comparable to the Bretton Woods meeting of 1944 to discuss world monetary reform, then there was general agreement that this was sensible; but the obvious and open attempt to hurt American interests, and the continued insistence upon preserving the personality of Europe distinct from that of America, together with an obstinate advocacy of the gold standard—this was not the language of the economists and the central bankers.

And in a France where certain of the traditional quarrels were beginning to fade away, where economic demands were being put forward without the disguise of political ideology, when people wanted to talk about peaches and sugar and minimum wages, the General's preoccupations often seemed far distant. As one writer had earlier put it, it was as if the France which General de Gaulle was talking about was not the France in which the French were living, nor the France in which they wanted to live.[14] And the economic appeal of his foreign policy was lessened when it seemed possible that the General was prepared to sacrifice economic advantages if the national interest demanded it. Industrialists, traders, workers, all demanded a more active economic policy and more productive investment, an end to a form of stagnation. M. Pompidou dismissed this as nostalgia for 'the fallacious facilities of inflation', and it was pointed out that he was closely associated with the Rothschilds. It was suggested that de Gaulle was too much influenced by the banks. Such a suggestion was also harmful for Gaullism.

14   Tour de France

The French nation is particularly hard to define in any simple way and this very characteristic of being hard to define is a most important element in its definition.   Paul Valéry

A PERCEPTIVE WRITER has said that for an Englishman the word 'French' denotes a nebulous, inscrutable essence viewed through personal reminiscences.[1] Such reminiscences are often not personal at all. They can be long-accepted ideas, perhaps put forward by some famous writer, perhaps thrown up by some particular event or series of events. And they continue to exist, like dead leaves pressed between the pages of a book. One has to be cautious about such ideas. Just as there is no greater discourtesy than flinging a nation's supposed characteristics in its face, so there is nothing so dangerous as explaining a country's history in terms of the alleged characteristics of the people who live there. There is no reason why one should pay any attention to Matthew Arnold's description of the French as having a passion for equality, or to Noel Coward's conviction that 'there's always something fishy about the French', or to a British newspaper's recent description of the French as 'a somewhat neurotic nation with a propensity for revolution'.[2] The authors of each of these judgements are only expressing the feeling that being French is different from being English, that French history is not the same as English history. One has to try, as objectively as one can, to make some sort of an assessment of what it is like to be French.

The attempts that have been made to draw a psychological portrait of the French have not been very satisfactory. In the famous books by André Siegfried, Jacques Rivière, Salvador de Madariaga and

Hermann Keyserling, the abstractions are interesting in terms of a general discussion about France.[3] They can hardly be taken as a definition of the French. To say that the Frenchman is quick-witted, alert, rational, logical, and that he prefers his leaders to be men of intelligence rather than men of character (and this is usually said to be in contrast with the British), is only to define a certain type of French politician or *littérateur*, probably acting in a special way in particular circumstances. When politics consist of endless negotia-tions and shifting coalitions, then a certain type of intelligence is at a premium. To these abstractions is usually added the comment that the Frenchman is so logical and intellectual that he finds compromise difficult. This is strange since French politics have often been an endless series of compromises. In any case there is something a little complacent in Frenchmen explaining that the French are a difficult people to govern because they are so intelligent. German writers, such as Keyserling and Curtius, stressed the French lack of any pioneering spirit, their refusal to be adventurous; André Gide listed a number of phrases which he thought of as typically French (*'fallait pas qu'il y aille'*, *'comment peut-on être persan?'*, *'désormais je ne bouge plus et je serais cent fois mieux,'* *'cultivons notre jardin'*), all of which are of the stay-at-home variety; Professor Renouvin used to give a lecture called *'les traits essentiels de l'âme et du caractère français'* in a course on French foreign policy, and there he used to explain that psycho-logically the Frenchman was not interested in empires as were the British. And yet the French conquered a vast overseas empire at considerable cost to themselves and unlike any other European country they fought two ferocious wars in an unsuccessful attempt to hold on to it.

Of course the French themselves continue to talk and write about their national virtues and vices, and they continue to try and discover what habits, traits, tendencies and practices are essentially their own. Sometimes an imaginary Frenchman, Monsieur Dupont or Monsieur Durand, is made to carry the weight of these observations; sometimes it is the ordinary Frenchman, *'le Français moyen'*, *'l'agriculteur moyen'* and so on. But more often than not, the statement is direct and bold. *'Le Français a l'esprit judiciaire'*, *'le Français n'a pas le sens civique'*, '*le Français est individualiste*', '*le Français cherche toujours à comprendre*', '*le Français se méfie de l'autorité*', '*dans chaque Français il y a un Bona-parte qui sommeille*' and so on. Countless examples could be given. They are to be found in all the newspapers and they are frequently to be heard in cafés. They have probably been intensified by the vast machine of *bavardage* that is French radio and television, and they must certainly have been encouraged by General de Gaulle's preoccupation with the nation and what he calls *notre caractère*. It seems likely too that this sort of speculation about what *le Français* is really like will have been encouraged by the current success of public opinion polls and *enquêtes* of all sorts.

But what is one to make of all this? Some flashes of intuition and some revealing truths are undoubtedly buried in this clutter of clichés and undusted assumptions. But the only real conclusion that one can draw from the process is that the Frenchman seems to be particularly self-conscious, and that this may well denote a certain lack of self-confidence, a feeling of uncertainty about himself and his associates. Perhaps it represents a search for some sort of identity.[4] But one must not follow him into this quarry of confusions, where a national characteristic is derived from a moment in history. It is not so correct to say that the Frenchman has '*l'esprit révolutionnaire*' or '*l'esprit frondeur*' as it would be to say that there are times in French history when there is a tradition of revolutions or Frondes. Some-times there is a confusion between national characteristics and social patterns. The Frenchman is not born with a particular and national reluctance to pay taxes, but the fact that for many years French busi-nesses, farms, shops and cafés were run by one man assisted by his family made the whole process of assessing these units for direct taxation one of unusual difficulty. Invariably there is over-simplifica-tion. The Frenchman is not Catholic; the Frenchman is not anti-clerical. He is in fact both and there are many different forms both of Catholicism and of anti-clericalism, some of which are deter-mined by geography.

To try and understand a nation is to try and understand its culture. One has to identify the social customs and symbols of its society. And, trying to uncover the symbols of French society, surely a starting-point is the war memorial, the *monument aux morts*. This is one of the few features which is common to the whole of France, since every commune has its *monument aux morts* and many communes have brought together memorials to the three wars, 1870, 1914 and 1939. These memorials are only part of a wider significance. There are names in French history which are as sharp as swords or which are etched on a national consciousness. One cannot believe that the scars of Verdun can ever be eradicated, or that names such as Château-Thierry, Péronne, Albert, Bapaume, Amiens, will cease to have a particular poignance. And yet these battlefields of eastern or northern France are only part of a greater whole. France is overwhelmed by history. *'Vieille France, accablée d'histoire'*, writes General de Gaulle; *'le Français a le sens historique'*, says the man in the café. The yardstick of history never leaves the Frenchman. Teaching in schools, and school text-books, are the obvious and universal method of maintaining an historical awareness. But in France, the names of the streets (rue François Premier, rue Bonaparte, rue du 29 juillet, rue du 4 septembre, avenue Thiers, Place Verdun, Boulevard de la Libération), of the lycées (Henri IV, Turgot, Pasteur, Guizot, Mallarmé), the national ceremonies (14 July, 11 November, 25 August, 18 June) and the whole paraphernalia of official ceremony and decoration, serve to embroider a powerful historical sense.

Guizot remembered that his mother knelt and prayed when she heard of the death of Robespierre; countless thousands read about the days when a little man in a green-grey coat led French soldiers halfway around the world; General de Gaulle's mother recalled her parents weeping when they learned that Bazaine had capitulated; the streets of Paris are adorned with plaques to mark the places where men died fighting against the Germans in the Liberation. Every occasion in France calls forth its historical analogy. Revolutionaries think of barricades and the Commune; organizers of movements think of the Estates-General; instances of tyranny arouse references to 2 December and Napoleon III; injustice conjures up the formidable name of Dreyfus. In 1947 at a time of great social crisis, to protest against the government's anti-strike measures, the communist paper *l'Humanité* came out with a headline saying that it was worse than Charles X (*'Pire que les lois de Charles X'*, a reference to the ordinances that sparked off the revolution of 1830).

France may not have a cultural hero such as Shakespeare or Dante or Tolstoy, but it is possible to find a number of political heroes, such as Joan of Arc, Louis XIV, Robespierre, Napoleon, Jaurès, Pétain. The cult of Joan of Arc has varied according to the fortunes of France; it seems to be in moments of defeat, after 1870 or 1940, that recourse is made to her. It has been suggested that often the hero is associated with some particular virtue, such as the purity of Joan of Arc (or the simplicity of the peasant girl, as Jaurès preferred to see it), the organizing ability of Napoleon, the cheerfulness of Joffre.[5] It is interesting to note that the greatest success in children's books in the last few years is the Astérix series about the Gauls and their resistance to the Romans.[6] General de Gaulle not only reflects these sentiments ('nothing struck me more than the symbols of our glories; night falling over Notre Dame, the majesty of evening at Versailles, the Arc de Triomphe in the sun, conquered colours shuddering in the vaults of the Invalides')[7] but he has reinforced them as he makes a point of saluting the statue of Clemenceau in the Champs Elysées and as André Malraux cleans and restores the historical monuments of Paris.

If Emile Zola was struck by the uniqueness of the English language in spelling the personal pronoun as a capital letter, so one can notice the frequent use, in French, of *'la France'*. When Winston Churchill broadcast that Germany had surrendered and that the war in Europe was over, he concluded with the words, 'Forward Britannia! Long live liberty! God save the King!' This was quite exceptional in English. But few French statesman would make a speech of any significance without saying *'Vive la France!'* Debates in the Assembly are filled with references to whether *'La France'* can do this or that. When Bazaine was on trial and accused of treason, he defended himself by saying that there was no regularly constituted government to obey, but the president of the court replied, 'There was France' (*'Il y avait la France'*). One of the most moving stories by Daudet tells the story of the school in Alsace which is about to be taken over by the Germans, and the schoolmaster gives the last lesson in French. At the end, he takes a piece of chalk and with all his strength he writes on the blackboard, 'Vive la France!' There is not an official speech made at a funeral, but what the orator assures the bereaved that it is not only they who mourn, 'mais c'est la France . . .' It is said that when Madame de Pompadour was in bed with Louis XV she called him France.

Of course, this attitude to the past has not always been so enthusiastic. There have always been those for whom the *monument aux morts* is simply a monstrosity and who would sing with Georges Brassens,

> *En dépit de ces souvenirs qu'on commémor'*
> *Des flammes qu'on ranime aux monuments aux morts*
> *Des vainqueurs des vaincus des autres et de vous*
> *Révérence parler tout le monde s'en fout.*

They are filled with shame rather than with pride at the name of Verdun and they would rather the war had not taken place at all or that it had not been directed by incompetent generals. Within the patriotism of the governing class there is always the hope of decoration or of promotion, no matter how bad the situation (in Courteline's play *Les Ronds de Cuir*, when a civil servant finds the murdered body of one of his colleagues, his immediate reaction is to apply for the murdered man's job). This incentive to patriotism has always been lacking amongst peasants and workers. It is not uncommon for them to see the glories of France as so many sacrifices that they have made with their blood and so much of their money that has been spent.

But often, whilst rejecting this aspect of a common heritage, Frenchmen have another ideal. If they are thinking in terms of humanity, for example in terms of the ordinary people of Europe trying to find some organization which will free them from the menace of wars ('à la piétaille des humbles Européens manque toujours sa patrie', as one of them has said),[8] it is customary for them to think of France as having some special role to play in striving for these great achievements. They think of French culture and French intelligence as having a particular relevance. Sometimes they are most sensitive to the importance of the French language and they show concern lest it should be penetrated by foreign words and phrases, seeing in this the degradation of a language which they think has had a great influence on universal culture, and fearing that the 'esprit de création' of the French will be affected.[9]

The French, then, are made up of different groups, as are all peoples, but they possess a particular sense of the past, even if they reject or adapt it. The past is often dramatic, because France has lived dangerously; and living with that past, the French continue to play their parts.

The French who developed this historical sense were a relatively declining population. From the end of the eighteenth century to 1945 the population of France grew from 27 millions to 47 millions, whilst the population of Europe as a whole had tripled. In 1800 15 per cent of Europe's population were French, in 1950 less than 8 per cent. In France, as in all European countries at this time, there was a movement to the towns, but in France the movement was particularly slow. The Revolution of 1789 affirmed peasant property, industry developed only slowly, the losses of the 1914 war were felt on the land and the economic crisis of the 1930's discouraged movement to towns. Hence on the eve of the 1939 war there were still slightly more French workers engaged in the primary sector of agriculture, forests and fishing than in the secondary sector of industry or the tertiary sector of services and liberal professions. With the notable exception of Paris, towns tended to remain small and only grew in regions where there was an obvious economic incentive, such as the coalfields of the north, the steel-producing region of the east, or the Lyons region where a variety of industrial, agricultural and commercial activities were brought together.

Often the towns did not develop, and continued without much change their former artisan or marketing functions. The countryside often remained unchanged from the days of Louis-Philippe, when Balzac said it looked like 'a tailor's pattern card'. Those who had gone to the towns maintained their contacts with the countryside and always carried within them much of their province. They remained close to the world of the peasant and to a peasant mentality. As the peasant feared for his crop, and spent his life, as the saying was, denying himself things so that he could eat after he was dead, so the worker feared his employer and the manufacturer feared competition and revolution, and so everyone came to fear German invasion. Distrustful of each other, dependent on the government, yet at the same time resentful of its demands, the French became an elderly population facing the future with apprehension. Generation followed closely on generation and carried on the preoccupations of its predecessor.

It is customary to suggest that since the end of the last war the French have changed (some would put the change as occurring a little earlier or a little later). And it is claimed that they have changed because the situation in which they find themselves has changed. The birth-rate has gone up, the mortality rate has declined and immigration has been high. Consequently the French population has increased more in the seventeen years from 1946 to 1963 than it did during the preceding century—from 40,503,000 to 47,573,000. It now stands at over 50 millions and the rate of increase remains high. This change has come too late to modify the large proportion of elderly people in the population (in 1971 it is estimated that this will be 13 per cent), but it has already produced an increasing number of young people (it is estimated that in 1971, 40 per cent of the population will be under the age of 21). The movement from countryside to town has accelerated. Whereas between 1900 and 1914 something like 40,000 men and women were leaving agriculture every year, in the immediate post-war years it was 80,000 to 90,000; since then the movement has become even more intense. There were 4,300,000 *agriculteurs actifs* on the land when de Gaulle came to power; by 1967 there were 3,200,000; by 1970 another 600,000 will have left.[10] In 1900, 30 per cent of the population lived in communes of less than 1,000 inhabitants; now almost a quarter of the population lives in towns of more than 100,000.

It is easy to say that as the urbanized Frenchman moves further and further away from his peasant background and mentality, the old mistrusts become out of place. There is no reason why the

France of the Caravelle, the Citroen DS and ID, the tidal generator of the Rance, the pipelines of the Sahara, the nuclear power stations, the modern railways and a thousand other technical masterpieces should face the future with apprehension. The French of the Ecole Nationale d'Administration, of the Plan, of the living quarters of the *Grands Ensembles*, with their *résidences secondaires*[11] and their national institution of holidays, do not know the unease of their ancestors. One English writer has already expressed the fear that the French are becoming 'less French',[12] and as a careful plan is worked out to take industry and various sorts of activity into the provinces, as towns like Grenoble, Toulouse, Rennes, Amiens, become lively, prosperous cities with teeming universities and dynamic municipalities, one wonders where is the relevance of the old historical culture? The *monument aux morts*, it is said, can have no place as a symbol and the muddy massacres of 1914 can mean no more to the generations of today, less dependent on their parents for their culture, than the names of Magenta and Solférino. The *Uhlans* of 1870, the *Boches* of 1914 and the *occupants* of 1940 are all equally distant and replaced by the tourists of the 1960's. Just as the historical and informative names of the Paris telephone exchange (Gounod, Chénier, Balzac . . .) have been replaced by mere numbers, some would have it that the effort of national identification through history is now otiose and the French are part of the new, mass society.

R. H. Tawney once said that in a country where the social organization is as tough and tradition as powerful as in England, 'national habits are not altered even by an earthquake'.[13] The same might be true for France. The transformation might not be as great as some would have us believe. Many of the French continue to live in small towns, many of which are really only large villages. In spite of being prefectures or sub-prefectures, or having various commercial functions, they retain the old rhythm of the countryside, the old somnolence of the provinces, in some respects even the old mistrust of the outsider. In terms of politics, culture, social structures, one wonders whether there has been much change.

In spite of the entertainment value of the cinema, the radio and the television, it is striking to see the old ambulatory circus and fairground coming into these small towns and functioning as usual. The need to attract tourists causes every municipality to hang on to what is old and picturesque, and to emphasize rural quaintness rather than progress and activity. In spite of what sociologists like to call *le take-off consommationniste* and 'contemporaneism', the improvement of means of communication and the broadened access to the world outside, there is little revolutionary change in mentality. It is as if the upshot of it all has been the steady *embourgeoisement* of new areas of society. The bourgeois ideals, the family, the demand for privacy, the children's desire to imitate their parents and to share the same achievements, all persist. It is as if the whole population has become characters in a bourgeois novel. And we know that it is easy for the new men of the towns, the men who think only in terms of efficiency, themselves to become immersed and conservative in their own preoccupations, which are sometimes not so different from the small-town politics they are replacing.[14]

One of the characteristics of traditional France was the predominance of Paris. Gravier's famous book, *Paris et le désert français*, first published in 1947, was an important influence in suggesting that the political and economic stagnation of France was due to the way in which Paris sucked the life-blood of the rest of France. Although the 1968 statistics suggest that the growth of the Paris region has been less than was anticipated, nevertheless the population of the region has gone up from 8,400,000 to 9,500,000, nearly a fifth of the whole population of the country. People talk of it having a population of 14,000,000 in the year 2000. In spite of great efforts (or perhaps because of a mistaken approach, for it has been said the process of decentralization has itself been centralized), Paris remains a concentration of the wealth, skills and powers of France, and when the Fifth Plan was under discussion, the provinces protested that they were only given what Paris had left—the familiar complaint of the old days.[15] This long continuity of development is possibly the explanation for the phenomenon which the geographer Demangeon saw in the 1930's and which the urban historian Chevalier claims to see today: namely that in spite of all the very real variety of Paris life, there is a unity which one can call the Parisians, fitting into an urban personality, living lives that resemble the lives of past generations of Parisians.[16]

Perhaps the most notable characteristic of the French as they were seen traditionally was their diversity. It was for this reason that they were a difficult people to govern. Now the talk of mass society would suggest that all these diversities had been ironed out, perhaps into a sleek sheen of prosperity. But it seems that the changes that have taken place have increased and complicated this diversity. Perhaps they have increased, for example, the contrasts between those areas of France that are dynamic and those that are static. It is said that Gravier should now write new books, *Toulouse et le désert méridional* and *Bordeaux et le désert aquitain*, since the developments of these towns have impoverished areas not far distant from them. The migra- tion of labour from the countryside has meant that whole areas are condemned to poverty, areas where only the old live. The process of migration represents a movement of suffering however logical it may be to the planner. There remain large areas of peasant poverty, such as the south side of the Massif Central, a great part of Brittany, the Pyrenees, parts of Lorraine, Champagne and Franche- Comté, the Morvan near to Burgundy. Perhaps sociologists are too fascinated by the presence of television sets (which in any case are rare in these areas). Even although a gleaming set may stand on an old wooden table, near to the fading picture of the grandfather killed at Verdun, the life remains primitive and hard, the sense of alienation probably increased by this communication with the different world that lies outside. Those who stay on the land will increasingly organize themselves so as to defend their interests, faced as they are with the rival dangers of low productivity (for some of the small, under-capitalized farmers) and excess production in almost every form of crop.

This rural poverty is matched by the poverty of perhaps two million workers who live on the minimum wage, which is fixed by the gov- ernment and which in 1968 could be calculated as the equivalent of about forty pounds a month. There are the old, who have one of the lowest pensions in western Europe. There are the small shop- keepers, who have been driven out of business by the big stores.

There are those who are badly housed or not housed at all, living in shanty-towns or muddy lots of waste ground. All this is *La France pauvre*, and it adds up to a great many human beings.[17] The French social security scheme has the advantage over the British system that it allows greater freedom in visiting doctors and consulting specialists. But it is a bourgeois advantage. The doctor has to be paid. Only afterwards can one be re-imbursed (up to 80 per cent, or conceivably more) and an enquiry has shown that in one research group, 39 per cent of those questioned claimed to have been at some time unable to call a doctor because they could not pay him.[18]

Those who are housed in the *Grands Ensembles*, places like Sarcelles or Massy-Antony in the Paris region, great monstrosities of 'new suburbs' rather than 'new towns', have become one of the favourite preoccupations of the sociologists. They find the sort of complaints that are common to all re-housing schemes, and they find inadequacies of planning, mistakes, and shortcomings which are partly to be explained by lack of resources. But it is interesting to see how often the complaint is of boredom (this particularly applies to the women; '*Madame Bovary dans les grands ensembles*' is a frequent suggestion) and of being cut off from a sense of the past. The absence of a church or of a cemetery (possibly of a *monument aux morts*?) seems to symbolize this, just as the absence of any boulevard for idle strolling on a Sunday or in the evening, or the absence of the traditional-style cafés, means a real and resented cessation of a necessary social activity. It seems that those who bring with them some element of a traditional culture, such as Catholicism or left-wing politics, can develop or intensify this culture, and it is in this way that they can adapt themselves.[19] However, the Frenchman's ideal lies a long way from the Grand Ensemble, or the great blocks of municipal flats. The popularity of the *pavillon*, the small house, sometimes extraordinarily small, and tiny garden, seems to extend to everyone (except architects) and one has only to look at the advertisement columns of newspapers to see how this inter-war trend continues. It is sometimes given a rather sentimental name, Sam Suffi (meaning *ça me suffit*, that is enough), Papachou, Douce France, Eden, Escale, Le Calme, Relaxe, Wigwam (although names of provinces are also to be found, such as Alsace, le Pays d'Artois, and many Breton names) and it is not uncommon for it to be patrolled by a dog.

It is widely believed that differences between the classes are less marked in France than in England. This is because the French aristocracy, while still in existence, plays no political role and has only a restricted social importance. The absence of any British-type public-school system or private university foundations reduces (at least in theory) the avenues of privilege, and children of different social classes rub shoulders in the lycées and faculties. Perhaps most important of all for the casual English observer, a country which has known innumerable politicians with heavy southern accents cannot have the notorious British concern with the social implications of accent. The ubiquity of the café, an open and outward-looking place, means that the more closed systems of hotel lounges, or public houses with different bars and prices, or country clubs, cannot prevent a natural mingling of social groups.

All this is true enough, and the changes that are taking place, the decline of the rural notabilities, and the fact that different classes see the same television programmes and tend to dress in similar ways, all ought to make for a greater social egalitarianism. But it is not true that France had such a striking social equality in the past, and all observers are agreed that within the competition of the consumer society, many of the old frontiers are being reinforced. There is no equality of opportunity and although it is difficult to get up-to-date figures, it used to be said that the son of a higher civil servant had eighty times more chance of entering a university than the son of an agricultural worker, forty times more than the son of an industrial worker and twice as good a chance as the son of a middle-grade civil servant. In terms of class consciousness, of belief in future prospects, marriage, culture or even many of the items of current consumption such as cameras and record-players, one can see complicated patterns of class differences emerging.[20]

One of the great fears of some Frenchmen has for long been the fear of being dominated by American culture. To some extent this fear has been modified by the British pop invasion. To the long-standing enthusiasm for American films (and often for American stars who seemed particularly un-French) was added the impact of endless American television serials and the pop music of the powerful Anglo-American industry. But in spite of this the French pop song seems to have retained a great deal of traditional French qualities, and these traditions have been powerful enough to have dominated the many non-French stars who have made a success in France (like Jacques Brel, Adamo, the singing nun Luc Dominique, Dalida, Petula Clarke).

French songs have traditionally reflected something of what was going on in French life. In the days of the Popular Front, the songs of Charles Trenet, with their emphasis on the open air, blue skies and freedom, expressed some of the exhilaration of the holidays-with-pay achievement; after 1945 the songs of Yves Montand reflected much of the period, songs about industrial workers, about suburbs or about memories of the resistance. More recently Enrico Macias (from Oran) has sung about the feelings of the Algerian settlers who have come to live in France ('*Non, je n'ai pas oublié*'); Jean Ferrat sings about the agricultural workers and their emigration to Lyons or Valence ('*La Montagne*'); Antoine had a song which mentioned the pill at a time when many French people were becoming 'pill-conscious' ('*Contre-Elucubrations problématiques*'); Richard Antony sang about the war in Vietnam, and there have been innumerable songs about the *mauvais garçons* who, under different names, have been so prominent in France (Johnny Halliday is perhaps the best-known singer of this type of song).

But at the same time as there is this traditional topicality, many of the songs could have been composed many years ago. Often to traditional accompaniment, the same old images of skies, flowers, countryside, peace, dreams, Paris (at any hour of the day or night) jostle with the same old rhymes (*rêver/trouver/pensée/aimée*; *nuit/pluie/Paris*; *enfance/chance/silence/dimanche*; *toujours/amour/jour,* and a song of Adamo's even adds *troubadour*). English songs when translated, as many of them are, take on a particularly French quality. Paul McCartney's 'Those were the days' becomes '*C'était le temps des fleurs*. And with all this rather simple, and some would say bad poetry, there is the influence of a genuine poetic tradition, Léo Ferré sings Aragon's poetry, and two genuine popular poets. Brassens and Prévert, have had a considerable influence. Often pop songs in France have more than a touch of surrealism about them (as Charles Trenet's used to have before the war) and there is sometimes an anti-bourgeois touch (as in several of Brassens' songs, 'Bancs publiques' for example). The humour can be quite sophisticated. The song 'Mini-mini-mini' sung by Jacques Dutronc contains the line 'C'est mini Dr Schweitzer', a reference to a not very well-known play, 'C'est minuit Dr Schweitzer'.[21]

Perhaps it is appropriate that the French pop world seems to be a world of individual stars rather than one of groups. This would fit in with the old adage about the Frenchman being an individualist. It is not unlike the attitude to the cycling race, the Tour de France, which used to arouse enormous enthusiasm, and where it was not the team that counted in the public eye so much as the individual rider. And often it was not the best rider who aroused the most interest. The public could grow tired of the skilful Louison Bobet, and showed an interest in riders who had particular characteristics. There was Robic, who was hard and difficult, Hassenforder who was eccentric, Fachleitner who was from the south and unpredictable, Koblet, 'le pédaleur de charme', and Abd el Kader Zaaf, who earned an undying fame because he once helped himself too liberally to white wine during a race.

Part of a Frenchman's historical sense lies in his awareness of his culture, his conviction (or even assumption) that this culture is superior to any other. So there is often a sense of shame about television. It is said that someone from the upper classes will invariably specify, when asked about television, that he watches it with discrimination.[22] Others complain that the popularity of the games where one can either win or lose money is the translation of the peasant mentality to the screen, and others express their sense of shame when they have to notice the popular success of some particularly vulgar comedy.[23] So it is particularly interesting to note that the spread of television has been accompanied by the policy of the *Maison de Culture*. Very much the concern of André Malraux, these institutions are meant to carry both traditional and modern culture to the ordinary people, especially outside Paris. The MDC are the joint responsibility of government and municipality and they have always aroused controversy. They have had a slow beginning, since only a handful have been built (although a hundred were originally planned) and many of them have run short of both money and of municipal good will.

But the real problem of trying to integrate society and the creative and intellectual culture which most of the directors of the MDC admire, is that in France there is a traditional gulf between intellectu-als and the public. This is all the more curious because French intellectuals have frequently seen themselves as playing a public role, either as the conscience of the public or as its pedagogue. Writers such as Sartre and Camus used a variety of means of expres-sion in order to get at the public; they wrote plays, novels, articles, and in the case of Sartre, films and political speeches as well. But they are always intellectuals, a class apart. They are always conscious of the distance that separates *les intellectuels* from other groups, and they are sometimes rather satisfied that this separation should be there. The attitude of the intellectuals will never coincide entirely with the attitude of other social and political organizations. Further-more, during the nineteen-sixties what one can call the *avant-garde* culture withdrew increasingly into abstract theories and into an overwhelming apprehension of anguish. The new novel, the new cinema, the new theatre, all stressed confusion, transience, incomplete-ness. In a world which is neither sympathetic nor absurd, but which is simply there, the mind seeks to catalogue the objects of the geometrical landscape.[24]

It is not surprising that there should be little contact between such preciosity and any but a small minority of French society. Even more were the theories of structuralism, which a number of intellectuals were formulating at the same time, beyond the under-standing of most. After all, bourgeois Parisians go to plays which deliberately seek to shock them by a display of sexual violence and perversity, and are apparently unaffected by them. There is a French tradition that culture is complementary to life as well as being the expression of it, and in cultural life, as elsewhere, one sees the success, ful compartmentalization of affairs.

But there are attempts being made to achieve contact between the different categories, and the Maisons de Culture have to be seen as part of these attempts, as is the present intellectual concentration on the social sciences and on communications. It comes as a shock to many to realize that France is so badly equipped with public lib, raries, that some 57 per cent of the population allegedly never open a book and that the number of illiterates called up to the forces is increasing.[25] But perhaps it is on the popular level that one can see most clearly the desire for contact and for communication. Perhaps the cult of the holiday is an example of this. This cult, or obsession, is long,standing and popular songs about Sundays and about the annual trip to the country and seaside are numerous. With the French one has the impression that this is more than the usual modern concern with leisure. It seems to represent the need to escape, or apparently to escape, from the constrictions of ordinary society. The French form themselves temporarily into a new community.

Perhaps one can see something of the same tendency in the vogue of the *tiercé*. Here, in order to win money, one has to pick the first three horses in a designated race, usually run on a Sunday. The bets are placed in specially licensed cafés and both this process and the discussion of the results are great occasions of 'togetherness'. Again, momentarily this time, a new society is created. Perhaps one of the reasons for the decline in the popularity of the Tour de France (although there are many other reasons) is that the Tour itself came to the different towns and villages. The present wish is for the audi, ence to move, to re,group and to participate.[26]

There is also the extraordinary sentimentalism of many popular papers and magazines. That the cyclist Walkowiack should have promised his father, a working man, that he would never have to work again if he won the Tour de France, seemed unbelievably fine. But when it was rumoured that Johnny Halliday had behaved badly towards his father, then his popularity seemed to suffer a momentary eclipse. People sought in other people's behaviour a sign of a world where everyone was good. Perhaps the interest in other countries' royal families suggests a hankering after a different order of society.

There are three means whereby most societies are held together—religious, political, and administrative. In contemporary France all three seem inadequate.

It is said that 94 per cent of French people are baptized into the Catholic church and that about 30 per cent of French adults perform their religious observances at Easter. But these figures vary geographically, certain regions, such as the west, the mountainous regions and the north being more religious than others. The figures vary socially too, since the working classes are less religious than the more bourgeois sectors. Then, in whatever class, women attend church more regularly and in greater numbers than men. The Catholic Church therefore affects only a portion of the population. Others continue to regard it as a divisive and bad influence. Although the Catholic Church has been proving its powers of adaptation in a striking way, it would be a bold man who would say that religious quarrels are things of the past and that the 1959 law, which enables public money to be spent on Catholic schools (which educate 18 per cent of the population) will not become the subject of further controversy.

French participation in political activity tends to be low. An important section of the population does not bother to apply for an electoral card and is not on the electoral lists; in 1958 these could have numbered between two and a half and three millions. Of those who can vote in elections, there are always a great many who abstain; in parliamentary elections between a third and a quarter, in municipal elections probably more. The number of people who are members of a political party is very low. The communists, the largest party in this respect, once claimed to have 400,000 members, but this figure has almost certainly dropped. It is thought that only about one-fifth of the industrial workers are members of trade unions, although peasant farmers and agricultural workers have probably a more than 50 per cent membership of their various organizations.

Administratively speaking, France is a centralized state, and the jacobin and bonapartist tradition of an army of officials covering the country, ultimately responsible to the central government, remains constant. Ever since Tocqueville it has been assumed that political instability should be balanced by administrative stability. But out of 38,000 communes (the smallest and basic unit of the administrative system) 24,000 have fewer than 500 inhabitants. Many of them are deserted and there have been cases of *mairies* being used as *résidences secondaires*. The department is also thought to be too small, and in economic terms meaningless. The whole process of administration seemed to become impossibly complicated and ineffective. In 1964, the 95 departments were grouped into 21 regions. Everywhere there was the realization that further reform was necessary. But if one removed this framework of administration, these vertebrae, what then would hold the French together?

There is thus an awareness of change, and there is a consciousness of new uncertainties. But change is not all-pervading. As is usually the case with France, there is much that is constant; new elements are added, but the old features remain. In 1944, when the war was still on, General de Gaulle met his old rival from the days of Algiers, General Giraud. 'How things have changed,' remarked Giraud. De Gaulle agreed that things had changed, but looking at the people, he doubted whether the French had changed (*'je doutais que ce fût le cas pour les Français'*).[27]

15   Revolution again

Tous les régimes basés sur un pouvoir personnel finissent toujours mal. Celui-ci n'échappera pas à la règle.   Pierre Mendès-France

THE EVENTS OF 1968 came as a shock to most people. That they should have come as a surprise to the government is not unexpected. The government was never particularly well-informed, and never showed much ability to co-ordinate its activities once the surprise had been assimilated. The would-be putsch of the generals in Algiers in 1961, like the strength of the opposition to de Gaulle in the presidential elections of 1965, were incidents which caught the government unprepared, and in the case of the first at least, some members of the government were uncomfortably near to panic. Doubtless this is a sign of the extent to which the government was distant from public opinion, or a confirmation of M. Mitterrand's argument that a one-man government was bound to be inadequate. But it is surprising that this crisis should have come as a shock to all observers. One of the most acute of them, Viansson-Ponté of *Le Monde*, had even written that France was bored.

In fact, the crisis of the régime was evident for everyone to see. Politically speaking, the government was still with the disappointing election results of 1967. The Chamber then elected had always had 'a vocation to be dissolved' (as General de Gaulle later put it), but he could not dissolve it before March 1968. In the meantime there was a good deal of unease among Gaullists. Those of the left regretted that there were not more social measures and pointed out that M. Pompidou's promise that important social reforms would be instituted once France had become a completely prosperous country was like saying that justice would reign only when justice was reigning. It was the politics of Ubu-roi. And a more conservative section of the Gaullists regretted that there was still a great deal of state control and interference, which, together with high taxation, kept the economy from progressing. They looked more sympathetic-ally towards the independent Gaullists and Giscard d'Estaing, whose small group's political importance had been increased by the government's need for its votes, and who seemed to presage an even-tual split amongst the Gaullists.[1] And behind all these political disputes, with everyone searching for a possible majority, there lay two considerable sources of disquiet: the one institutional, since all the questions which had been opened by the new nature of presiden-tial elections remained unsolved; and the other personal, since more and more the problem of 'après-Gaullisme' appeared, and the possible successors to de Gaulle viewed each other in the light of this eventual competition. Pompidou, Debré and Giscard d'Estaing were the front candidates but there must have been others who thought that the future held possibilities for them.

The whole political outlook became more uncertain when the deputy from Polynesia withdrew from the UNR (because the govern-ment was not giving him satisfaction in their attitude towards Poly-nesia). With two other deputies who had been counted in the major-ity but who were potential dissidents, the government lost its over-all majority. The dispute between Pompidou and Giscard d'Estaing made the possibility of a government defeat all the more real and there were a good many rumours in circulation. It was widely reported that whatever happened de Gaulle would never accept communists in the government, and there were hints of illegality. M. Christian Fouchet had been moved to the Ministry of the Interior and it was thought that he was all set to play a 'strong man' role. People began to ask themselves whether, with or without de Gaulle still at the Presidency, the Gaullists would accept a vote in the Assembly and simply hand over power to the next government just as M. Laniel did in the days of the Fourth Republic. Even without a govern-ment defeat, there was the fear that the government could find itself paralysed.[2]

An attack on the communists had been expected, since the election of 1967 suggested that they had become too respectable (possibly as a result of de Gaulle's own eastern European policies) and that people had been too ready to vote for them.[3] Although all observers had stressed the continuing and fundamental differences that existed between the communists and the Federation,[4] the beginning of 1968 saw an extension of their co-operation into a very restrained joint programme. Communist strength, especially in the Paris region, had been re-affirmed in local elections (the election to the *conseils-généraux* of each department) in November 1967.

Thus with the public-opinion polls showing in favour of M. Mitterrand's popularity, and with continued uncertainty about General de Gaulle's personal intentions (a common story going about was that he had accepted to be a candidate in 1965 on the understanding that he would remain in office for two or three years only), the political climate was at best speculative, at worst morose. The government did not assist its own cause by the somewhat brutal manner in which it presented its budget, reduced the value of social-security benefits and introduced a scheme to bring in advertising on the national radio and television networks. Nor was the economic climate encouraging. There was a steady rise in unemployment, and by the end of January the figure of half a million out of work was being quoted (whereas 380,000 had been given in October). Domestic consumer demand remained low, trade to the other member countries of EEC fell (except to Italy), investment within France was sluggish, and in general terms there was the impression that French economic development was almost grinding to a halt. It was in this sphere that Giscard d'Estaing was able to be most critical, and it must have been partly to forestall him, as well as being worried by stagnation, that the Finance Minister, M. Debré, introduced a series of measures to stimulate economic recovery. These measures of January 1968, which included a reduction of taxation and an increase in some social benefits, and which made available additional credits for housing and for industrial expansion in certain areas, were to be supplemented by further reflationary measures in June should they prove inadequate.

It was thought typical of de Gaulle's republic that the one area where economic strength was undeniable was that of the gold and foreign exchange reserves. Not everyone thought that such a sizeable part of French wealth should consist of ammunition for the General's expected onslaught on the dollar and the world monetary system. One of the most notable publications of 1967 was Jean-Jacques Servan-Schreiber's *Le Défi Américain*, which became a best-seller, with the biggest sales of any French book since the war.[5] The argument put forward was that American investment in Europe was proceeding at such a rate that Europe was threatened with something like colonial status. And de Gaulle's famed anti-Americanism was shown by this book to be an irrelevance. The Americans were able to dominate, not because of the power of the dollar (90 per cent of the needed capital was raised in Europe) but because they have the ability to organize production and technology. It was in these fields that de Gaulle's contribution was said to be harmful rather than helpful. To withstand the American challenge it was necessary to have a federated Europe, including England, which would be able to proceed to an economic and technological expansion comparable to that of the Americans. It was precisely this Europe which de Gaulle was opposing.

In all these ways therefore, if it is not correct to speak about a crisis in France, by the end of 1967 and the beginning of 1968 there was certainly a long-standing and profound malaise. And nowhere was this more acutely felt than in the French universities, where the malaise was the equivalent to a crisis. By the beginning of the academic year there were over 500,000 students in the different French faculties, almost double the numbers that had existed in 1962. And although these numbers had been expected by the Fifth Plan, their unequal distribution had not been foreseen. Faculties of Law (where economics and social science are taught) and Arts had increases of 33 per cent and 30 per cent respectively over the preceding year, whereas there was only a 12 per cent increase in the Faculties of Science. This disproportion aggravated for Law and Arts the already desperate situation with regard to teachers and buildings. The Sorbonne, which had 40,000 students, had asked for

390 new teaching posts but had been allotted only 72, and similar examples could be given throughout the country. Many universities both in Paris and in the provinces had no new buildings to accommodate the increased numbers.

Perhaps the gravest aspects of the situation were underlined by a number of commentaries made at the 'rentrée' of October 1967, including a press conference by the minister, M. Peyrefitte.[6] One was the small number of students who would actually succeed in passing all their examinations. Of those who were hoping to take the preparatory certificate in medicine, only 50 per cent would pass and would be allowed to proceed to the first year of a medical course, and again only half would be expected to pass their first-year examination. Of all students in their first year only 25 per cent could be certain of completing their course successfully. And when they had completed the course, there was a problem of employment. An increasing number of students, especially from the Faculties of Law and Arts, found that there was no way for them to use the subject which they had studied. And the minister made it clear that in his opinion there were two necessary reforms. The one was to impose some control on university entry, and make it more difficult for people to enter university. The other was profoundly to alter the whole structure of university teaching, so as to get better results. (And it could be added here that the shortage of university teachers was not merely the result of government parsimony, it was also because there were not enough people equipping themselves with the degrees that were thought necessary. The usual one for a non-professor was the *agrégation*, which was a competitive examination, the numbers passing being deliberately kept low, and the usual qualification for a professor was the *doctorat d'état*, a mighty piece of research which necessarily took many years to complete.)

But the minister did not speak in any more precise terms. On the subject of a selection system limiting university entrance he merely asked the university authorities to reflect and declared that the debate was open. Therefore, the worst form of crisis was developing, in which conditions were intolerable for everyone, in which the whole university structure was officially called into question, and in which the government was not giving any clear leadership. Some university authorities, who had for years been complaining about the inadequacies of official policies and who had chafed at their own powerlessness, since all decisions were taken by the ministry in Paris, gave signs of being rebellious when they refused to admit any more students, putting a ban on new admissions.

It was not surprising that this sense of crisis was shared by the student body. French students had been politicized for a long time, having been concerned with the Algerian war and with compulsory military service, and having always had a number of organizations which fought for their scholarships and for particular student rights. In 1967 and 1968 these student organizations assumed greater importance. They were reinforced by being part of an international movement of protest, youth throughout the world protesting about Vietnam, atomic weapons and the many injustices of the capitalist system; but within France itself they were spectacularly reinforced by the political system's lack of effectiveness. An organized group is always more powerful when the society within which it operates is losing its sense of coherence and purpose. This was the case in France.

It was in this atmosphere that a series of student protests made their mark. There were manifestations for the right of men and women students to visit each other in their hostels ('la mixité' was the battle-cry); there were demonstrations against inadequate material and against teaching methods, taking the forms of strikes and sit-ins; there were brawls with right-wing students as the left wing became more prominent and insisted on giving a more prominent place in university life to the class struggle and to the particular heroes of the moment, Che Guevara and Régis Debray; there was a rejection of some of the most sacred parts of the system, namely the examinations. Twice the new university in the suburbs of Paris, the Sorbonne-Nanterre, had to be closed. On 3 May a big demonstration in the Sorbonne itself was broken up by police and over 500 students were arrested. This was the start of the real crisis.

The revolution of 1968, or 'les événements de mai-juin' as others prefer to call it (as there used to be historians who refused to call the

English revolution of 1640 a revolution but insisted on the term 'rebellion'), can be studied in three phases. There was firstly the student phase. This movement was able to gain force, both in Paris and in the provinces, because it now had a number of precise aims: the withdrawal of the police from the Latin Quarter, the re-opening of the Sorbonne and the release of the arrested prisoners. The brutality with which the police used their truncheons and tear-gas aroused public sympathy for the students, both from the bourgeois elements of the population, who saw their sons and daughters being shamefully treated, and from the workers, who usually detested the police anyway. The minister for Education failed to grasp what was happening and he made no impact at all when he claimed that the disorders came from a small minority, since he could not then justify the continued closure of the Sorbonne, which he insisted on keeping closed in spite of some conciliatory moves by the Rector. In the absence of the Prime Minister, who was in Afghanistan, there was no other government spokesman, and opposition leaders (however uncertain they were about student violence) attacked the government's incompetence.

The student movement reached a climax on the night of Friday 10 May. Supported by the younger population of the *lycées* and by a proportion of teachers, encouraged by signs that the government was weakening, the students constructed barricades and in the early hours of the morning fought a pitched battle with the police. After a struggle of extraordinary ferocity, by 6 a.m. nearly 400 students and police had been wounded, and uncounted hundreds of students were having their wounds treated by their own organizations and by the public. Parts of the Latin Quarter looked exactly like a battlefield. Hundreds of cars had been destroyed or badly damaged, but the destruction to property did not shock opinion as much as the spectacle of police violence and government ineptitude.

And it was clearly a battle which was about to recommence and to spread. On the Saturday students occupied the Sorbonne Faculty of Arts annexe at Censier, the students of Strasbourg occupied their university and claimed that it was autonomous, and the trade-union leaders called for a strike and demonstration on the following

Monday, 13 May. It was said that 13 May 1968 would be more significant in French history than 13 May 1958.

The return of the Prime Minister saw an immediate attempt to stop this movement. Within a short time of his arrival, he broadcast to the nation and accepted all the student demands. He also arranged that the manifestation of 13 May would not be subjected to any interference by the police. This intervention brought about a remarkable change of atmosphere, and it was almost in a mood of *kermesse* that some 800,000 demonstrated on the Monday. There was no violence even when, at the end of the demonstration, the students occupied the Sorbonne. Nor was there any violence when, two days later, they occupied the Odéon theatre (also in the Latin Quarter). The student movement had passed from action to discussion and had become *'une fête verbale'*. General de Gaulle left Paris on 14 May for an official visit to Romania. M. Pompidou said that he understood the anguish of modern youth and referred to a 'crisis of civilization'.

The second phase of this movement began almost immediately General de Gaulle had left. On 14 May a number of workers occupied the factory of SudAviation in Rennes. At the same time workmen struck at the Renault factory at Cléon, near Rouen, and when they found that they could not persuade all the workers to join them, they brought production to a standstill by occupying the works. This strike spread to other Renault works at Flins and at BoulogneBillancourt in the Paris suburbs. Once again the technique of the lockin was used. Within a week more than nine million were on strike and the whole of France was paralysed. There was not a sector of French life which did not take part in the movement, from lawyers, doctors, undertakers and astronomers to theologians, footballers and dancers of the FoliesBergères. Everyone demanded more money and more say in the direction of affairs.

General de Gaulle cut short his stay in Romania and returned to Paris on Saturday 18 May, but whilst it was widely expected that he would address the nation, he did not do so. He was only reported as saying *'La réforme, oui; le chieenlit, non!'* ('Reform, yes; bedmessing, no!') and a broadcast which had already been arranged for the following Friday was not brought forward. A motion of censure had been posed and the Assembly was due to debate it on Wednesday. It was therefore normal for the President to await the result of the vote. But in reality the President was hoping to calm the situation, to impose his own rhythm on events. On the Tuesday, the Prime Minister started his attempts to organize a vast wage negotiation, accepting from the start a considerable series of increases.

But it was not easy. In radio discussion Giscard d'Estaing had spoken of the need for society to change, and Edgard Pisani, former minister of agriculture, had said that the student movement had had the virtue of posing fundamental problems which had to be discussed. The left-wing Gaullist, Capitant, had gone even further and had blamed the government for the troubles, and some of the most timid members of the UNR were protesting at the apparent inactivity of the government. One of them, René Caille, was to claim that there had to be a complete change in the manner and method of government. The censure motion was eventually defeated by 11 votes, several members of the Democratic Centre having decided to support the government, as did the followers of Giscard d'Estaing (the latter having made a somewhat waspish speech referring to Eliza Doolittle's desire to be treated better).[7] The atmosphere was not improved by a return of violence in the Latin Quarter, following the government's announcement that Daniel Cohn-Bendit, who figured as the leader of the student movement and who had gone to Germany, would not be allowed back in France. (Although born in France, Cohn-Bendit had German nationality.)

On Friday 24 May General de Gaulle made his long-awaited speech. But on this occasion it was a failure. Neither his appearance nor his message gave any comfort or inspiration. He announced that a referendum would be held, he asked for the government's economic and social reforms to be approved (and here he brought in the notion of participation, of profit-sharing and co-management of affairs, although in the vaguest way), and he said that if the referendum were not successful he would retire. An anonymous author wrote on the wall of the Sorbonne, 'it has taken him three weeks to tell us in five minutes that within a month he will do what he hasn't been able to do in ten years'. And in those parts of Paris where there was not bloodshed and it was possible to sing, the crowds sang 'Adieu de Gaulle'.[8]

The meeting with the unions and employers began the next day, Saturday 25 May, in the Ministry of Social Affairs, rue de Grenelle. The atmosphere was not good since the possibility of General de Gaulle's withdrawal from the scene was in everyone's mind, and therefore the question was asked, would any agreement signed with Pompidou be effective? But throughout a weekend of hard negotiations a draft agreement was hammered out. Questions of wages, the working week, allowances, retirement, old people's pensions, all these vital questions of workers' rights were arranged. This was the biggest agreement since the Liberation, and Pompidou was selfconsciously triumphant when he announced it to the nation early on the morning of Monday 27 May. But by midday the situation had been reversed. The rank and file of the unions, the strikers themselves, rejected the agreements. Conscious of their power, they looked to a political victory as well as to a series of social benefits. Both de Gaulle's speech and Pompidou's Grenelle agreements were failures.

On the Monday night a massive meeting was held at the Charléty Stadium in Paris. The only important political figure there was MendèsFrance. It seemed that in the confusion of strikes and student unrest a possible solution was the formation of a MendèsFrance government which would look after the transition from one régime to another. M. Mitterrand supported this idea, whilst insisting that he would be a candidate in the presidential elections. On the Wednesday the usual cabinet meeting was cancelled. General de Gaulle left Paris, supposedly to go to Colombeylesdeuxéglises for a quiet meditation. His failure to arrive there, since he had in fact gone to Mulhouse and to BadenBaden, aroused the greatest expectation. It was widely assumed that he would retire, and both MendèsFrance and Giscard d'Estaing saw themselves forming governments prior to new elections.

But it was not to be. At 4.30 on the afternoon of Thursday 30 May, speaking only on the sound radio and sounding determined and vigorous, General de Gaulle announced that he would not resign, nor would Pompidou. The referendum was cancelled and elections were to be held. Within a few minutes the communist party accepted this procedure. The idea of revolution slumped; only the students protested ('*Elections trahison*') together with the independent socialists. Revolution disappeared and was replaced by the normal constitutional procedure, which begins the third phase of the movement.

The electoral campaign opened in a most unusual situation. De Gaulle had denounced international communism as the danger that France was facing. Few people took this seriously. But the success with which a Gaullist demonstration was organized on the night of 30 May suggested that Gaullist organization had never been lacking, even though it had been slow in getting under way. The cry against communism was popular, since many French people understood it imperfectly and feared its possible role in a future France. There was no attempt to minimize the gravity of the events that had just taken place; on the contrary, the violence of the student revolutionaries was possibly exaggerated. After voting on 23 and 30 June, the UNR won a most handsome victory. Gaining an absolute majority by some 51 seats, the Gaullists reinforced the myth of the permanent relevance of Gaullist rule. They won some 295 seats, whilst Giscard d'Estaing also improved his prospects by winning 64 seats. Within a short time de Gaulle was able to discuss philosophical and political matters on the radio and to re-cast his government by replacing Pompidou by Couve de Murville. It seemed that the worst moment of Gaullism had been surmounted. Out of the despair had come an extraordinary victory that had remedied the 1967 elections and the depressed period of politics that followed them. The seemingly endless adventure of Gaullism was entering yet another phase.

Naturally, there is a lot that one has still to learn about these events. A number of important details remain mysterious. For example what were the relations between de Gaulle and Pompidou during the crisis? Or what exactly happened on 29 May when de Gaulle disappeared and when journalists had the opportunity of making the hilarious statement that they had lost General de Gaulle? It is established that he saw a number of army leaders, certainly General Massu and probably his son-in-law General de Boissieu. But even those who have written the most imaginative accounts of May 1968 have been reticent about this particular episode.[9] Nevertheless, in spite of some ignorance of detail one is obliged to assess the significance of what happened. And already the types of explanation which are being put forward are in the tradition of the explanations offered for French revolutions. It has been said that everything was attributable to foreign plots and plotters, and the role of the half-German and Jewish Cohn-Bendit has been useful to this interpretation. The minister of the Interior in Couve de Murville's government has made a number of insinuations and there have been rumours about the unusually healthy state of student union funds. A corollary to this version of the conspiracy theory is the communist belief that the police deliberately provoked the students and that *agents provocateurs* were at the barricades urging a confrontation that they thought would be disastrous for the students.[10] A different form of explanation sees the whole affair as an accident and puts the blame on the incompetence of the authorities (and of course it is noticeable that the three ministers responsible, Joxe, who was acting Prime Minister during the absence of Pompidou, Fouchet and Peyrefitte all lost their jobs). Or, in still different manner, one can interpret these events as part of a world crisis arising from the structure of modern capitalism, factors which are so general that it is almost useless to speculate on the details of a particular con-frontation.[11]

It is noticeable that just as these explanations approximate to the traditional ways in which French revolutions are usually interpreted, during the events of May everyone was very self-consciously playing a role. The idea of overthrowing the government by another 13 May on the tenth anniversary of 13 May 1958 impressed everyone, but bigger analogies were soon sought. The capture of the Sorbonne was the fall of the Bastille; the barricades were the barricades of 1848; this great upsurge of aspiration and heroism was the Commune of 1871 (and a *son et lumière* of the Commune was hastily improvised and shown in Montmartre, followed by a discussion). Retrospectively, it is the Russian revolution of 1905 which has become the favourite comparison, 1905 being the prelude to the real revolution.[12]

But ought one to think about these events of May and June as a revolution at all? This question resolves itself into two other questions: to what extent was the régime near to collapsing? Why was it that the government won the elections so convincingly?

Looked at in one way there is no reason to think that the régime, or for that matter the government, was ever near to collapsing. As a communist spokesman put it, the Sorbonne was not the Latin Quarter, the Latin Quarter was not Paris and Paris was not France. There was no real danger of food and petrol running short, and with few exceptions, violence was confined to the students and to a minority of them. The essential institutions of the state remained. But looked at in another way the contrary is true. Once again the vulnerability of power in France was strikingly proved.

The best historical comparison would be the incident of 1836, when a telegraphic message was received by the government of Louis-Philippe, stating that Prince Louis Napoleon, the future Napoleon III, had arrived in Strasbourg and was acting with the support of a certain army officer. The message then stopped, and the telegraphist explained that fog had interrupted the communication. The king, the royal family and some of the government spent the night in the palace, uneasily impatient for information. A special despatch the next day told them how Louis Napoleon's attempted uprising had ended in ridicule. But what is important is that the government had been worried and had taken seriously the news that a young adventurer was trying to stir up trouble. It thereby revealed its lack of confidence in its own powers of survival, and one could say that every French government is acutely aware of its own fragility.

It seems certain that during May a number of experienced politicians and administrators were convinced that the government could not continue and a number of them began to act on that assumption. We have General de Gaulle's word for it that he seriously contemplated resignation.[13] Had this resignation taken place then it is more than probable that the whole nature of the régime would have been called into question, and although this might not have been the 'revolution' of the theorists, there would have been something very revolutionary about it.

It could be argued that it was this very revelation of the precariousness of power that influenced the elections. The opposition to de Gaulle was considerable; the uneasy alliances which made up the politics of Gaullism were crumbling; the supporters were critical rather than loyal. But once the real possibility of overthrow had been seen, then there was a rallying of support. It was not simply that property had been destroyed and that people did not understand Cohn-Bendit's talk about violence on the streets being the equivalent of years of violence inflicted on the workers in the factories. It was also as if there were two de Gaulles. The one was a partisan leader who was the object of criticism, of ridicule (it was said that he would set up a Free French government in Romania) and of an impatient detestation; but the other was the national leader to whom the nation responded when he denied that he would abdicate. 'The ambition and hatred of discarded politicians' ('la haine des politiciens au rancart' as de Gaulle put it) did not have the same appeal, and Mendès-France lost his seat at Grenoble to Jeanneney, the minister who had introduced the much resented social security reforms. It is as if there are two political consciousnesses in France, the one partisan and the other national.[14]

But it is interesting to reflect on some of the details of this revolution. The one figure who was nearest to emerging and taking power was Pierre Mendès-France. His name was put forward many times as a possible solution. His reputation as an honest and uncompromising man was one that ran through the political spectrum, and he was the only man to be popular with the students. He had been absent from power since 1956 and he could in no way be held responsible for the chaos of 1968. He was independent and courageous, someone who belonged to no party and who was perhaps aggressively above the egocentric scheming of the ordinary politician. All this is to say that there is a similarity between the claims made for Mendès-France in 1968 and those which were made for de Gaulle in

1958. There was something solitary about both men, emphasized by the *'traversée du désert'* that each had undergone. The difference between them lay less in differing appreciations of their prestige than in Mendès-France's own failure to act decisively and effectively.

The students raised a number of ideas which were widely discussed. They repeatedly showed their dislike of the established political parties and of the parliamentary system. They never showed the slightest enthusiasm for the official leader of the opposition, Mitterrand. And this disdain for the political élite was very Gaullist. They rejected Parliament and parliamentary elections, suggesting vague schemes of a more direct and intimate contact between those who ruled and those who were ruled. Except where these notions dissolved into anarchism there is a strange echo of some of the ideas of de Gaulle and his desire to consult the people directly. Differences of opinion grew between workers and students when the workers on strike seemed only to be interested in their immediate revindications. The students claimed that they despised those workers who were prepared to accept a permanent position of authority in return for a few supplementary francs. General de Gaulle too had been known to express his contempt for such mundane considerations (he told his minister of Food after the Liberation that some day the French would have to think about something other than bloaters). The student rejection of a consumer society is not such a long way from de Gaulle's belief in man's profound *'insatisfaction'* and some of the anti-capitalism of the students found an echo in the Gaullist dream of a pan-capitalist society. De Gaulle's Bergsonian conception of a world in constant change was not altogether out of place during the events of May. More precisely, many of the students (and the independent socialists) were particularly violent in their rejection of the communist party ('nothing gave me so much pleasure as to be at the head of a demonstration with all that communist filth in the rear' was Cohn-Bendit's reported comment on 13 May). De Gaulle, too, was hostile to a party which had accepted Stalinist (i.e. foreign) control and the whole direction of the Gaullist election campaign was against a so-called communist plot.

Therefore, paradoxical as it may seem, there was a certain *rapport* between the movement of protestation and Gaullism. And perhaps the essential is this: the revolutions of 1958 and 1968 have more in common than that they were both sparked off by students, both based on utopic constructions which no one seriously considered to be permanent (French settler power in Algeria, student-power in France), and both eventually dominated by the same man. In reality the connection between these two revolutions is that they are the same revolution. Within different circumstances, one can see France in search of a political system which will respond to the needs of French society. The Third and the Fourth Republics provided a political culture that was fitted for a largely unchanging society. Political élites were the products of small-town politics and small-scale business. New generations persisted with the issues that had seemed important to their predecessors; they fitted into an administra- tive system which they did not reform but which they made more complex; they faithfully defended the interests of their respective groups. But 1958 was an attempt to break out of this, to find some- thing new and more effective, to find something national.

That there should have been a similar upheaval ten years later is a sign that Gaullism has been a disappointment, that the old political structures persisted and that General de Gaulle appeared increasingly as an ordinary conservative leader. The protest of 1968 was essentially the same protest against inadequate political systems. The sympathy that was at first felt for the students, the enthusiasm with which all sections of the community pressed their demands for reform, and the sense of liberation which seems to have reigned during some of these days, all were testimony to this desire to find a new structure. This desire for something new had shown itself in the intensity with which people had fought the new-style presidential elections in 1965, and in the success of certain young candidates on both sides during the 1967 general elections.[15] But in 1968 as in 1958 the only possibility of constructing something new seemed to lie in General de Gaulle. The opposition parties represented the real grievances of certain groups; but their organization, their ideas, their self-conscious divisions, all represented the political atmosphere of the Third and Fourth Republics. It was not to them that youth, conscious of its importance but uncertain of its future, was going to turn. Nor were they likely to attract the mass of those who were alarmed by the violence of divisions within France and who sought security.

The communist party had faithfully observed and reported on the social injustices of the Fifth Republic, and shortly before the events of May the central committee had said that conditions had never been so bad.[16] Although somewhat surprised by the size and tempo of the worker movement (the workers having learned more quickly than their leaders that the students had given an example of how to make the government give way), they had negotiated for better wages and they had hoped that their prolonged strike would bring the Pompidou government down. But they had distrusted the in-surrectionary movement of students who, in their eyes, had neither the necessary organization nor the proper appreciation of the class struggle to launch a real revolutionary movement. The communist party foresaw the revolution, at least in the first instance, as arising out of a democratic vote. Whereas Maurras said 'by any means, even legal', the communist party seemed to be saying that it would act only by legal means. It made great play during the elections of de Gaulle's visit to army leaders and of the threat of armed force that this implied. It sought to reassure rather than to animate, it suggested a going back rather than a move forward. And it was neatly caught out. It had not yet shed its revolutionary and sectional past so as to become a truly national party. It had so lost its revolu-tionary fire that it has now been classed as yet another of those French political parties which started out on the left but which have steadily moved to the right.[17]

The government, led by Couve de Murville, started out with great confidence. It inaugurated a policy of economic expansion as a means of overcoming the economic effects of the strikes and of the wage increases. Under the responsibility of the new minister of Education, Edgar Faure, a sweeping bill for educational reform of the universities was prepared, which would give greater autonomy to the Faculties and which would associate students with university administration (as well as creating supplementary Faculties). The minister of the Interior, Marcellin, whilst preparing security means to provide against further disturbances, was also at the centre of a planned regional reform. It was expected that equally profound measures to ensure worker participation in industry would also be announced. General de Gaulle seemed vigorous and self-confident, and he seemed to retract none of his former policies or utterances.

Three events modified the extent of Gaullist victory. The one was the expression of discontent amongst the UNR. At a conference held at La Baule, the UNR expressed reservations at the reforms prepared by Edgar Faure. That the two ministers responsible for the two sectors of immediate importance, Education and the Interior, should be outsiders rather than proper members of the UNR was a subject of great complaint, and that the architect of the electoral victory (or so he was regarded), Pompidou, should no longer be a member of the government at all was bewildering to many now self-confident Gaullists. An article in *La Nation* spoke of the need for the party to supervise government action (24 September 1968), and an incident in the Assembly between the Secretary of the party, Robert Poujade, and M. Faure suggested that there could be many difficulties. The greatest pressure had to be exercised on the party before they accepted the university reforms.

The second event was the Soviet intervention in Czechoslovakia in August 1968. Followed as it was by an apparent increase in Russian bellicosity, it rendered de Gaulle's policy of friendship towards Soviet Russia more difficult and it retarded the evolution of some national form of communism in eastern Europe. Although anxious to play down the significance of Soviet action (and M. Debré referred to it as an accident), the French government was forced to envisage that NATO might well gain a new lease of life. The increase of Soviet naval strength in the Mediterranean, and the fear that an agreement with Algeria could give them use of the base of Mers-el-Kebir, was a subject of even more lively French alarm.

But the greatest blow was economic. From September onwards a number of financial observers pointed to the remarkable prosperity of the West German mark and the question of whether the mark should be revalued upwards, whilst other currencies, including the franc, should be devalued, became a matter of intense discussion. Within France a steady pessimism began to grow. It seemed that there would be fresh outbreaks of student violence when the universities reassembled in November, out of dissatisfaction with the Faure reforms or because of the confusion in which many universities seemed to be plunged. Economically speaking, much of the activity had been of a re-stocking nature and once this was over there was prospect of a slump. It was common gossip that the schemes for participation would not get off the ground, and whether these plans were or were not pressed, it seemed that only dissatisfaction could come for them. A proposed reform of the Senate displeased many of the local *élites*. And in these circumstances, speculators, many of whom were French, began to prepare for a devaluation of the franc, a move which gathered momentum until by mid-November there was an international financial crisis of the first order. After a European bankers' meeting in Basle it was confidently expected that the franc would be devalued in order to restore its competitivity, and many saw, or hoped for, a repeat of the 1958 devaluation.

But on 23 November the French government announced that there would be no devaluation and over the next few days a series of austerity measures were announced. De Gaulle, in a broadcast, threatened those who sought to recreate the disorders of May, which he blamed for the crisis. The nuclear programme was cut back and spending on many projects was reduced. The American government pledged its support for the franc and there was no secret in Paris that great expectations were entertained of a *rapprochement* with Mr Nixon.

Thus once again the situation had taken a sudden turn. From the near resignation of May had come the triumphs of June and July. But by November Gaullist policies seemed to be in ruins. The UNR was no longer docile, or convinced. There was the prospect of imminent social conflict in which de Gaulle would appear as the representative of the bourgeoisie against the people. The lessons of May suggested that there was bound to be further violence in the streets. The peasantry represented an almost permanent source of disquiet. In Europe French supremacy was threatened by German power and it was suggested that the recovery of Germany in political terms dated back to the great Common Market crisis of 1965. The policies towards both Russia and America needed revision. The franc was no longer the assured currency that it had been, nor were French prosperity and planning the great successes that they had once appeared. In constitutional terms, relations between the President and the Prime Minister remained undefined, and in personal terms *après-Gaullisme* came still nearer without there being any certainty as to what this would be. If ever there was a moment for General de Gaulle to show his cynical pessimism it was this. Perhaps he thought, with Anouilh's Créon, *'les bêtes, elles au moins, sont bonnes et simples et dures.'*

He has pursued his policies. At home it was announced that a referendum would take place in 1969 on the institutional reforms (the substitution of a council of technocrats for the Senate and a greater regional autonomy) in spite of the opposition of Giscard d'Estaing and many of the UNR. During January 1969, when the dispute between Edgar Faure and some of the UNR had become acrimonious, he showed no apparent interest in the matter. In foreign policy he showed a disposition to intervene in various conflicts, by sending arms to Biafra and by associating himself more decisively with the Arab states and with Soviet Russia in the Middle East, and stopping all arms supplies to Israel. Once again the desire to assert a French position abroad seemed to be paralleled by a certain conservatism at home. The leader of the centre party, Jacques Duhamel, protested at government by 'enigma and incantation' in the midst of 'incoherence and contradiction'.

The week-end of 23 and 24 November 1968 was a typical Gaullist happening. All France waited to see what he would do, waited to hear what he would say. Yet again he defied opinion, refused to give way, and vigorously asserted a policy which, against all expectations, had some immediate success. But it was not only a typically Gaullist event. It was also typically French. What other nation allows itself to be put perpetually in the position of an audience waiting on an actor? Does this not denote the condition of a nation as well as the personality of a man? On the one hand there are the divisions of France. In 1961 Pierre Mendès-France spoke of the prospect of civil war in France and the need to devise institutions and policies which would prevent it. On the other hand there is the idea of France. On 11 November 1968 General de Gaulle spoke of '*la flamme de la foi et de la fierté nationales*' which had been lit in the two world wars.

He concluded. '*C'est la même flamme qui inspirera au long de l'avenir, comme elle le fit au long du passé, l'âme de la France éternelle*'.

The dialogue is likely to continue.

During the early months of 1969 the government prepared a plan to divide France administratively into regions and to make the Senate a council for the discussion of economic affairs. General de Gaulle decided that this plan should be submitted to a referendum, and he announced that if the plan were rejected, then he would resign. He was criticized for this. It was said that he was utilizing the procedure of the plebiscite and acting with unnecessary gravity. His justification was that, even with a Gaullist parliamentary majority, his freedom was limited. Parliament might have emascu-lated regionalism; the Gaullist party might have split. De Gaulle could only use his customary method: to dramatize, to personalize and to threaten. Only in this way could he hope to force reforms on an uncertain and anxious nation.

On 27 April 1969 the majority voted against the referendum, and on the next day General de Gaulle resigned. It remains for his successors to find ways in which the mass of French people can identify themselves as a unity: it can be by institutions, by organiza-tions, by action or by the various forms of persuasion. But the need is there today, as it has been in the past. For France is a character in search of an author.

16   Postscript—June 1969

DURING THE YEARS when General de Gaulle was in power, the question most frequently asked had been, what will happen when the General is no longer there? This was not only a question of guessing at the name of his successor. It was also a matter of judging the whole future of the French nation. With the defeat of 27 April 1969, the General's resignation came quickly. There was evidence to show that he had anticipated the event; some have even suggested that he welcomed it. The laconic communiqué stating the fact of resignation, the subsequent silence and isolation in Ireland were in keeping with the General's own traditions. The capital of his reputation was maintained.

But in the past he has made it clear what his understanding of the future would be. If the regime of political divisions and powerful political parties returned, then France would return to the confusions, and possibly to the anarchy, of the preceding Republics. In a world filled with danger, France would not be equipped to face that danger. But if, on the other hand, France chose a leader who was a national leader, then the stability of the Fifth Republic's institutions would persist, and the other achievements of the Fifth Republic, as de Gaulle saw them (that is to say, France's high prestige in the world and level of economic prosperity), would also be maintained.

At first sight it would seem that the Gaullist conditions have been maintained. No one has contested the validity of institutions. And although candidates agreed that their style of government would not be that of General de Gaulle, they did not announce any intention of changing the constitution. Furthermore, although the presence of seven candidates seemed to token the return to the multi-party system of the past, in reality there were only two serious candidates for the presidency: the Gaullist candidate, Georges Pompidou, and the 'centrist' candidate, the President of the Senate and therefore the interim President of the Republic, Alain Poher. Both claimed that they would be Presidents of reconciliation, of unity, and of all the French people. The other candidates were fighting other battles: the Communists and the Socialists were disputing the leadership of the left, the Independent Socialists and the Trotskyists the leadership of new, and young, movements of protest and contestation. Both the opinion polls and the voting figures revealed a remarkable stability of the political structures, with the Gaullist vote remaining constant and solid. Any suggestions that M. Poher could cause masses of Frenchmen to renounce their earlier allegiances, and out of hostility to de Gaulle and enthusiasm for more gentle and modest policies vote for M. Poher, were soon revealed to be false. There were no panic moves; no landslides.

But yet at the same time a fundamental weakness has re-appeared. It is a weakness which has existed for a long time, which it was the mission of Gaullism to repair. This is the existence of sections of France which are irreconcilable. Perhaps the majority of the French are conservative. Perhaps about two-thirds vote for men who propose no great change in the organization of society. That is to say that whilst other countries might oscillate between left and right, in France the oscillation is between right and right centre. The French, as has been said, prefer those who close windows to those who open them. Although the Chamber (elected in 1968) could, constitutionally, have been dissolved in July 1969, no one seriously considered this possibility. The three traditional holiday months are sacred. However great the crisis, the Frenchman must have his holiday.

But there is another France. The France which shows a remarkably constant communist vote and which, in spite of its importance, sees itelf condemned to powerlessness and obliged to resort to the useless weapon of abstentionism. This is the France that demands social reforms. And there is another France, which refuses to accept a polarization into Gaullists and communists, and which proposes an alternative programme of progress. This is the France that demands technical reforms, and requires that institutions should function effectively.

Gaullism had sought to reconcile these diverse elements, and within a strong state, acting an important role on the world stage, Frenchmen would only remember that they were French. Like his friend Malraux, de Gaulle sought to reveal to men the grandeur that they possessed unwittingly. By 1968 he had largely failed. In spite of de Gaulle, Gaullism had come to represent only the conservative section. De Gaulle himself had accepted that Gaullism should play a divisive role, attacking the communists. The Gaullist state offered only administrative reform, not social justice.

Can M. Pompidou succeed where de Gaulle failed? Already the burden of recent French history presents further complications and the souvenir of the events of 1968 might become the source of recriminations amongst the Gaullists as amongst the left. There are those who suggest that the last six months of Gaullist power was a period of non-government, a *vacance de pouvoir,* when France slipped gently towards economic disaster, and the affirmation of German strength became progressively stronger.

Frenchmen will look for strong leadership; they will look for agility and intelligence in the treatment of their problems; they will look for stability as well as for progress; they will seek to defend their sectional interests and they will look for conciliation rather than for conflict. And, as M. Pompidou prophesied Gaullist victory, *'parce que nous aimons la France',* as M. Poher sought to justify *'une certaine conception républicaine et démocrate de la France',* as the communist M. Duclos had a vision of *'la France de la Révolution française',* so all Frenchmen will go on telling about France, *'la France'.* In this they have not changed.

Notes on the text

I THE BEGINNING

1 See, for example, the article by Paul-Marie Duval, 'Marseille retrouve les vestiges imposants de ses origines grecques', in *Le Monde*, 5 August 1967.

2 This is discussed in Dr Peter Lewis's article, 'The failure of the French medieval estates', in *Past and Present*, 1962. His book *Later Medieval France: the Polity* (1968) is a most important contribution to the understanding of French society on the eve of modern times.

3 G. Fourquin, *Les campagnes de la région parisienne à la fin du moyen âge* (Paris, 1964), pp. 61–3.

2 THE ANCIEN RÉGIME

1 E. Porschnev, 'The legend of the seventeenth century in French history', in *Past and Present*, No. 8, 1955.

2 Louis XIV did not inaugurate this ceremonial protocol. His father was married for three years before he consummated his marriage, when, it was said, his close friend Charles de Luynes carried him, protesting, to the Queen's bedroom. Protocol was never absent, and this odd procession was led by the *valet de chambre*, solemnly carrying a candle.

3 The most recent account of the reign is in John B. Wolf, *Louis XIV* (1968); this is concerned mainly with the diplomatic and administrative achieve-ments. Pierre Goubert, *Louis XIV et vingt millions de français* (Paris, 1966), studies the reign in its wider aspects. A remarkably lucid and penetrating analysis of eighteenth-century France is to be found in C. B. A. Behrens, *The Ancien Régime* (1967).

3 THE REVOLUTION

1 One of the best ways of understanding this is to read the well-known book by Pieter Geyl, *Napoleon, For and Against* (1949; Penguin edition, 1965). Perhaps the best way of understanding the Revolution is to delve into the monumental work by Richard Cobb, *Les armées révolutionnaires* (Paris,

1961–3). One should also consult the same author's article on the revolutionary mentality in *History*, 1957.

4 POST-REVOLUTION

1 The most convenient accounts are Alfred Cobban, *A History of Modern France* (1965 edition), and Gordon Wright, *France in Modern Times* (1962).
2 See the discussions in *La Décentralisation* (Aix-en-Provence, 1964).
3 The whole question of French demography has been studied many times. Pouthas, *La population française pendant la première moitié du XIX siècle* (Paris, 1956) is detailed, although his figures are not always accurate. See particularly Ariès, *Histoire des populations françaises et leurs attitudes devant la vie depuis le XVIII siècle* (Paris, 1948).
4 These questions, with bibliographical references, are discussed in Kindle-berger, *Economic Growth in France and Britain 1851–1950* (1964).

5 THE YEARS OF DESPAIR

1 These mutinies have often been the cause of speculation. One can now recommend Guy Pedroncini, *Les mutineries de 1917* (Paris, 1967), and the special number of the *Revue d'histoire moderne et contemporaine*, Vol. XV 1968.
2 See Douglas Johnson, 'Austen Chamberlain and the Locarno agreements', in *University of Birmingham Historical Journal,* 1961.
3 Claude Fohlen, *La France de l'entre-deux-guerres* (Paris, 1966) is an excellent general account, while Albert Sauvy, *Histoire économique de la France entre les deux guerres* (2 vols., Paris, 1966–7) is a remarkable analysis.
4 On the Stavisky affair, see Maurice Chavardès, *Le 6 février 1934* (Paris, 1966). On the Popular Front see the published version of the colloquium, *Léon Blum, chef de gouvernement* (Paris, 1967).
5 For an interesting account of intellectuals during the period (which, curiously enough, makes no mention of Gide), see Stuart Hughes, *The Obstructed Path* (New York, 1968).

6 THE SECOND WAR

1 The best account of the 1940 campaign is Major L. F. Ellis's *France and Flanders 1939–1940* (History of the Second World War; 1953), and there are many others which consider these events, such as John Williams, *The Ides of May* (1968) and Guy Chapman, *Why France Collapsed* (1968). For a recent consideration of the German break-through, see G. Beau and L. Gaubusseau, *Dix erreurs: une défaite* (Paris, 1967).
2 The whole question of the armistice is extremely complicated. Perhaps Henri Michel, *Vichy: Année 40* (Paris, 1966) is the first book to consult, but

amongst the many sources one should mention the article by Louis Marin, 'Contribution à l'histoire des prodromes de l'Armistice', in *Revue d'histoire de la deuxième guerre mondiale*, June 1951.

3 The most complete account of Vichy is that by Robert Aron, *Histoire de Vichy* (Paris, 1954), but the collection of texts, with a perceptive commentary by Jacques de Launay, *Le dossier de Vichy* (Collection Archives; Paris, 1967) contains a great deal of material.

4 For a consideration of de Gaulle's attitude to the Popular Front, there is an interesting passage in André Malraux's so-called *Antimemoirs* (1968), pp. 93-4, which reports a post-war conversation between de Gaulle and Léon Blum and describes de Gaulle's bitterness.

5 The principal source for the story of Gaullism is obviously the memoirs of General de Gaulle. *Histoire de la France Libre* by Henri Michel (Collection Que sais-je?; Paris, 1963) is most useful.

6 The Resistance has been most carefully studied by Henri Michel, *Histoire de la Résistance en France* (Collection Que sais-je?; Paris, 1950) and *Les Courants de pensée de la Résistance* (Paris, 1962), but one understands things better if one turns to a political analysis, such as H. Denis, *Le comité parisien de la Libération* (Paris, 1963), or to an account of opinion, like C. Bellanger, *Presse clandestine* (Paris, 1961).

7 THE POST-WAR WORLD

1 *Mémoires de guerre*, Vol. II, p. 306.

2 Robert Aron, *Histoire de la Libération* (Paris, 1967), pp. 655 and 723, suggests that some 40,000 were killed, but it has recently been suggested that this figure is a considerable exaggeration.

3 This is the opinion expressed by Mme Georgette Elgey, *La République des illusions (1945-1951)* (Paris, 1965).

4 The communist party since the war has been studied by Jacques Fauvet, *Histoire du parti communiste français*, Vol. II (Paris, 1965), and by Annie Kriegel, *Les communistes français* (Paris, 1968).

5 For the RPF, see Christian Purtschet, *Le Rassemblement du Peuple Français* (Paris, 1965).

6 The most recent study of the war in Indo-China, which always considers what is happening both in France and in Indo-China, is to be found in the volumes of Lucien Bodard, *La Guerre d'Indochine* (3 vols., Paris, 1965-7). Jules Roy has written on the French defeat, *La Bataille de Dien-Bien-Phu* (Paris, 1963), as have Jean Lacouture and Philippe Devillers, *La Fin d'une guerre: Indochine 1954* (Paris, 1960).

7   The question of France and the institution of Europe has been studied many times. Raymond Aron and Daniel Lerner, *La Guerre du C.E.D.* (Paris, 1956) is an interesting case-study, whilst Alfred Grossner, *La IV République et sa politique extérieure* (Paris, 1961) is more general. Books on French planning also abound, and will be referred to later.

8   See André Armengaud, *La Population française au XX siècle* (Paris, 1965).

9   There are several books on Mendès-France. For his government see Pierre Rouanet, *Mendès-France au pouvoir* (*18 juin 1954 – 6 février 1955*) (Paris, 1965).

8   THE REVOLUTION OF 1958

1   For an account of the plots and conspiracies which surrounded 13 May, there are two books which contain a lot of detail, presented somewhat sensationally: Merry and Serge Bromberger, *Les 13 complots du 13 mai, ou la délivrance de Gulliver* (Paris, 1959), and J. R. Tournoux, *Secrets d'Etat* (Paris, 1960). Viansson-Ponté has written interestingly about the conspiracies in *Le Monde*, 14 and 15 May 1963, whilst J. Ferniot, *De Gaulle et le 13 mai* (Paris, 1965) is excellent. The reflections of the editor of *Le Monde*, 'Sirius' (Hubert Beuve-Méry), *Le Suicide de la IVe République* (Paris, 1958), and the recollections of one of the activists of Algiers, Alain de Sérigny, *La Révolution du 13 mai* (Paris, 1958) are amongst the best contemporary documents. In general, see de la Gorce, *De Gaulle entre deux mondes* (Paris, 1964).

2   André Malraux writes, 'I remember General de Gaulle's answer to the question "When did you think you would return to power?" "Always..."' (*Antimemoirs*, trans. Terence Kilmartin, 1968).

3   For some evidence of those who thought that de Gaulle would be a partisan of keeping Algeria French, see Alain de Sérigny, *op. cit.*, pp. 143*ff.*; Jacques Soustelle, *L'Espérance trahie* (Paris, 1962); and for particular reference to Michel Debré's assurances, Georges Bidault, *Résistances* (Paris, 1967), pp. 219*ff.*

4   In a reference to Louis-Philippe's father, Philippe Egalité, who had been an early supporter of the 1789 Revolution, it used to be said that Louis-Philippe was both of the royal blood and covered in it.

5   The phrase is by Jacques Fauvet.

9   THE GENERAL

1   The essay *France Herself Again* by the Abbé Ernest Dimnet had been written for an English audience and published in 1914.

2 For details of de Gaulle's military career see de la Gorce, *De Gaulle entre deux mondes*; David Schoenbrun, *The Three Lives of Charles de Gaulle* (1966); and J. R. Tournoux, *Pétain et de Gaulle* (Paris, 1964).

3 For various photographs see the little book by Lacouture, *De Gaulle* (Paris, 1966). The English novelist Anthony Powell writes, 'Persons at odds with their surroundings not infrequently suggest an earlier historical epoch' (*The Valley of Bones*, 1964, p. 76).

4 It is said that one of the books which he read and re-read during these years was the second volume of Tocqueville's *La Démocratie en Amérique*. For reference to de Gaulle's bullying tactics see Sir Edward Spears, *Two Men Who Saved France* (1966), pp. 148ff. See also his letter to Bidault, in which he says, '*Depuis que nous sommes malheureux, ce que nous avons fait de plus fructueux fut en même temps ce qui provoque les plus violents orages*' (*Mémoires de guerre*, III, p. 506).

5 '*Au fond, comme chef de l'Etat, deux choses lui avaient manqué: qu'il fût un chef; qu'il y eût un Etat*' (*Mémoires de guerre*, III, p. 23).

6 'It must, indeed, respond to the cravings felt by men who, imperfect themselves, seek perfection in the end they are called upon to serve. Conscious of their own limitations and restricted by nature, they give free rein to unlimited hopes, and each, measuring his own littleness, accepts the need for collective action on condition that it contribute to an end which is, in itself, great' (*The Edge of the Sword*, trans. Gerard Hopkins, p. 60).

7 'I wished to establish that the state . . . was returning, first of all, quite simply, to where it belonged' (*War Memoirs*, II, trans. Richard Howard, p. 304).

8 This is told by Georges Bidault. There are many other examples of such a preoccupation with the details of protocol. During the negotiation with the Algerian leaders de Gaulle gave instructions to the French representatives not to shake hands with the rebels. For the New Year celebrations of 1969 de Gaulle was ostentatiously silent with the Israeli ambassador, and obviously friendly to the Lebanese representative.

10 PRESIDENT AND PARLIAMENT

1 For accounts of the constitution see Dorothy Pickles, *The Fifth French Republic* (1962); P. M. Williams and M. Harrison, *De Gaulle's Republic* (1960); Pierre Avril, *Le Régime politique de la V République* (Paris, 1964); and J. Blondel and E. D. Godfrey Jr., *The Government of France* (1968 edition).

2 Pierre Viansson-Ponté, *Les Gaullistes* (Paris, 1961).

3 Charles de Gaulle, *Mémoires de guerre*, III, p. 126.

4 See the article 'La tête et les jambes', in *Le Monde*, 7 November 1961.

5 Avril, *op. cit.*, pp. 247*ff*.

6 François Mitterrand, *Le Coup d'état permanent* (Paris, 1964), p. 139.

7 These questions can be studied in the excellent book by Jean Charlot, *L'UNR: étude du pouvoir au sein d'un parti politique* (Paris, 1967), but see two revealing articles, by Christian de la Malène in *La Nation française* (4 August 1960), and by Francis Leenhardt in *Démocratie 59* (26 November 1959).

II ALGERIA

1 For a general survey of some aspects of Algerian development see Douglas Johnson, 'Algeria: some problems of modern history', in *Journal of African History*, 1964.

2 Two books in English give useful surveys of this period in French and Algerian history: Edgar O'Ballance, *The Algerian Insurrection 1954–1962* (1967) and David C. Gordon, *The Passing of French Algeria* (1966). The authority for thinking that de Gaulle had resigned himself to accepting Algerian independence is de la Gorce.

3 *Le Monde*, 27 March 1962. Bazaine was the French marshal who had surrendered to the Prussians at Metz in 1870.

4 *Le Monde*, 20 March 1962.

12 FRANCE IN EUROPE AND THE WORLD

1 *Le Monde*, 29–30 April 1962; *Le Figaro*, 28 April 1962.

2 *Manchester Guardian*, 10 July 1957.

3 For a survey of de Gaulle's attitude towards European unity see Roger Massip, *De Gaulle et l'Europe* (Paris, 1963).

4 The text of de Gaulle's letter of 24 September 1958 has never been published although it has been summarized in *Le Monde*, 28 October 1960. Eisenhower's reply was given in hearings before the sub-committee on national security in *U.S. Senate, 89th Congress*, 15 August 1966, Part 7, Supplement (Washington, 1966), pp. 230–1.

5 Mr Edward Heath made this specific claim in a speech to the Council of Western European Union on 10 April 1962. Quoted in Susanne J. Bodenheimer, *Political Union: a Microcosm of European Politics 1960–1966* (Leyden, 1966).

6 *Combat*, 12 April 1965.

7   See J. R. Tournoux, *La Tragédie du général* (Paris, 1967), p. 330.
8   '*J'ai tâché de servir seulement la France. Eux l'ont servie aussi, mais ils n'ont pas servi qu'elle et, même, ils n'ont pas servi elle, d'abord. Que ce soit un grand malheur national, j'en suis bien d'accord avec vous. Combien la France serait en meilleur point si toute la force d'ardeur et d'action qu'ils constituent ne s'employait, ne se dévouait qu'à la chose national, quel que soit leur idéal social!*' De Gaulle to Vercors, 19 February 1956, published in *Le Monde*, 30 August 1967.
9   *Mémoires de guerre*, III, p. 53.
10 See the article by Stéphane Erasmus in *China Quarterly*, April-June 1964.
11 W. W. Kulski, *De Gaulle and the World* (Syracuse, 1966), in a careful study, suggests that de Gaulle's policy has had little effect upon the events or the situations.

13 GAULLISM EVOLVES

1   The editor of *Le Monde* commented, '*rarement la théorie du pouvoir absolu a été exposée avec plus de complaisance*' (2–3 February 1964).
2   These matters are discussed in Jean Lecerf, *La Percée de l'économie française* (Paris, 1963) and also in the *Economist*, 18 May 1968.
3   There is a large bibliography on the subject of French planning. The PEP pamphlet, *French planning: some lessons for Britain* (1963) and J. and A./M. Hackett, *Economic Planning in France* (1963) are to be recommended. There are some interesting remarks in Andrew Shonfield, *Modern Capitalism* (1965).
4   It has been argued that there is no causal relationship between the establishment of the Common Market and the rapid growth of its members, and that one should argue the other way round, that it was the high rate of growth of Continental Europe which stimulated trade between members of the Common Market. In the case of France it was a question of her reaping the benefit of the rapid increases in production which occurred between 1953 and 1957. See Alexander Lamfalussy, 'Europe's Progress: Due to the Common Market?' in *Lloyd's Bank Review*, October 1961.
5   This point is made in Claude Gruson, *Origine et espoirs de la planification française* (Paris, 1968), p. 220.
6   Professor Peter Worsley says so in *The Trumpet Shall Sound* (2nd edition, 1968), p. xi.
7   '*Ah! si le général de Gaulle avait parlé il y a trois semaines comme il l'a fait hier, nous n'aurions pas eu ce deuxième tour*' (*Le Figaro*, 14 December 1965).
8   An interesting interpretation of the Presidential elections is to be found in R./G. Schwartzenberg, *La campagne présidentielle de 1965* (Paris, 1967).

A more detailed local study by Paul Bauju and André Valentino, *Atlas de l'élection présidentielle de 1965: département du Rhône* (Lyons, 1968) shows that while Lyons itself voted for de Gaulle, Villeurbanne voted for Mitterrand.

9 See Valéry Giscard d'Estaing's letter to the mayors of France in *Le Monde*, 16 July 1966. Two articles, amongst many, which discuss the implication of the presidential elections are Alain Lancelot, 'Les résultats de l'élection présidentielle', in *Projet*, February 1966, and Pierre Avril, in *Le Régime politique de la V République* (2nd edition, Paris, 1967).

10 So anxious was de Gaulle that his talk would be the last of the eve-of-poll messages to be heard by the electorate, that he asked M. Edgar Faure to abstain from taking part in a late-night discussion to be broadcast by Europe No. 1. This M. Faure did. General de Gaulle also made it plain that he reserved the right to intervene between the two ballots should it be necessary (*Le Monde*, 3 March 1967).

11 See the articles by René Capitant and Louis Vallon in *Notre République*, 17 March 1967.

12 François Goguel, 'Les élections legislatives de mars 1967', in *Revue française de science politique*, June 1967.

13 This subject is treated in John Newhouse, *Collision in Brussels* (1967).

14 '*Nous subissons un nationalisme intégral. Celui du temps des grands crises. Nous qui aspirons aux grands détentes.*' Georges Izard, *Lettre affligée au général de Gaulle* (Paris, 1964), pp. 17, 32.

14 TOUR DE FRANCE

1 Christopher Campos, *The View of France* (1965), p. 13.

2 *Daily Telegraph*, 11 July 1968.

3 André Siegfried, *A Study in French Nationality* (1929); Jacques Rivière, *Le Français* (Paris, 1924); Hermann Keyserling, *The Spectral Analysis of Europe* (1925); Salvador de Madariaga, *Englishmen, Frenchmen, Spaniards* (1932).

4 When I was a student at the Ecole Normale Supérieure, there was a game (which probably reflects the influence of some Third Republic lycée teacher) which sought to attribute national characteristics in particular (and sometimes unusual) circumstances. One series went like this: one German is a scholar, two Germans are a duet, three Germans are a war; one Englishman is an island, two Englishmen are a boxing match, three Englishmen are a colonial expedition. There was always considerable disagreement about the characteristics of the French. One version ran, one Frenchman is a cuckold, two a political argument, three are three

political parties. But this was challenged by a version which said three is a *ménage à trois*. Ought one to conclude from this that the French are particularly proud of their political and sexual customs?

5 Gabriel Le Bras, 'Psychologie de la France', in *Revue de psychologie des peuples*, 1952.

6 *Astérix* has just been translated into English, which has surprised some Frenchmen since they thought that Astérix was reserved for *'une certaine idée de la France'*. See Robert Escarpit, 'Astérix for two' in *Le Monde*, 28 November 1968. Does one assume that in these stories the Romans are really the Americans?

7 *Mémoires de Guerre*, Vol. I, pp. 1–2.

8 Jean Guéhenno, 'Si l'Europe trouvait son âme', in *Le Figaro*, 19 July 1966.

9 The most famous discussion of this is in Etiemble, *Parlez-vous franglais?* (Paris, 1964), but there is a revealing article by the economist Alfred Sauvy, 'Renovation du français', in *Revue de Paris*, 1963. Several committees and organizations have been set up for the defence of the French language and one of them has proposed the establishment of a word bank storing French words which can be used for new technical purposes.

10 François H. de Virier, *La Fin d'une agriculture* (Paris, 1967).

11 The cult of the *résidences secondaires*, for weekends or holidays, is now said to be as great as the cult of the motor-car. It is estimated that by 1970 there will be 1,700,000 in France, some would say many more. See the opening pages of Simone de Beauvoir, *Les Belles Images* (Paris, 1966).

12 John Ardagh, *The New French Revolution* (1968).

13 R. H. Tawney, *The British Labour Movement* (New Haven, 1925), p. 33.

14 See Edgar Morin, *Commune en France* (Paris, 1967) and *Tendances et Volontés de la Société Française* (Paris, 1966). The general comment on the extent of urban change is my own conclusion rather than that of the authors here referred to. For an aspect of relations between the *bourg* and the farms see Claude Grignon's article in *Revue française de sociologie*, 1968.

15 *Le Monde*, 1–2 September 1968.

16 Demangeon, *Paris, La Ville et sa banlieue*, quoted in Chevalier, *Les Parisiens* (Paris, 1967).

17 Pierre de la Gorce, *La France pauvre* (Paris, 1965).

18 *New Society*, 22 December 1966. The 1967 reforms increased contributions and decreased benefits.

19 Henri Lefèbvre, 'Les nouveaux ensembles urbains', in *Revue française de sociologie*, 1960. Ardagh (*op. cit.*) visited the same site some time later and found conditions much improved.

20 Darras, *Partage des bénéfices* (Paris, 1966); this is a collective work. Tradition-ally, it was easy to designate social classes in France. For example, the in-sistence in Mauriac's *Nœud de vipères* on the mother *'qui avait porté le foulard'*.

21 In the French pop world there is a good deal of intellectual sophistication and one wonders how many listeners appreciate it all. Equally one wonders how many of the supposed ten million readers of *Astérix chez les Bretons* appreciate the jokes about the British, their accents, etc.

22 Darras, *op. cit.*, p. 127.

23 Pierre Sabbagh, *Les perles de la télévision* (Paris, 1963); Maurice Clavel, 'La France de Guy Lux et de Pierre Sabbagh', in *Le Nouvel Observateur*, 26 July–1 August 1967. For the statement that every Frenchman is an individualist and wants to have his own television service see the statement by the then Director of the service, Wladimir d'Ormesson, in *La Croix*, 7–8 August 1966.

24 Zwedei Barbu, 'Chosisme: a socio-psychological interpretation', in *The European Journal of Sociology*, Vol. IV, 1963. See the critical appraisal by Pierre de Boisdeffre, *La cafetière est sur la table* (Paris, 1968).

25 *The Times Literary Supplement*, 23 November 1967.

26 But perhaps the audience did participate in the Tour de France to some extent. I used to live by a steep hill near to Rouen and I noticed that when the Tour was on people used more often to ride to the top.

27 *Mémoires de guerre*, III, p. 20.

15 REVOLUTION AGAIN

1 On the subject of Giscard d'Estaing's relations with the majority, see the interview that Pompidou gave to *l'Express*, 4 September 1967. François Mauriac, now a devoted supporter of de Gaulle, wrote in his Bloc-Notes of Giscard, *'Il se fait une certaine idée de Giscard d'Estaing qui n'est pas petite'*, and foreseeing the divisions of the Gaullists and the triumph of the 'gauche classique', he concluded, *'Je ne le verrai pas et ce sera ma dernière chance . . .'* (*Le Figaro Littéraire*, 4 September 1967).

2 This was the opinion of René Capitant, *Notre République*, 12 October 1967.

3 See Alfred Grosser, *Le Monde*, 25 October 1967.

4 Raymond Barillon, *La Gauche en mouvement* (Paris, 1967).

5 This was translated into English as *The American Challenge*, 1968.

6 *Le Monde*, 21 October, 1967.

7 A number of those in the centre groups were to be rewarded for having supported the government. In the forthcoming elections they did not have any Gaullist opponents.

8 Innumerable books and articles have already been written about these events. Patrick Seale and Maureen McConville, *French Revolution 1968* (Penguin Special, 1968) gives a particularly clear account of the student organizations.

9 For example, Christian Charrière, *Le Printemps des enragés* (Paris, 1968), p. 339-40, is particularly reticent about this.

10 See René Andrieu, *Les communistes et le révolution* (Paris, 1968).

11 Malraux spoke in such terms on Europe Numéro 1. For a sociological explanation of the events see Alain Touraine, *Le mouvement de mai* (Paris, 1968).

12 See Bensaid and Weber, *Mai 1968: une répétition générale* (Paris, 1968).

13 In his television interview with Michel Droit.

14 This point is argued with great subtlety by Pierre Fougeyrollas, *La conscience politique dans la France contemporaine* (Paris, 1963).

15 See Maurice Duverger in *Le Monde*, 9 March 1967.

16 *L'Humanité*, 19 April 1968.

17 In the *compliment* of the new edition of René Rémond, *La Droite en France* (Paris, 1968), Vol. II, p. 439.

Acknowledgments

Bildarchiv Foto Marburg, 5, 8; Caisse Nationale des Monuments Historiques, 9; French Embassy, London, 21-24; Giraudon, 3, 6, 7, 10; Keystone, 14, 15, 19; Edition Lapie, 2; Janet March-Penney, 27, 28; Phillips Collection, Washington, 12; Paul Popper, 17, 18; Radio Times Hulton Picture Library, 25, 26; S.N.C.F., 20; Walters Art Gallery, Baltimore, 11; Photo Yan, 4

Select Bibliography

Duby, G., and R. Mandrou, *A History of French Civilization* (trans. J. B. Atkinson), New York, 1964, London, 1965.

Wallace-Hadrill, J. M., and J. McManners (ed.), *France: Government and Society*, London and New York, 1957.

Latouche, Robert, *From Caesar to Charlemagne*, London, 1968.

Boussard, Jacques, *The Civilisation of Charlemagne*, London, 1968.

Bloch, Marc, *Feudal Society* (trans. L. A. Manyon), London and New York, 1961.

Lewis, P. S., *Later Medieval France*, London, 1968.

Mandrou, R., *Introduction à la France moderne, 1500–1640*, Paris, 1961.

Treasure, G. R. R., *Seventeenth-Century France*, London and New York, 1966.

Cobban, Alfred, *A History of Modern France*, 3 vols., Harmondsworth, 1965.

Wright, Gordon, *France in Modern Times, 1760 to the Present*, London and New York, 1962.

Thomson, David, *Democracy in France since 1870*, 4th ed., Oxford, 1964.

Chapsal, Jacques, *La vie politique en France depuis 1940*, Paris, 1966.

Bernard, Philippe-J., *La France au singulier*, Paris, 1968.

Who's Who

AURIOL, Vincent (1884–1968). Lawyer and financial expert. Socialist deputy for Haute Garonne in the 1920's. Leader of the opposition in 1934; two years later took cabinet office under Léon Blum. Elected first President of the Fourth Republic in 1947.

BABEUF, Gracchus (1760–97). Political agitator (through his paper *Le tribun du peuple*) and terrorist plotter under the Directory. Arrested in 1796 on the eve of a planned uprising, and guillotined a year later. He was among the first to propound socialism as a practical policy, and thus a forerunner of the revolutions of 1848 and 1871.

BEUVE-MÉRY, Hubert (b. 1902). Director-general of *Le Monde*, in which he writes influential leading articles under the pseudonym 'Sirius'. Was active in the Resistance.

BIDAULT, Georges (b. 1899). Historian, and pre-war editor of *L'Aube*. Chairman of the national resistance council during the occupation. Appointed minister of Foreign Affairs by de Gaulle in 1944, and variously held that post or the premiership 1945–53. Vigorously supported the cause of French Algeria.

BLUM, Léon (1872–1950). Leader of the Socialist party from 1919, and three times Prime Minister. Helped to form the Popular Front (1934), and as Prime Minister 1936–7 followed a policy of non-intervention in the Spanish civil war. After the defeat of France in 1940 he voted against the grant of special powers to Pétain. Arrested and interned by the Vichy government, he was tried at Riom, handed over to the Germans and imprisoned at Buchenwald. After liberation he returned to Paris, resumed the leadership of the Socialist party, and was a caretaker Premier pending the election of Auriol as first President of the Fourth Republic.

BOULANGER, Georges Ernest (1837–91). General, and would-be dictator. After a military career he became minister of War in 1886. He became the leader of a wide spectrum of those seeking revenge for the defeat by Germany in 1871. His supporters ranged all the way from the pretender, the Comte de Paris, to the anarchists. Eventually his movement grew to such a size that the government had to suppress it. He fled to Belgium, and committed suicide.

BRASSENS, Georges (b. 1921). Composer and singer. Discovered by Patachou in 1952; since then has appeared in many night-clubs and in films. Among his own songs are 'Le Gorille', 'Le Parapluie' and 'La Complainte des filles de joie'.

BRIAND, Aristide (1862–1932). Eleven times Premier. Originally Socialist but broke with them in 1906 and in 1910, as Premier, he smashed a rail strike by calling up reservist strikers. After World War I, as foreign minister, he negotiated the Locarno Pact (1925), which paved the way for German entry into the League of Nations, and signed the Briand-Kellogg Pact, renouncing war as an instrument of national policy.

CAMUS, Albert (1913–60). Novelist, essayist and dramatist, Nobel Prize winner in 1957. Associate of Sartre but parted with him over the attitude to adopt towards communism. His most important work is *La Peste*, a modern parable on the collective responsibility in the face of evil, exemplified by an outbreak of bubonic plague.

CHABAN-DELMAS, Jacques (b. 1915). Joined General de Gaulle in London; served on Free French National Committee. After the war was elected to the Chamber, and to the mayoralty of Bordeaux. Leading member of the UNR (Union pour la Nouvelle République). President of the Assembly since 1958.

CHARLEMAGNE (742–814). King of the Franks and Emperor of the Romans. Son of Pepin the Short; acceded (768) jointly with his brother, who died in 771. Crowned Roman Emperor in St Peter's, Christmas Day 800. By the end of his reign he had extended the borders of his kingdom from Barcelona to Schleswig-Holstein, and from Ushant to Vienna.

CHARLES X (1757–1836). Younger brother of Louis XVIII, whom he accom-panied when he returned to France on the restoration of the monarchy in 1814. Succeeded his brother, 1824. Appointed a number of increasingly unpopular governments, culminating in the extreme royalist ministry of Armand de

Polignac (1829). The three-day 'July Revolution' of 1830 cost him his throne, which passed to Louis-Philippe, of the younger branch of the Bourbons.

CLEMENCEAU, Georges (1841–1929). Politician and journalist, appointed Premier by President Poincaré in 1917, in the darkest days of the war; he led France to victory (the troops called him 'Père-la-Victoire') and presided at the Versailles Peace Conference.

COLBERT, Jean-Baptiste (1619–83). After the death of Mazarin, became Louis XIV's minister of marine, the interior and finance. Much the strongest and ablest of Louis's ministers, he greatly increased the revenues by reforming the tax structure, imposing tariffs and encouraging colonization.

COURCEL, Geoffroy, Baron de (b. 1912). French ambassador to Great Britain since 1962. Chef de Cabinet to General de Gaulle in London, 1940–41; worked with him in Algiers and, later, as regional commissioner for the liberated territories. Held various important posts in France, then Secretary-General to the Presidency 1958–62.

COUVE DE MURVILLE, Maurice (b. 1907). Escaped from France in 1940; member of Free French National Committee, Algiers, 1943. Held various senior ambassadorial posts from 1945 to 1958, including Washington and Bonn. Appointed minister for Foreign Affairs 1958, Premier 1968.

DALADIER, Edouard (b. 1884). Premier 1938–40, he co-operated with Chamberlain in the Munich agreement. Taking over the ministries of Defence, War and Foreign Affairs, he led France into the 'phoney war'. His government fell in March 1940, and though briefly a member of the Reynaud cabinet he was dismissed in June, when France fell. He and Léon Blum were indicted at the Riom war-guilt trial in 1942, where they vigorously attacked Pétain (the trial was suspended after a few months).

DEBRÉ, Michel (b. 1912). Served in the Resistance; joined de Gaulle in Algiers. Leading member of UNR (Union pour la Nouvelle République). Prime Minister 1959–62, minister for Finance 1965–1968, minister for Foreign Affairs from 1968.

DEFFERRE, Gaston (b. 1910). Socialist candidate for the Presidency, 1965. Member of the executive committee of the underground Socialist party during the occupation. Member of the Chamber of Deputies. Director of the Marseilles daily *Le Provençal*, Mayor of Marseilles, minister under the Fourth Republic.

DÉROULÈDE, Paul (1846–1914). Writer and politician; vigorous propagandist against the Third Republic and in favour of revenge for the defeat of France by Germany in 1871. Founded the ultra-nationalist 'League of Patriots' and campaigned in support of General Boulanger.

DREYFUS, Alfred (1859–1935). Jewish army officer, convicted by court-martial in 1894 of passing military information to Germany, and sent to penal servitude on Devil's Island. His case, which rested on forged evidence and was bedevilled by anti-semitism and military stubbornness, split France into two bitterly opposed camps. Emile Zola, Clemenceau and Jean Jaurès campaigned on his behalf, and eventually the scandal was righted when the true culprits, Major Esterhazy and Col. Henry, were revealed. Dreyfus was released, vindicated and restored to his rank in 1906, and served in World War I.

FAURE, Edgar (b. 1908). With de Gaulle in London and Algiers. On the War Crimes tribunal at Nuremberg. Radical Socialist Deputy and minister. Prime Minister 1955–56. Professor of law at the University of Dijon and sent on various missions by General de Gaulle. Minister of Agriculture 1967, minister of Education 1968.

GAILLARD, Félix (b. 1919). Leading Radical and finance expert. Prime Minister, 1957–58.

GIDE, André (1869–1951). One of the most influential writers of the twentieth century. In a sense it is true to say that his whole output is autobiography and self-revelation (*Journal*, 1949; *Si le grain ne meurt*, 1926). Helped to found the literary review *Nouvelle Revue Française*. Nobel Prize for literature, 1947.

GIRAUD, Henri (1879–1949). General and politician. Captured by the Germans in 1940, he escaped to Switzerland in 1942 and returned briefly to Vichy France. In November 1942 he made his way to Algiers, where he took command of the French army in Africa, also assuming civil powers when Admiral Darlan was assassinated. Subsequently was persuaded by Churchill and Roosevelt to merge his forces and government with de Gaulle's Committee of National Liberation, of which he was co-chairman until April 1944.

256

GISCARD D'ESTAING, Valéry (b. 1926). Finance minister in the governments of Debré and Pompidou until 1967. Leader of independent Gaullists.

GODARD, Jean-Luc (b. 1930). Leading film director. His most famous films include 'Au bout du souffle', 'La Chinoise', 'Week-End'.

GUIZOT, François (1787–1874). First Professor of Modern History at the Sor-bonne. Elected to the Chamber of Deputies in 1830, and after the July Revolu-tion in that year became minister of the Interior under Louis-Philippe. Was minister for Public Instruction in several governments, Ambassador in London, and from 1840 to 1848 was the dominant influence in government. After the 1848 revolution he returned to history. He was a leading Protestant.

HERRIOT, Edouard (1872–1957). Mayor of Lyons 1905–47 and leader of the Radical-Socialist party. Successively Senator and Deputy from 1910 to 1940 without giving up the mayoralty of Lyons, and held many ministerial posts. Accused Pétain (1942) of violating the constitution; resigned from Legion of Honour. Interned in Germany 1944–45. Elected President of the National Assembly, 1947.

JAURÈS, Jean (1859–1914). Leader of the Socialist party before World War I and founder of L'Humanité (now the Communist organ). Tried to avert the outbreak of war but – though he said that if war came, French socialists would fight for France – he was assassinated by a fanatical nationalist on 31 July 1914.

JOAN OF ARC (1412?–31). French national heroine and patron saint (canonized by Benedict XV in 1920). When the English and Burgundians were masters of all France north of the Loire, and Henry VI of England claimed the French throne, a Domrémy peasant girl, inspired by 'heavenly voices', gained access to the Dauphin, inspired his troops and raised the siege of Orléans (1429). The victory of Patay the same year enabled the French to recapture Reims, where the Dauphin was then crowned as Charles VII. Captured by the Burgundians, Joan was turned over to the English, tried as a heretic and burned at the stake.

LAFAYETTE, Marquis de (1757–1834). Joined the American Revolutionary army in 1777. Served at the seige of Yorktown and was present at the surrender of Cornwallis. Returned to France, joined the reform party and was a member of the Estates-General in 1789. Commanded Paris National Guard after the

257

fall of the Bastille, and was a principal author of the Declaration of Rights. Supported Napoleon in the Consulate, but eventually became estranged from him and retired to the country. Opposed Napoleon after the 100 Days and demanded his abdication. Favoured restoration of the Bourbons but was actively opposed to Charles X. Commanded National Guard in the revolution of 1830, helped to put Louis-Philippe on the throne.

LAVAL, Pierre (1883–1945). Politician and lawyer, moving from socialism through republicanism to fascism and collaboration with the Germans. Held a number of cabinet posts between the wars, moving steadily towards appeasement of the fascist powers. With Sir Samuel Hoare of Britain (Hoare-Laval Pact, 1935), he worked to ensure that Italy would be given a free hand in Abyssinia. Headed the Vichy government under Pétain. Tried after the war on charges of treason, convicted and shot.

LECANUET, Jean (b. 1920). Leading Social Catholic, candidate for Presidency, 1965.

MALRAUX, André (b. 1901). Novelist and art critic; minister of state for Cultural Affairs since 1958. Fought with the Republicans in the Spanish civil war, and served in the resistance movement. His best-known novel is *La Condition Humaine* (1933). His *Antimémoires* (1967) are a prime source for recent French history and for *gaullologie*.

MAURIAC, François (b. 1885). Novelist, dramatist and journalist. Nobel prize for literature, 1952. His novels are usually set in the Bordeaux region, and their theme is the conflict between sensual passion and a conventional middle-class background. Characteristic novels are *Le Baiser en lépreux* (1922), *Le Nœud de vipères* (1932), and *Les Chemins de la mer* (1939).

MAURRAS, Charles (1868–1952). Poet and publicist; propagandist for royalism, Catholicism and fascism. Joined 'Action Française' at the time of the Dreyfus case and was a leading anti-Dreyfusard. Advocated a Catholic, royalist France. Collaborated with the Germans; condemned to life imprisonment in 1945 but released on health grounds just before his death.

MENDÈS-FRANCE, Pierre (b. 1907). Radical Deputy 1932–40. Served with de Gaulle in London and Algiers. Prime Minister 1954–55. Negotiated Geneva agreements, dividing Indo-China into North and South Vietnam. His style of government was strongly personal, with 'fireside chat broadcasts à la Roose⁄velt; his brisk, technocratic methods aroused such wide hostility that his ministry lasted only 8 months. Has consistently opposed de Gaulle since 1958. Defeated in elections of 1958, he returned to Parliament as an independent Socialist in 1967, but was defeated in 1968.

MITTERRAND, François (b. 1916). Lawyer and Deputy (Rassemblement Démocratique). Founder of the Prisoners' Aid Society. Political director of *Le Courrier de la Nièvre* (and has represented the Nièvre in the Senate and Chamber). Minister of the Interior in the Mendès⁄France government, 1954–55. Leader of the opposition to de Gaulle. Was candidate for Presidency in 1965.

MOLLET, Guy (b. 1905). Schoolmaster. Served in the Resistance. Elected Deputy, 1945, and secretary⁄general of the Socialist party, 1946. Prime Minister, 1956–57 (at the time of the Suez war). Minister of state, 1958–59. Deputy and one of the leaders of opposition to General de Gaulle.

MONNET, Jean (b. 1888). Banker, who has held a large variety of posts as financial, economic or industrial adviser to governments, from World War I to the 1950's. Came to London after the fall of France; served on British pur⁄chasing commission in Washington and on Free French committee of national liberation in London and Algiers. Author of the 'Monnet Plan' for the moder⁄nization and re⁄equipment of French industry. Pioneer of a united Europe.

MONTAND, Yves (b. 1921). Franco⁄Italian actor and singer, famous for such songs as 'C'est si bon', 'Venez donc chez moi', 'Sakoura', and for films such as 'Wages of Fear', 'Sanctuary' and 'Aimez⁄vous Brahms?'

ORTOLI, François⁄Xavier (b. 1925). Lawyer: civil servant specializing in legal and financial affairs. Was *chef de cabinet* to Georges Pompidou when he was Premier. French representative on the Franco⁄Italian conciliation commission, 1952 (where his Corsican birth helped). Represents the government on the board of the semi⁄nationalized news agency Havas. Minister of Finance, 1968.

PÉTAIN, Philippe (1856–1951). Marshal of France. Defender of Verdun (1916) and French C.⁄in⁄C. on the Western Front. War Minister, 1934. Ambassador to Spain, 1939–40. Vice⁄premier in the Reynaud ministry, 1940, becoming Premier onReynaud's resignation. Arranged French surrender, and became Head of State in the Vichy government, with dictatorial powers.

Convicted of high treason in 1945, sentenced to death, but General de Gaulle (to whose son Pétain had stood godfather), commuted the sentence to life imprisonment.

PFIMLIN, Pierre (b. 1907). Has been a minister in almost every government from Liberation to the Fifth Republic. Deputy (MRP) for the Bas-Rhin and mayor of Strasbourg. He has represented France in, and presided over, the Assembly of the Council of Europe. Prime Minister, May 1958.

PIAF, Edith (1915-1963). Singer, actress and cabaret artist. Her seemingly untrained yet completely professional performance will live in the memory. Famous for songs like 'La vie en rose', 'Ne pleurez-pas milord', 'Je ne regrette rien'.

PISANI, Edgard (b. 1918). Senator (Democratic Left) for Haute-Marne, 1954-61. Minister of Agriculture in Debré and Pompidou governments until 1967. Although a Gaullist, voted against Pompidou government in May 1968. Defeated at elections.

POMPIDOU, Georges (b. 1911). On General de Gaulle's staff, 1944-46. Member of the Constitutional Council, 1959-62. Director of the Rothschild Bank from 1956 until his appointment to the Premiership in 1962. Succeeded as Premier by Couve de Murville, 1968.

POUJADE, Pierre (b. 1920). Founder, in 1955, of a right-wing movement of protest against big business, taxation, technocracy and central government, and for the small man in trade, industry and agriculture, and the 'good old days'. At first achieved quite a following, but his essentially negative, unconstructive appeal did not last long.

POUJADE, Robert (b. 1928). Secretary of the Gaullist party.

PROUST, Marcel (1871-1922). The foremost French novelist of the twentieth century. His *magnum opus* is the 7-section novel cycle *A la recherche du temps perdu* – basically an immensely detailed, complex account of one man's discovery of his own artistic vocation.

REYNAUD, Paul (1878-1968). Last Premier before the collapse of France. Had held various ministerial posts 1930-40. Minister of Finance, 1939-40, under

Daladier, whom he succeeded in March 1940. When the German attack came in May he replaced General Gamelin as C./in/C. by Weygand, brought Pétain into the cabinet and made General de Gaulle under/secretary for War. Trans/ ferred the seat of government to Tours, then to Bordeaux. Resigned 16 June, when Pétain demanded an armistice. Tried at Riom, 1942, and deported to Germany. After Liberation, was a member of the second constituent assembly, and a Deputy (1946–62).

ROBBE/GRILLET, Alain (b. 1922). Novelist. Noted for extended, detailed descriptions of material objects, as a means of demonstrating the indifference of the inanimate world to man, and thus freeing him from the tragic sense. His novels include *La Jalousie* (1957) and *Le Voyeur* (1955). Wrote film scripts *L'Immortelle* and *L'Année dernière à Marienbad*.

ROBESPIERRE, Maximilien (1758–94). Leading orator of the Revolution. After the execution of Louis XVI he was elected to the Committee of Public Safety and became chief spokesman of the Revolution. Supported the Reign of Terror and was eventually overthrown by a coalition of those who had had enough of the Terror and of his own increasing absolutism. Guillotined, 28 July 1794.

ROCHET, Waldeck (b. 1905). Secretary/general of the Communist party since the death of Thorez. Specialist in agricultural questions; director of the journal *La Terre*. Deputy, and chairman of the Communist group in the Assembly.

SARTRE, Jean/Paul (b. 1905). Existentialist philosopher, novelist and play/ wright. Took part in the resistance movement 1941–44. Became founder and editor of *Les Temps Modernes* in 1944. Awarded Nobel Prize for literature in 1964 but declined it. His plays are the most effective exposition of his philo/ sophy, e.g. *Les Mouches* (1943), *Huis Clos* (1944), *Les mains sales* (1948), *Le Diable et le Bon Dieu* (1951), and *Les Séquestres d'Altona* (1959).

SCHUMAN, Robert (b. 1886). A junior minister in the Reynaud government, 1940. Arrested by the Gestapo and imprisoned, but escaped and served in the Resistance. After Liberation, was a member of both constituent assemblies and of the national Assembly, held various ministries including Foreign Affairs, and was a leader of the MRP (Mouvement Républicain Populaire). Author of the 'Schuman Plan' for the pooling of European heavy industrial resources.

SERVAN-SCHREIBER, Jean-Jacques (b. 1924). Foreign political editor of *Le Monde*, 1948–53. Now editorial director of the weekly *L'Express*.

TATI, Jacques (b. 1908). Film actor and director. Creator of highly individual film comedies, e.g. *Jour de Fête, Les Vacances de M. Hulot, Mon Oncle*.

THIERS, Adolphe (1797–1877). Prominent supporter of Louis-Philippe, and twice Premier in his reign. Arrested by Napoleon III at the time of the coup d'état in 1851. Led the opposition to the imperial régime, and protested, on the grounds of unpreparedness, against the declaration of war in 1870. Negotiated peace with Germany, 1871, and suppressed the Commune. Elected first President of the Third Republic, 1871.

THOREZ, Maurice (1900–64). Secretary-general of the Communist party from 1930. Deputy, 1929–39. Called up in 1939 but left his unit when the party was banned, and was sentenced to death *in absentia* for desertion. Amnestied, 1944, and returned to France. Member of both constituent assemblies, and held cabinet posts under de Gaulle (1945–46) and as vice-premier (1946–47). A hard-line Stalinist, even after the rise of Khrushchev. Died in a Soviet ship *en route* to Yalta for medical treatment.

TRENET, Charles (b. 1913). Singer, prolific song-writer ('Y a d'la joie', 'Narbonne mon amie' etc.), novelist (*Un noir éblouissant*) and film actor.

VALÉRY, Paul (1871–1945). Poet and philosopher. Joined Mallarmé's group, 1891 (and married his daughter). In 1917 published his first great poem, *La Jeune Parque* (dedicated to André Gide), and in 1922 an important collection, *Les Charmes*. Influenced by Mallarmé, particularly in his feeling for the music of words. Elected to the Academy, 1926.

VERCORS. Pseudonym of Jean BRULLER (b. 1902), caricaturist and writer. Wrote and published, during the occupation, the novel *Le Silence de la Mer*. Was one of the founders of 'Editions de Minuit', a famous underground publishing house.

Index

Numbers in italic refer to illustrations

ADAMO, SALVATORE, 210
Adenauer, Konrad, 156, 161
Africa, Equatorial, 52, 96; French
  territories in, 96, 125, 140–141;
  Western, 52, 96
agriculture, 181–2; policies, 192
Aigues-Mortes, 11
Aix-en-Provence, 11
Albert, battle of, 200
Albigensian heresy, 15
Alesea, battle of, 11
Algeria, 47, 52, 92–3, 100, 101–2,
  124; Louis XIV and 23; de Gaulle's
  policies for, 137; war in, 95–8, 107,
  109, 118, 140ff.; see also De Gaulle
Alibert, Raphael, 69
Almereyda, suicide of, 56
Alps, 9, 12
Alsace, 9, 19, 45, 47
America, 29, 66, 165–8, 234
American alliance, 194
American culture, 209–10
Amiens, 205; battle of, 200
Ancien Régime, 28, 31
Annam, 53
Anne de Bretagne, 17
Aquitaine, 9, 12
Aquitaine, Duke of, 13
Arab-Israel war (1967), 121, 195
Arabs, de Gaulle's association with,
  237; in Algeria, 142, 144; in
  France (AD 732), 12, 15
Aragon, Louis, 211

Ardennes, 9, 65
army, in Algiers, 145; in World War
  II, 64–5; mutinies in (1917), 55–6
Assembly, see Chamber of Deputies
Astérix, 201
Atlantic alliance, 194
atomic bomb, French, 158
Auriol, Vincent (see Who's Who,
  p. 253), 86, 87, 108, 139
Austrasia, 12
Auvergne, 69
Avignon, 81

BABEUF, GRACCHUS (see Who's Who,
  p. 253), 29
Balzac, Honoré de, 50, 203
Bank of France, 31
Bao Dai, Emperor, 90
Bapaume, battle of, 200
Barthélemy, Joseph, 126
Bazaine, Marshal, 201
Beauce, 10
Belgium, 45, 64
Ben Barka affair, 189
Ben Bella, 142, 143, 146; release from
  prison, 150
Berbers in Algeria, 142, 144
Bergson, Henri, 118
Bernanos, Georges, 85
Beuve-Méry, Hubert (see Who's
  Who, p. 253), 152
Biafra, French arms to, 237
Biaggi, Jean Baptiste, 150

263

Proust, Marcel (*see* Who's Who, p. 260), 62
Puys, 9
Pyrenees, 9, 207

QUINET, EDGAR, 43

RACINE, JEAN BAPTISTE, 20
railways, 46, 50, 172
referendum, 189; of 1958, 86, 104; of 1962, 154, 177; of 1968, 224; of 1969, 235
religious disputes, 17, 44, 55
Renault light tank, 57
Renault motor-works, 84, 223
Rennes, 51, 205
Renouvin, Pierre, 198
Republican Front, 95
Resistance movement, 68, 77–8, 81, 82; reserve army formed, 78; sabotage of firearms, 78
Réunion, 141
Revolution, of 1789, 49, 50, 203; of 1830, 38, 41; of 1848, 41; of 1958, 97, 231; of 1968, 219–36; *see also* French Revolution
Revolutionary legislation (1791), 44
Revolutionary war, 47
Reynaud, Paul (*see* Who's Who, p. 260–1), 64, 65, 66, 67, 77, 114, 120, 133; transition from Third to Fifth Republic, 125
Rheims, 12, 15
Rhine, river, 12
Rhône aircraft factory, 84
Rhône delta, 9
Ribot, Alexandre, 55
Richard, Jacques, 138
Rigaud, Hyacinthe, 20
Rivière, Jacques, 197
Robbe-Grillet, Alain (*see* Who's Who, p. 261)
Robespierre, Maximilien (*see* Who's Who, p. 261), 29, 200, 201
Robic (cyclist), 211
Rochelle, Drieu le, 69

Rochet, Waldeck (*see* Who's Who, p. 261), 188
Rocque, Colonel Casimir de la, 69
Roman influence, 11, 12
Romier, Lucien, 69
Roosevelt, Franklin D., 66, 74, 82, 114, 120, 158, 165
Rouen, 12
Rouvre, 11
R.P.F. (Rassemblement du Peuple Français), 89, 109, 116, 122, 137; and de Gaulle, 89, 121
Russia, 168, 233, 237; alliances with France, 53–4, 163–5

ST LOUIS, 44
Salan, General, 101, 103, 148; replaced in 1958, 144–5
Salengro, Roger, 61
Sarajevo, 53
Sarcelles (new suburbs), 208
Sarrail, General, 55
Sartre, Jean-Paul (*see* Who's Who, p. 261), 78, 175, 212
Savoy, 45
Schuman, Robert (*see* Who's Who, p. 261), 91; as foreign minister, 156
Second Empire, 43
Second Republic (1848–51), 41
Seine, river, 12, 18
Servan-Schreiber, Jean-Jacques (*see* Who's Who, p. 262), 219
Sétif, 141
Siegfried, André, 197
social customs, 199–200
social security reforms, 192
social system, 51, 76, 201
Socialist congress at Tours, 58
Solférino, 205
Sombart, Werner, 49
Sorbonne, 219, 228; closure of, 222
Sorbonne-Nanterre, 221
Sorel, Albert, 117
Soustelle, Jacques, 98, 99, 102, 131, 137; dismissal of, 146; influence of, 138
Spaak, Paul-Henri, 156